Media Representations of September 11

Edited by Steven Chermak, Frankie Y. Bailey, and Michelle Brown

Crime, Media, and Popular Culture

PRAEGER

Westport, Connecticut
London

Library of Congress Cataloging-in-Publication Data

Media representations of September 11 / edited by Steven Chermak, Frankie Y.
  Bailey, and Michelle Brown.
      p. cm. — (Crime, media, and popular culture)
  Includes bibliographical references and index.
  ISBN 0–275–98044–8 (alk. paper)
    1. September 11 Terrorist Attacks, 2001—Press coverage. 2. September 11
Terrorist Attacks, 2001—Public opinion. 3. Mass media—United States. I.
Chermak, Steven M. II. Bailey, Frankie Y. III. Brown, Michelle, 1971– IV. Series.
HV6432.7.M43 2003
973.931—dc21   2003053639

British Library Cataloguing in Publication Data is available.

Library of Congress Catalog Card Number: 2003053639
ISBN: 0–275–98044–8

First published in 2003

Praeger Publishers, 88 Post Road West, Westport, CT 06881
An imprint of Greenwood Publishing Group, Inc.
www.praeger.com

Printed in the United States of America

The paper used in this book complies with the
Permanent Paper Standard issued by the National
Information Standards Organization (Z39.48–1984).

10 9 8 7 6 5 4 3 2 1

Copyright Acknowledgments

The author and the publisher gratefully acknowledge permission for use of the following
material:

Excerpts from a telephone interview Randy Frances Kandel held with David M. Rosen.
Used with permission.

Contents

Series Foreword

This volume marks the launching of an exciting new interdisciplinary series on Crime, Media, and Popular Culture from Praeger Publishers. Because of the pervasiveness of media in our lives and the salience of crime and criminal justice issues, we feel it is especially important to provide a home for scholars who are engaged in innovative and thoughtful research on important crime and mass media issues.

This series will focus on process issues (such as the social construction of crime and moral panics), presentation issues (such as the images of victims, offenders, and criminal justice figures in news and popular culture), and effects (such as the influence of the media on criminal behavior and criminal justice administration).

With regard to this latter issue—effects of media/popular culture—as this preface was being written the *Los Angeles Times* and other media outlets reported that two young half-brothers (ages 20 and 15) in Riverside, California, had confessed to strangling their mother and disposing of her body in a ravine. The story was attracting particular attention because the brothers told police they had gotten the idea of cutting off her head and hands to prevent identification from a recent episode of the award-winning HBO series, *The Sopranos.* As the *Los Angeles Times* noted, this again brought into the spotlight the debate about the influence of violent media such as *The Sopranos,* about New Jersey mobsters, on susceptible consumers.

In this series, scholars engaged in research on issues that examine the complex nature of our relationship with media. Peter Berger and Thomas Luckman coined the phrase the "social construction of reality" to describe the process by which we acquire knowledge about our environment. They and others have argued that reality is a mediated experience. We acquire what Emile Durkheim described as "social facts" through a several-pronged process of personal experience, interaction with others, academic education, and, yes, the mass media. With regard to crime and the criminal justice system, many people acquire much of their information from the news and from entertainment media. The issue raised by the report above and other anecdotal stories of "copycat" crime is how what we consume—read, watch, see, play, hear—affects us.

What we do know is that we experience this mediated reality as individuals. We are not all affected in the same way by our interactions with mass media. Each of us engages in interactions with mass media/popular culture that are shaped by factors such as our social environment, interests, needs, and opportunities for exposure. We do not come to the experience of mass media/popular culture as blank slates waiting to be written upon or voids waiting to be filled. It is the pervasiveness of mass media/popular culture and the varied backgrounds (including differences in age, gender, race/ethnicity, religion, etc.) that we bring to our interactions with media that make this a particularly intriguing area of research.

Moreover, it is the role of mass media in creating the much discussed "global village" of the twenty-first century that is also fertile ground for research. We exist not only in our communities, our cities, and states, but in a world that spreads beyond national boundaries. Technology has made us a part of an on-going global discourse about issues not only of criminal justice but of social justice. Technology places us to events around the world "as they happen." It was technology that allowed Americans around the world to witness the collapse of the World Trade Center's Twin Towers on September 11, 2001. In the aftermath of this "crime against humanity," we have been witnesses to and participants in an on-going discussion about the nature of terrorism and the appropriate response to such violence.

In this first volume in our new series, we have brought together scholars from a wide range of disciplines to examine the role of mass media in the social construction of reality in the wake of an event such as September 11 that affected all us in profound ways. This volume is only the first in a series that we expect to be both timely and significant.

Frankie Y. Bailey and Steven Chermak,
Series Editors

1

Introduction

Many occupational worlds are generally closed to outsiders, but life in the firehouse is sacrosanct. Like other occupations where death, serious physical injury, and fear are weaved into the fabric of the work, *being* a firefighter requires a tireless commitment to group solidarity. Firefighters adhere to a red code of silence—whereby they can talk only to others like themselves about what it means to fight fires. Their lives are interwoven not only by the loyalty to one another but because they live, work, play, and exist together. Their world has unwritten rules, codes, and customs, and a unique language, and their commitment to solidarity shields firehouses from bureaucratic, political, and other outside influences. Distinguished journalist-historian David Halberstam writes:

Firemen live in a world apart from other civilians. The rest of the world seems to change, but the firehouses do not. This is, in fact, as close to a hermetically sealed world as you are likely to find in contemporary America: It is driven by its unique needs, norms, and traditions, some of which are inviolable.... A great deal of the tradition and the coherence is family-driven, with generation after generation supplying men to the department. It is almost as if there is a certain DNA strain found in firefighting families.[1]

Their "hermetically sealed world" was ripped violently open on September 11, 2001.

The 9-11 terrorist attacks were against the people, the principles, beliefs, and the way of life that is American. The celebration of the many heroes of

September 11 helped people process the loss, restored faith and confidence in society, connected people together in unexpected ways, and provided justification for a significant response. A mayor, the passengers of United Airlines Flight 93, other flight attendants, law enforcement officers, good Samaritans, and even fictional creations all attempted to provide hope to what was a hopeless situation. Although these heroes were significant, the firefighter was probably the most important hero used in the aftermath of September 11. This was not a newly created icon because the "firefighter as hero" had long been established. Being a victim of a fire is a great fear, and firefighters voluntarily rush toward what we fear to conquer it and save lives. Nearly 350 firefighters died on September 11, fulfilling their promise to put others' lives before their own. It was, however, the events that occurred that day, and then how various media presented firefighting, that gave a renewed significance to their position as hero. Most accounts, although there were a few controversial exceptions, celebrated the life of the firefighter.

Halberstam's probing account of the firehouse, and the lives and deaths of 12 of the 13 men assigned to Engine 40, Ladder 35 near Lincoln Center in Manhattan who responded to the World Trade Center on September 11, is perhaps the most revealing and emotional of the published works. But many more images, accounts, and insights were published. The following list provides a snapshot:

- Gary Varvel, in the editorial cartoon "Fallen Heroes," published in the *Indianapolis Star* (September 16, 2001), shows an Uncle Sam character walking away from the rubble of the World Trade Center carrying a firefighter in his arms.
- Photographs of New York City firefighters were among the most frequently disseminated. Two of the most powerful of the many photographs were those of three firefighters hoisting the American flag on a pole at Ground Zero and another of firefighters draping the flag over a wall at the Pentagon.
- There were several thousand tribute Web sites created that included poems, pictures, dedications, songs, and prayers for firefighters.
- The consumer was bombarded with firefighter collectibles, including stamps, coins, key chains, toys, books, posters, pictures, and souvenirs. The consumer could have installed a firefighter thematic image on his or her computer, bought the "Image of Hope Firemen Figurine," the "We Will Never Forget Collector Plate," or the "Firemen with Angel Figurine," or read one of the many books, photo compilations, or tribute magazines dedicated to firefighters.
- Films, videos, plays, and television specials explored life as a firefighter, as well as the emotional trauma caused by the events. For example, *The Guys,* a film adapted from a play written by Anne Nelson, a professor of journalism at Columbia Uni-

versity, is about a fire captain in search of the words to write the eulogies for fire-fighters who died in the World Trade Center.

- "Into the Fire" and "The Rising," songs on Bruce Springsteen's critically acclaimed album, capture the very powerful reality that firefighters were walking up the stairs toward the fire as everyone else was trying to get out.

This book is about how various media elevated specific meanings and ignored other readings when interpreting the events of September 11. These terrorist attacks are certainly among the worst events in American history. Their occurrence at a time when society is both consumed and connected by its media gave the events dramatic significance. It also opened the events up to the possibility of a wide range of conflicting interpretations. For news organizations, nothing else was important except events related to the attacks and the response to it. Newspapers, magazines, broadcast news, and the Internet published millions of accounts to define what happened. Popular culture outlets also participated in these definitional processes, as television shows referenced what happened, some movie releases were delayed because of the similarities between the fictional images and the realities of what happened, and singers/songwriters, poets, and novelists told stories in an attempt to make sense of what happened. We decided that the best approach to take stock of the wealth and breadth of images, ideas, and accounts available to be analyzed was to connect with scholars from different disciplines. The events of September 11 were seeping into some academic work, but we knew that other scholars, who long had an interest in understanding the constructed realities and the significance of the media world, would be struggling to make sense of what was being said and ignored in various media outlets about the tragedy. We were not disappointed: The chapters contained in this book provide a diverse range of perspectives exploring the role of the media in defining the events of September 11.

We had two broad goals for this project and asked the contributors to keep these in mind as they reacted to media coverage. First, we wanted to provide an understanding of the media's role in transforming the events of September 11. Two issues were important in this regard. We wanted to approach scholars who have analyzed a variety of media in their efforts to provide a broader cultural understanding of the issues and events of the world. The volume includes research of newspaper and television coverage, Internet Web sites, comic books, songs, advertising, tribute books, and compilations. We asked contributors to write about September 11, but we were not specific about the topic for exploration. The value in this general approach was that the contributors choose very different issues, occurring at different times, for their reflective work. For example, the foci of the contributors range from the mainstream news coverage that was presented within 24 hours of the planes hitting the towers to the long-term media struggles with describing Islam and Jihad, to an analysis of the songs and music used to explain what had happened. Second, we wanted to work with scholars who would be approaching the topic with different methodological and theoretical approaches. The contributors to the volume represent a wide range of disciplines, including criminology, criminal justice, sociology, law, American studies, communication studies, cultural studies, Germanic studies, and journalism. We hope this is one of the issues that will give this volume lasting significance, because it is both instructive of the different theoretical and methodological approaches used to understand media images and highlights the need to cross-pollinate ideas across academic disciplines.

Although we have organized the chapters into three parts, there are many overlapping issues across the entire volume. The chapters included in Part I highlight theoretical perspectives used to understand the realities created by the media. These chapters provide an understanding of why the media emphasized certain readings and ignored other explanations of September 11. The four chapters included in Part II focus on how the news media presented, archived, and memorialized the attacks. These chapters also show the range of content-related methodologies that researchers use to analyze and understand media texts. The four chapters in Part III focus on the representations of September 11 in popular culture and demonstrate how fictional and real media accounts overlap as well as collide. Across this section, we witness the struggles that artists encountered in their attempts to make sense of September 11 within the cultural conventions of particular narrative structures.

PART I: THEORETICAL OVERVIEW

September 11 is precisely the kind of event that defies representation. And yet it is through media coverage that the day was primarily experienced and understood by its various cultural audiences. At the extreme ends of representation, where attempts at mediating such subjects as murder, genocide, war, and the Holocaust are made, we encounter what Austin Sarat calls "the limits of our ability to 'know,'" where "we can and do watch others die without being able to capture death's meaning or significance."[2] As media scholars, we run up against the questions of what it means to experience such a tragedy primarily as a media event and, by consequence, what effects media images have upon understandings and explanations of September 11. There is, of course, a bitter, undeniably tragic reality to September 11. This is also, as John Fiske asserts, a reality, like all realities, that can still be accessed "only through discourse, and the discourse that we use determines our sense of the real. Although discourse may not produce reality, it does produce the instrumental sense of the real that a society or social formation uses in its daily life."[3] Media images are significant points of study in part because the manner in which they construct the social realities that we live by and through is not self-evident. And yet, as the authors across this volume will make clear, it is primarily by way of the media that the cultural significance of September 11 was determined. They will also assert that at these ends, within these limits, the politics of representation have become most intensified and acute. Their questions converge, when their arguments do not, in considerations like the following: What is the role and function of media in times, like September 11, of national and global crisis? How do various forms of media engage this role and to what effect? What, precisely, is at stake in the images that media produce? The chapters that make up Part I of this volume are theoretical blueprints and instructional road maps for how these kinds of questions may be engaged, important discussions of the effects of September 11 upon what it means to do media studies as well as exemplars of how various kinds of media may be explored analytically.

These authors assemble around a powerful point of consensus: September 11 has been narrativized by way of the media into a primary, recognizable discourse, one with a distinct logic—a clear beginning (September 11, 2001), forceful middle (war), and moral end (democratic victory). They concur that these dominant media narratives express a distinctly "superficial quality" (Strawson) and a "puzzling unanimity and even monotony" (Breithaupt). Marked by the emergence of "dominant hegemonic agendas of super-patriotism and militarism" (Mukherjee) and the offering of "a fairly limited world view, one that tends to support a dominant political ideology" (Campbell), they find the national narrative of September 11 to be one of containment modeled through moral impulse, the repression of dissent, and healing ritual. This consensus is grounded, however, in an even more powerful theoretical assertion: that within and without the monolithic tendencies of mass media exist fissures and fragmentation, contests and debates, active struggles over the meanings of September 11 that, because they are largely obscured by more dominant modes of representation, have barely begun to be engaged. For these authors, this is precisely where the work of media studies and the analysis of images of September 11 begin.

As this volume predominantly focuses upon Western and particularly American media, John Strawson's contribution, "Holy War in the Media: Images of Jihad," engages the troubling absence of Muslim perspectives. In his examination, the very terms at the center of the 9-11 tragedy are subject to debate and the nature and parameters of that debate are powerfully influenced by a global media. In his analysis, September 11 is precisely the kind of event that can potentially unleash cross-cultural grapplings with the stereotypes that accompany essential ideas and values at the center of cultural, religious, and transnational identity politics. In this specific instance, the term of focus is Jihad. In Strawson's map of the media's navigation of this debate, contests are played out in which assertions and oppositions directed at Muslim stereotypes are mobilized by, through, and against specific kinds of coverage by key media outlets. We witness how embedded within the popular and international conceptions of Jihad are often vastly disparate notions about the nature and meanings of Islamic governance, jurisprudence, and self-identity.

Roopali Mukherjee's piece, "Between Enemies and Traitors: Black Press Coverage of September 11 and the Predicaments of National 'Others,'" continues this analysis of the politics of othering by way of an examination of black press coverage of September 11. Her chapter is a consummate application of discursive analysis, where, through the systematic identification of key themes in a number of regional black newspapers across the United States, she carefully maps the role of black media outlets in complicating emergent national narratives of September 11. The complex ambivalence at the heart of black press coverage of September 11, framed by both assent and dissent, exposes essential contradictions and contests at work within and without what Mukherjee identifies as the contemporary hegemonic discourse of "super-patriotism." Here, she demonstrates how the danger of the dominance of such an ideology and mode of representation is not simply that it leads to a tolerance of "racisms that would under other circumstances be cloaked and more subdued," but, as her research meticulously illustrates, that its terms are historically and culturally grounded within multiple kinds of discourses centered upon racial otherness. It is within such a framework that she offers a strategy for understanding the tensions and predicaments that Muslim and Arab citizens may potentially find themselves caught up in.

In "Commodifying September 11: Advertising, Myth, and Hegemony," Christopher Campbell provides a seamless sampling of textual analysis as applied through Stuart Hall's now classic discussion of "encoding/decoding" from British cultural studies.[4] Campbell analyzes the advertising industry by way of a broad overview and one particular case study, the widely celebrated Anheuser-Busch Clydesdale commercial. With striking parallels to Mukherjee's research, Campbell's work (1) reveals the primacy of cultural myth and discourse in the representation and commercialization of September 11, (2) maps the manner in which the advertising industry's mobilization of these mythologies effectively sublimates dissent and opposing worldviews, and (3) discloses a specific mode of methodological inquiry. His multiple and conflicting readings of one particular mass media event demonstrate how a single cultural artifact may serve as a vortex of social inquiry and public debate, in his particular case, at the strange intersection of consumer society and the emotive, mythic discourse of September 11.

The final chapter of this section of the volume, Fritz Breithaupt's "Rituals of Trauma: How the Media Fabricated September 11," is marked by its theoretical innovation and implications. Breithaupt introduces trauma theory as a template through which to understand how alternative frameworks for understanding September 11 and its perpetrators came to be closed off. In his examination of documentary footage and photo anthologies on September 11, Breithaupt maps how trauma in fact becomes "the central axis of storytelling" across various forms of media. His analysis provides a fascinating discussion of how media processes mimic and reproduce the experience of trauma. Within this framework, he points to many of the core mechanisms of 9-11 representation and how these often morally sensitive and ethical conventions nonetheless culminate in an insistence upon American innocence by way of a "traumatized" American public. In such a world, the media hold out an empty promise of healing and transcendence, while "The Image takes the place of the consciousness that 'trauma' therapy aims for."

PART II: NEWS TEXTS AND CULTURAL RESONANCE

The news media play a particularly significant role in responding to, recreating, and constructing historic events for several reasons. First, there is an expectation that the news media represent the public at such events. The public was starved for information and interpretation—citizens wanted to know what had occurred, who was able to do such damage, and what additional risks existed. People turned to various media, and when Internet Web sites shut down because of the congested traffic, users went to other sources. With this expectation comes the enormous responsibility that the media will uncompromisingly fulfill its role as informant and watchdog of society. Second, the news media was important because of their access to the places of destruction. The distribution of technology within society has provided an astonishing number of accounts. Third, news media have positioned themselves to offer nonstop and seemingly comprehensive coverage. The events were recorded and relived as broadcast stations halted all other programming, newspapers expanded in length to provide written accounts, and media organizations immediately began packing additional information on their Web sites.

The chapters presented in this section focus on news media coverage at different points in time: From news accounts on September 11 (Reynolds and Barnett) and September 12 (Wykes), to anniversary coverage (Wykes), to newspaper articles attempting to memorialize the events (Damphousse, Hefley, and Smith), to the archiving of news stories on Internet Web sites (Brown, Fuzesi, Kitch, and Spivey). Although the research methods used in this section vary, the findings presented by the authors overlap in intriguing ways. Taken together, these chapters reveal a connectedness between news outlets, where the reading and interpretation of events is reprocessed in a narrow manner. They demonstrate that officials appreciate the power of the news format and use news as a way to manage and communicate their interests to the public. Finally, they discuss how specific frames, such as patriotism, unity, and trauma, were promoted to describe September 11, and argue that these frames worked well because they resonated with broader cultural ideals.

The Reynolds and Barnett chapter that leads this section focuses on media coverage presented on September 11. This chapter provides results from a qualitative analysis of the verbal and visual frames portrayed in the first 12 hours of CNN's coverage. Their meticulous methodological approach, using the transcripts to best examine what was being said and juxtaposing those comments against the images being displayed, provides a revealing account of the frames emphasized in what has arguably become the most important news outlet in times of crisis. In addition, this chapter helps us understand the significance of the "breaking news" format of news media. The authors demonstrate that it is here that the foundation for providing specific readings of events is immediately constructed. With the constant repetition of the planes striking the towers being portrayed, they find that the media started to contemplate how best to respond to terrorism and the solution was narrowly defined: The "plethora of keywords, images, sources of information, sentences and thematic elements that, in the end, created a powerful, dominant frame—that a U.S. military–led international war would be the only meaningful solution to prevent more terrorist attacks." They show that the media and key political officials promoted three thematic clusters that resonated with a broader dominant ideology: war and military response, unity, and justification. These clusters combined to "create the impression that war was inevitable and necessary to combat the horror and devastation that Americans had just witnessed."

In the second chapter in this section, Brown, Fuzesi, Kitch, and Spivey explore how news media enhance their presence by publishing accounts on the World Wide Web. Brown et al. use a qualitative content analysis to map the themes, packages, and discursive elements related to news coverage on the

Internet. Historically, news media have been constrained by the presentational requirements of the medium, such as the length of time of a broadcast or the number of pages available to a daily newspaper. The Internet has altered these constraints and provides the opportunity to educate, inform, and provide alternative readings and diverse perspectives of events. The authors find, however, that the archival collection of information about September 11 "mimics more popular and accessible news media." More important, and similar to the conclusions of the Reynolds and Barnett chapter, they document that both format and cultural practice influenced the archival representations of September 11. They conclude: "Mainstream Internet news agency sites serve many functions, but perhaps most clearly, in this context, they attempt to create a particular historical order out of the chaos of September 11. The multiple accounts (visual, audio, and textual) that mix personal and national tragedies and reactions serve to preserve the memory of September 11 as the single most shocking and tragic day in American history, but one that Americans rapidly overcome through the deep mythographic reserves of cultural heritage and a unified impulse toward war."

In the chapter, "Reporting, Remembering, and Reconstructing September 11, 2001," Maggie Wykes provides a comparison of September 12, 2001 newspaper accounts to one-year anniversary news coverage. Wykes analyzes the news accounts published in the British nationals as "a way of interrogating British journalism." She explains: "I have read the newspaper articles on September 11 as discourse or as extended, multilayered metaphors wherein the material form is given powerful and resonant thematic meanings and values according to the culture of the reader." Wykes's conclusions about the news accounts published the day after the attacks are stunningly similar to Reynolds and Barnett's analysis of CNN's breaking news formats and Brown et al.'s analysis of Web sites: "the British press, even those papers most often in opposition or disjunction, was relatively uniform in the parameters of explanation it offered audiences: this was war; the enemy was Islamic terrorism, personified by bin Laden, and all of us in the West were united in our rectitude and vulnerability." Her explanation for this uniformity includes reference to the mutual dependence on particular sources, the tendency of the national press to attempt to unify in times of crisis, an abandonment of the tendency to trivialize, and a reliance on news values "steeped in cultural resonance." Also, she concludes: "September 11 demanded journalism. It epitomized, totally, everything that constitutes news. It was relentlessly a threat to Western/white power so fitted to the theorized meta-political agenda of the U.K. press; it required little more than mere description to tell the story in clear, simple, populist, salable terms—hence the heavy use of images; and it complied to many of the specified news values in relation to knowledge about news values." In her examination of the anniversary coverage, however, she finds that such uniformity was beginning to disappear and that the news media provided very few critical accounts of the effects and impacts of the American response to bin Laden and terrorism.

The final chapter in this section by Damphousse, Hefley, and Smith examines the memorialization of the 9-11 attacks. Damphousse et al. highlight why contemporary society almost immediately memorializes tragic events, why memorials are important, and analyze how the news media have become the vehicle to promote the construction of memorials. The authors use a very intriguing methodological approach as they examine both the narratives used to memorialize the 9-11 attacks and the individual and official sources promoting specific narratives. The authors provide two interesting comparisons. First, they compare the similarities between the narratives used to memorialize the Oklahoma City bombing and those related to the 9-11 attacks. Although defining these as very different types of events ("acute" v. "chronic"), they find that many of the narratives used in the building of the Oklahoma City memorial were used in post-9-11 coverage. They also discover, however, that because the nature of events was very different, a broader and more complex array of narratives was presented in the news media to memorialize September 11. The narratives used in news stories about the memorials are similar to the frames and thematic packages uncovered in the other chapters in this book. Second, they compare the sources and the narratives used to memorialize the three primary sites of the attacks: the World Trade Center, the Pentagon, and the Pennsylvania crash site. Since each site had "a different story to tell," the primary narratives presented in the news media and the sources that advocated for specific narratives for each location were different.

PART III: POPULAR NARRATIVES

While the newsworthiness of September 11 provoked an immediate and vast coverage across various kinds of news media formats, other kinds of media faced a different set of challenges. American cinema, for instance, experienced a distinct lag in representation, with many films temporarily shelved due to the close proximity of their fictional narratives to the actual events of the day. This line between fiction and reality became the source of a good deal of artistic energy and frustration, serving as an essential focal point in the struggle by the producers of popular culture to make sense of September 11. The contributions that make up the final section of this volume mark a pivotal conclusion, moving us beyond the traditional parameters of media study and social inquiry into the more nebulous realm of the popular. As these essays exemplify, September 11 incited an unusual moment of self-reflexivity and critical engagement within popular culture as commercial entertainment industries, individual artists, and cultural participants struggled to find ways to engage and render comprehensible September 11. As Randy Kandel writes: "The diverse narratives of the immediate events, the planes hitting the buildings, the buildings burning, the people crossing bridges covered with ash, resonate with an effort to document the surreal, and to emotionally assimilate the unthinkable…a popular cultural production that defies the literal fragmentation of human bodies and steel towers, parallels the real unity of New Yorkers in crisis, and mimics the questionable and querulous national unity of the moment." As institutions and performers that predominantly ground their work in the fictional spaces of the cultural imaginary, many found themselves at the limits of their medium, struggling to find a way in which to properly address the events of September 11. In this final section, each author presents us with a particular case study of precisely this kind of engagement, an assessment of "the relevancy of art to the explosive times in which we live" (Hamm). Each also simultaneously provides an innovative illustration of important new research topics and trajectories in media studies.

American culture has recently experienced a strong resurgence of superhero imagery. From Batman to X-Men, Spiderman to the Incredible Hulk, superheroes have reentered various kinds of popular discourse, including film, television drama, and animated cartoons. Amid the complicated constructions and invocations of heroism after September 11, Jarrett Lovell and Amy Nyberg excavate the origins of superhero imagery and map its transformations in comic book discourse. Lovell's piece provides an innovative analytical performance that maps the struggle to define which superhero best fits the ideological contours of a post-9-11 America. Focusing upon the characters of Superman and Captain America, Lovell historically plots the emergence of each and the relationship of history to the nature of their symbolism and the values they represent. In the process, he accounts for the way in which September 11 made problematic the conventions of representation and cultural expectations surrounding the Superman icon successfully enough to account for the sudden discursive rise of Captain America. Lovell asserts that "perhaps more than any other form of media, comic books are dependent upon iconography to communicate ideology to a mass audience." His chapter culminates in a fascinating moment of ideological dissent within the Captain America series when the medium is forced to confront the question of what happens in the acute rupturing of superhero iconography in a post-9-11 world.

Amy Nyberg continues this line of analysis in her piece, "Of Heroes and Superheroes," where she examines the 9-11 tribute comic books. Here, she finds that superheroes are largely absent, replaced instead by first-person accounts of September 11 by those at Ground Zero, friends and families of loved ones, and average Americans. Like Lovell, she asserts that "the superhero narrative structure and genre conventions did not readily lend themselves to telling stories of September 11." Nyberg instead maps how the horrible reality of September 11 runs counter to the essential conventions of superhero narratives, initiating a deconstructive impulse within comic book discourse where the imagined universe of superheroes is simply not sustainable in the immediate aftermath of a post-9-11 America. Instead, the structural limits of the superhero are exposed, and only slightly recuperated, when merged with images of the real and mortal heroes of September 11. The traditional story of fictional superhero "triumph cannot be reconciled with the reality of September 11 and therefore is abandoned, unfinished, because we know the 'real' story."

This image of the ruptured narrative is elaborated in Randy Kandel's chapter, "Narrative Reconstruction at Ground Zero," by way of her personal 9-11 experience—and participation in three occupational subcultures, those of mystery writers, legal anthropologists, and administrative law judges. Kandel highlights the predominant metaphor for experiencing September 11—"storying" by way of the individual narrative. At the center of her work is a focus on the ways in which September 11 challenged and reaffirmed professional and self-identities at a historical moment that marks "the end of ordinary narrative." Her discussion traces how transformations across various kinds of communities culminate in a unique popular narrative with important distinctions and conflicts, as well as shared points of commonality. New York mystery writers discuss various aspects of September 11 and its impact upon their craft, including its immediately prohibitive effect upon the development of fictional worlds and a renewed sense of moral imperative within their writing. Legal anthropologists respond similarly, questioning the central questions and missions of their discipline and the proper role each should play in the unfolding of a post-9-11 world. Kandel writes of these groups that "Both write stories as metaphors of experience." Her analysis of the stories of administrative judges is somewhat different. Here, in the bureaucratic workspace of the New York Taxi and Limousine Commission, judges "did not look through their professional lenses to story their own personal or professional bridge across the September 11 aftermath. When the ordinary stories disappeared, and the work became routinized, the court became only a workplace, where coworkers could share their personal stories of who was where when." In the end, Kandel's essay raises the important question of how different kinds of work cultures invite varying levels of cultural participation and story-building with respect to an event like September 11.

In the final chapter, Mark Hamm provides an impressive survey of the prolific response by the music industry to September 11, where, as Hamm writes, "the sheer magnitude of this music is one measure of its consequence." Organized in three parts, Hamm's analysis includes an examination of the history of American standards and pop hits in commemoration processes (natural disaster in 1927 Mississippi; racial violence in 1935 Florida; and Pearl Harbor, 1941); an assessment of the vast wave of material written and produced in reaction to September 11 (including a series of tribute albums); and a discussion of various tracks released on September 11 and their uncanny relationship to events of that day (as specifically apparent in the lyrics of Bob Dylan's *Love and Theft* album). In this engagement, Hamm discusses the spectrum of post-9-11 music in its varying degrees of complexity, sentimentality, and social significance. Across a sampling of various songs, genres, and topical aspects, Hamm argues that the best performances "generally enhance our understanding" of September 11, are "more eloquently written and more coherently conceived," and "help move people toward catharsis." He concludes his piece with an elaboration of this kind of cultural production in practice, Bruce Springsteen's much-heralded *The Rising* album.

CONCLUSION

The chapters in this volume provide an understanding of how the attacks of September 11 have been presented in different cultural forms. We are certainly aware that these attacks and the aftermath continue to be presented by the media and processed by the public in intriguing ways. The number of different accounts intensified immediately before and on the one-year anniversary, but news reporters, songwriters, filmmakers, artists, advertisers, and commentators continue to offer new constructed truths about these events that are worthy of analysis. This volume starts a discussion leading to a better understanding of the impacts of these representations, and the contributors' theoretical and methodological insights will be particularly valuable to scholars who are interested in dissecting the accounts of this and other similar historic events.

I

Theoretical Overview

2

Holy War in the Media:
Images of Jihad

John Strawson

Jihad is a very powerful word
—Zeyad Yasin, CNN Interview, June 6, 2002[1]

The Western media's portrayal of all things Islamic has proved to be enor-
mously complex since September 11. The familiar Orientalist images of
Islam[2] as a backward, cruel, and yet exotic religion have jostled with genuine
attempts at multicultural treatment and instrumental political expediency
toward Muslim communities in the West and significant allies beyond. The
shock of September 11 destabilized assumed orders and revealed discourses as
well as political power as tantalizingly fragile. I will argue in this historical
moment the media became an important forum through which contested
images of Islam were circulated, which fragmented the homogenous Orientalist framework and offered new points of departure for the exploration of
even notoriously difficult areas of Islamic jurisprudence such as Jihad.[3] Zeyad
Yasin's commencement speech at Harvard University on the topic of Jihad
provides us with a useful lens through which to view the changes.

Did September 11 signal a new stage in an Islamic Jihad against the West?
This question was inevitable once it was established that Osama bin Laden
and the al-Qaeda network were its perpetrators. As the media both asked and
attempted to answer that question, the issue of what Jihad exactly is became
central. The fanatical Muslim warrior threatening civilization has been an
enduring image in the West since the Crusades.[4] This ancient theme had been
given a current edge through Huntington's clash of civilizations theory, in

which Jihad as "holy war" appears to have become an inevitability.[5] In this account, essentialist cultural conflicts could both explain September 11 and serve as a warning for perhaps worse to come. Islam and the West's collision course could not be avoided. However, this analysis would prove far too simplistic in a world where key Muslim states were seen as essential allies in U.S. President George Bush's war on terrorism. If Saudi Arabia, Egypt, the Gulf States,[6] Turkey, and Pakistan were to become key players alongside the United States and Britain, the view of an inevitable "holy war" between Islam and the West was at least an inconvenient one. That the media formed a nexus of communication between politicians, religious leaders, and Islamic experts before the general public weaved a discourse between the well-known Orientalist discourse and the more edgy multicultural one.[7]

The reaction to Zeyad Yasin's Harvard commencement speech, originally entitled "My American Jihad," allows us to track the delicate line that the media followed in dealing with the issue. Yasin, a 22-year-old biomedical student, appears to have wanted to square the circle between American and Islamic values. For Yasin, "both the Quran and the constitution teach ideas of peace, justice and compassion.... Each of these texts, one at the heart of my religion and the other at that of my country, demand a constant struggle to do what is right."[8] Yasin's speech, given nine months after September 11, argued that the concept of Jihad has been corrupted and should be understood on many levels as a struggle for:

[S]elf-purification and awareness, public service and social justice. On a global scale, it is a struggle involving people of all ages, colors and creeds, for control of the Big Decisions: not only who controls what piece of land but more importantly who gets medicine and who can eat.[9]

Yasin's definition of Jihad as a struggle posed in terms of personal morality and social justice is a common understanding of Jihad in many Islamic circles. It is entirely consistent with the Arabic root of the word meaning "effort." This is clearly quite different from the militarist meaning of the term as used by al-Qaeda, and other extremist groups, who claim that Islam teaches that Jihad is a holy war.[10]

Yasin's use of the term "American Jihad" produced such a strong backlash that he was forced to change its title to "Of Faith and Citizenship." The conjoining of "Jihad" and "American" appeared to spark the controversy. As the Harvard speech became newsworthy, the media opened up the very debate that Yasin had wanted to provoke. "I wanted to try to reclaim the word 'Jihad' from the way it has been used and abused," he told ABC News the day before the speech. The ABC interview contained a description of Jihad "in its truest and purist form, the form that all Muslims aspire, is the determination to do right, to do justice even against your own interests."[11] Professor Richard Thomas, the chair of the commencement committee, explained why Yasin's speech was chosen:

It appealed because it began with a personal perspective of a Muslim-American, questioning whether he is fit as an American and as a Muslim. And then expanded that to include all of us in terms of the struggle it promotes and urges on all of us.[12]

However, the ABC piece then turned to the controversy and online petition campaign by Hilary Levey. Having heard the original title of the speech, Levey asked the university leadership, "[C]an you tell us if there is an explicit condemnation of violent jihad or the invocation of jihad for terrorist purposes or by organizations that support terrorists?" Having received no satisfactory answer, she began to campaign for changes in the speech and obtained 3,600 signatures for her petition. Next, ABC, no doubt in the interest of balance, interviewed Jewish, Catholic, and Muslim students. Benjamin Gaiper, who is Jewish, commented, "I think it's impossible, in a post-9-11 world, to say that the word 'Jihad' is nonpolitical." A Catholic, Christopher Pierce, continued this theme: "What I think of, and what comes to mind, are thoughts of suicide bombings in the Middle East, or planes hitting the World Trade Center." The Muslim students all took a rather different tack. Nader Hasan thought the speech was "inspirational, it is motivational." However, he accepted that the term will mean different things to different people. Saif Shah Mohammed, also a Muslim, believed that the term had been hijacked and its original use in Islamic tradition undermined. Hasan summed up the Muslim-American dilemma post–September 11: "I understand the origin of the term 'Jihad' as a spiritual struggle to do the right thing. But I am also an American, and I live here and I know that Jihad has been misappropriated by many people. So I also think about the falling Twin Towers when I hear the word."[13] The piece ends with Yasin pleased that a wider audience had begun to consider several meanings of Jihad.

The ABC piece is an interesting package and presents a good range of popularly held views on what Jihad means. ABC's use of Jewish and Catholic interviewees may be essentialist in part, but the views expressed would be commonly held by many Non-Muslims. The discourse of the Muslim students is interesting as all three—Yasin, Mohammad, and Hasan—basically subscribe to the same outlook. First, there is the necessity to deal with September 11 as both Muslims and Americans. This, no doubt, is due in part to the way in which Muslims in the United States were forced on to the defensive after the events. The intriguing part of this is revealed in the second common outlook. This is an account of Jihad as originally a spiritual struggle that has been appropriated, abused, or hijacked by modern extremists.

The next day Yasin is interviewed on CNN by Daryn Kagan. Kagan pressed Yasin about American perceptions of Jihad post–September 11: "[D]o you understand that Americans, as they have been victims and have watched victims of terrorists groups that have adopted the word Jihad...have a different understanding of that word?" In this interview, Yasin's identity is being constructed as somehow un-American. However, Yasin managed to reassert his identity when he explained the aim of his speech: "I'm hoping people will get a sense of both unity between American-Islamic values—the idea that there is no contradiction between being a Muslim and being an American, that the values that we share are universal values, as well as trying to reclaim the word from the way it's been misappropriated."[14] Again, as Yasin had wanted, a major news service became part of the emerging debate about Jihad.

The story was also followed in the print media. The *New York Times* covered the story on June 1, 2002, with a piece on the dropping of "Jihad" from the title of the speech. The article gave much space to quotations from Yasin explaining his use of the term Jihad. However, key passages considered the two sides of the argument:

Mr. Yasin had said that the speech was intended to reclaim the original meaning of jihad as "struggle," and use it [to] rally his fellow graduates to fight against social injustice. Critics, however, said in a petition that the choice of the word more commonly used to mean "holy war" implied support for the terrorism of Sept. 11 and other violent acts committed in the name of Islam.[15]

This balance of arguments was tipped in favor of Yasin by an opinion article by Nader Hasan, who described himself as Yasin's "classmate and friend." "That single emotive word—jihad—has driven our usually civil campus into a frenzy," he wrote.[16] It is another example of openness that the *New York Times* published Hasan's piece. In letting Muslims speak for themselves, there appears to be a weakening of the Orientalist framework, which previously meant that Muslims were represented in a stereotyped manner. In Hasan's account, we hear the now familiar sentiments about Jihad. Unlike the terrorists of September 11 who characterized their actions as a holy war against the infidels, Yasin:

[W]ill be talking about a different jihad—one known to Muslims, but often lost in political discourse. In the Koran, jihad refers to the internal struggle with oneself to do what is right and does not entail violence. It is a universal ideal.[17]

Accepting that it would be "naïve not to recognize the semantic tension," he continued, "a virtuous religious word has been perversely used by the likes of Osama bin Laden and his followers and now conjures up images of planes crashing into buildings."[18] Again, we should notice the way in which Osama bin Laden is perversely using the term. Hasan continued by making a broader argument for why Yasin was right to reclaim the word Jihad:

... [I]f we were to deny Mr. Yasin his use of the word, we would lose an opportunity to right some of the wrongs we have committed since September 11. In the aftermath of the terrible attacks, our nation became a less tolerant place. Suddenly racial profiling of Muslims, Arabs and South Asians became a good idea; detaining immigrants without due process became a necessary evil; and Islam became the ideology of our enemies. Harvard, a bastion of liberal thinking, was not immune to this wave of anger. Columns vilifying Islam and the Muslims appeared in the Harvard student newspaper, and many classmates callously referred to Islam as a violent religion.[19]

This shift in tone continues as he reiterated the view that Muslim-Americans not only have grief for the victims of September 11, but also for the "hijacking of their faith." As he explains it, "the healing process means mourning those who were killed in the terrorist attacks as well as reappropriating our religion from those who do harm to it."[20] Thus, the public commencement speech became a moment not merely to educate non-Muslims but also for Muslims to educate themselves.

Mr. Yasin's address about jihad is a step towards reclaiming what is ours. Muslim-Americans need to do this bit by bit, word by word, to show our fellow citizens that America has nothing to fear from Islam. Tolerance never comes easily. It often means learning about concepts that might initially seem painful or hostile. Such learning may well begin on commencement day, when my classmates will find there is no reason to fear a Muslim talking about the meaning of an Arabic word.[21]

This interesting interplay between the loss of lives and loss of the faith has been a recurrent theme in this public discourse. In a strange sense the claim is being made that September 11 is a double tragedy for Muslim-Americans— perhaps a triple tragedy with the correctly referred-to rise in negative attitudes toward Islam and the curtailments of civil liberties. The commencement speech became the moment to address those multiple tragedies, as the Harvard audience was transformed into a representative of the United States. That this element is the discourse frequently present in the media is significant, because it is indicative of the porous character of the hegemonic American narrative.

Throughout this story, individual Muslims whether it is Yasin or his advocate, Hasan, are presented in the media as representative of Muslims and of Muslim opinion. Their views on the complex question of Jihad appear to be endowed with authenticity, which is mainly due to their identity. It is noticeable that Jihad is constructed by the Muslim informants as being (1) rooted in the Quran, (2) an internal moral struggle, (3) a peaceful activity, and (4) that these essentials have been perverted by Osama bin Laden and al-Qaeda.[22] That the media circulated these views of Jihad undoubtedly provided a platform for the free speech of the Muslims concerned. However, what exactly is the status of these views, coming as they do from students of biomedical sciences and the like?

This fact was picked up by Daniel Pipes, a regular columnist and controversial Middle-East expert for the *New York Post*, who placed Yasin's speech in a lurid light:

[I]magine it's June 1942—just a few months after Adolf Hitler declared war on the United States. At Harvard University, a faculty committee has chosen a German-American to give one of the three student orations at the festive commencement ceremony. He titles it "American Kampf" purposefully echoing the tile of Hitler's book, "Mein Kampf" ("My struggle") in order to show the positive side of "kampf."[23]

His comments: "Far fetched? Sure. But exactly this scenario unfolded last week at Harvard. Just replace 'German,' 'Nazi,' and 'Kampf' with 'Islamic,' 'militant Islamic' and 'Jihad'.[24] Warming to his theme, Pipes continued:

Yasin titled his talk "American Jihad," echoing Osama bin Laden's jihad against the United States. Yasin declared his intention to convince his audience of 32,000 that "Jihad is not something that that should make some one feel uncomfortable."[25]

Pipes then mobilizes what he described as the "authoritative *Encyclopedia of Islam* to deliver the killer blow to Yasin's arguments about non-violent Jihad. The *Encyclopedia of Islam,* he explained, defines Jihad as "military action with the object of the expansion of Islam," and, furthermore, it "has principally an offensive character."[26] The reader is now perplexed: Is she to believe the Muslims presented in the *New York Times,* or the *Encyclopedia of Islam*? Indeed, Pipes is keen to assert that, for an unexplained reason, Harvard University and Middle-East experts at American universities in general hide "the truth about Jihad." The reader must be now even more perplexed as Pipes portrays himself as the keeper of special knowledge about the Middle East and Islam, while other experts are to be regarded as highly suspect. In this turmoil the reader may wonder how the *Encyclopedia of Islam* became so "authoritative."

Pipes does at least attempt to address this problem in his longer article for *Commentary*, pithily titled "Jihad and the Professors."[27] In this highly polemical piece he continues the argument that most American Middle-East academics see Jihad as streaming at least from a peaceful origin, and that "the portrait happens to be false." According to his self-selected survey of over two dozen experts, he tells us only one really accords with his own views. He produces his own potted history of Islam, complete with the 78 battles of the Prophet Mohammad, the Muslim expansion to Spain and India within a century of his death, through the Ottoman conquest of Constantinople in 1433, right up to the "triumph of Uthman dan Fodio in West Africa (1804–1815)." This, he says, tells a story that Jihad is entirely entwined into the character of Islam—"jihad was part of the warp and woof not only of pre-modern Muslim doctrine but of pre-modern Muslim life."[28] To take a leaf out of the Pipes method, remove the reference to Islamic history and replace it with European history concentrating on the Crusades, wars of colonial conquest, slavery, the Holocaust, and apartheid. From that, a rather grim picture of the West might emerge.[29] Pipes's entry into the public discourse is usefully illustrative of the difficulties with the past Orientalist discourses. They appear brittle in the context of societies that are no longer (if they ever were) culturally homogenous. The political rhetoric and episodic constitutional reality of free speech, equality before the law, and inclusiveness make exclusionary cultural narratives increasingly effective. Media representations of Islam since September 11 have underlined the imperatives and capacity to recast the dominant discourse.[30]

Taking the theme from Yasin, the media presented the issue as a debate about whether Jihad is peaceful or violent. This is indeed Yasin's main intention: to undermine the image of Islam as a violent religion and social system. However, while his use of the term as a struggle for justice and to do the right thing is accurate, it is rather defensive to deny that Jihad has other meanings and uses. This has been hinted at, but never explained. The assumption appears to be that once you accept that Jihad has military content at all, then September 11 becomes an example of Jihad and thus a Muslim holy war against the United States. Indeed, this is how Pipes's logic works: he attempts to discredit all those who regard Jihad as nonviolent by referring to Islam's history of wars. In this argument, Muslims have a violent past that stretches back over 14 centuries, and this results in an equally violent present of which

September 11 is merely the latest of a long list of Jihads. In this account, Pipes transforms all violence by Muslims into Jihad. Islamic law, however, does offer a sophisticated discourse that reveals how crude Pipes's argument is.

Yasin's arguments about Jihad being a struggle for justice are indeed rooted in Islamic culture and law. One of the reported sayings of the Prophet Mohammad is "the greatest Jihad is to speak openly in front of the prince." This is seen as an early articulation of the right to free speech. This Jihad as a means of advancing human rights has been seen by Islamic writers and activists as a key Islamic contribution to the international human rights debate.[31] However, the sources of Islamic jurisprudence are not static; rather, they need to be subjected to careful interpretation.[32]

The discussion of Jihad in the media has a superficial quality, in that only the most general propositions are advanced and debated. This superficiality is a common feature of any media treatment of legal issues, particularly those with technical issues associated with a long history—and especially those connected with the unfamiliar legal system. Jihad involves all three. In attempting to place the discussion within an Islamic jurisprudential framework, it is necessary to stress that, like all legal systems, Islamic law has many schools and many trends. It is erroneous to think of Islam as a solid social category that generates one definite legal system complete with a finished unchanging legal content or doctrine.[33] It is also significant to stress that Islamic law has developed through definite historical process, and, like all history, it is also open to different interpretations.[34] Bearing these conditions in mind, any investigation of Jihad takes us to the emergence of the Islamic law in the eighth century,[35] and in particular to the emergence of a special branch known as the *siyar*, which deals with international legal relations.[36]

Despite its divine origin in the revelations in the Quran, Islamic law is constructed by human agency. *Shari'a* (literally "the path"), is developed through the interweaving of a series of sources beginning with the Quran but being supplemented by the *sunna* (the traditions of the prophet), *ijma* (consensus of the jurists), *qiyas* (analogical argument), and *ijtihad* (independent legal reasoning). These sources of law are identified and defined through the emergence of jurists as the post-Prophetic Islamic polities are established, especially in the late Ummayad and early Abbasid periods (particularly in the later half of the eighth century).[37] The formation of the caste of jurists, known as Mujtihids (or the *fiquah*), is thus the social institution through which jurisprudence develops. In the same way, juristic techniques are brought to bear on the interpretation of the Quran and the particular verses *(surat)* that are seen as particularly relevant to legal issues. As Khaled Abou El

Fadl argues, "the jurists had become the repositories of literary, text-based legitimacy."[38]

As Islamic international law *(siyar)* developed in its classical form, it constructed a view of the world divided between the Islamic and Non-Islamic powers, known in Arabic as the *dar al Islam* (the territory of Islam) and the *dar al harb* (the territory of war).[39] International legal relations were mainly seen through this worldview. The use of force was seen by the jurists as largely undesirable.[40] However, rather like contemporary approaches to the topic,[41] they attempted to create criteria that could be used to justify its use while at the same time developing a system of constraints.[42] As Majid Khadduri points out, most jurists agreed that the use of force, or Jihad, in the military sense could be justified in self-defense and could be used only for the purpose of spreading Islam.[43] The latter proposition becomes confused with the obligation of Muslims, individually and collectively, to spread Islam. In this sense, Jihad thus works at two levels: Muslims must make every effort to extend the influence of Islam, and governments must not use force for Non-Islamic purposes. It is perhaps at this point that governments for political purposes in the classical Islamic period conveniently dovetail the two propositions in order to provide an Islamic gloss for military actions. This is not unlike the manner in which governments throughout the past century have used religious authority and political values: to justify the use of force, to protect democracy and lives, or in the current period, to defeat terrorism. Islamic legal discourses in the field of international relations are as imbricated with politics as are those in the West.[44]

The development of the Jihad within the *siyar* is the result of the creation of a system of regulation for the use of force under the control of the political authorities. The classical works all make the point that the Jihad is a collective, but not universal, obligation. Not all Muslims have to take part in it, and indeed it is obligatory that some Muslims remain at home. Ibn Khaldun relies on the Quranic injunction that "and the believers should not all go out to fight. Of every troop of them, a party only should go out."[45] As this makes clear, Jihad is an organized mechanism and it requires the sanction and activity of the structured Islamic community—its government. Jihad as it has been used by Osama bin Laden and a whole host of self-proclaimed Islamist groups is thus not just a perversion of the idea of Jihad as a struggle for social justice, but is also being misused even in the military sense. Worse, it is quite clear that a carefully developed corpus of restraint prohibits the use of force against unarmed civilians and against other Muslims. Shaybani refers to the Prophet Mohammad's authority on this point: "Fight in the name of God and in the 'path of God.' Combat only those who disbelieve in God. Do not cheat or commit treachery nor should you mutilate anyone or kill children."[46] At other times, the Prophet also prohibits the killing of women and aged men.[47] What is central to this classical view of Jihad is the enemies against whom it is to be waged are polytheists. It is not against other peoples of the book, such as Jews and Christians—and the jurisprudence developed to include other believers such as Zoroastrians.

This issue of Jihad then is not a debate about whether it might encompass violence but rather how violence is regulated by international Islamic jurisprudence. This issue of regulation entirely escapes those who believe that an individual Muslim or any group of Muslims is able to use violence against the enemy with a divine sanction. As we have seen, this is far from the case. The *siyar* is itself a constraining influence on the behavior of the Imam, the political leader of the Islamic state. Jihad can only be waged by the authorities. It has to be said that knowledge of the *siyar* is limited among the Muslim general public, and relatively few scholars are seriously engaged in its study.

This is in part due to the way in which colonialism marginalized non-Western legal systems, and in particular any areas of the colonized law dealing with power and international relations.[48] An example of this can be seen in the way in which the British in India edited Charles Hamilton's translation of the Hedaya, the leading text of the Hanafi school of jurisprudence,[49] by omitting the chapter on the *siyar* from its second edition, which was published in 1870.[50] This English edition continues to circulate in India, Pakistan, Bangladesh, and Malaysia today, with the references to international law—including Jihad—removed. Indeed, colonization in much of the Muslim world, and the Europeanization of Islamic law in the Ottoman Empire and Persia at the end of the nineteenth century, saw the decline of Islamic legal reasoning and Islamic juristic concepts of power as Islamic law was reduced to mainly family and personal-status law and enframed within Western court systems (and in the case of the Ottoman Empire and Persia, within Western-type constitutions). For much of the twentieth century Islamic law appeared as essentially private law applied in *Shari'a* courts outside the main legal system. This inevitably gave the appearance that Islamic law was a customary system in the hands of some rather lowly judges at best. The Europeanization of law undermined the Islamic jurisprudence on governance *(siyassa)* and on international law *(siyar)* through removing the dynamic element of the Islamic legal system, the *fiquah,* the collective strata of jurists—not necessarily part of the judiciary, but located in civil society institutions such as universities. The breaking of Islamic power had a profound influence on the way in which Islamic law developed and also on the way in which it could be portrayed. Islamic legal authority could easily be portrayed in the mass media—and also in some academic works[51]—as a customary folkish system. As a consequence, the idea that Jihad was a power endowed in state authorities was replaced by self-styled Muslim leaders issuing *fatwas* declaring a Jihad against any opposing political force. This necessarily trivialized the carefully constructed jurisprudence in the *siyar*. Islamic law, whose authority was invoked when this "Jihad" was declared, was debased as it became a crass veneer for gang warfare and assignations.

Zeyad Yasin's speech, while not reconnecting the Islamic word to this rich Islamic jurisprudence, nonetheless created a debate. In a globalized world the story was picked and debated in Europe and the Islamic world.[52] It is interesting that the media coverage from the Islamic world was among the most critical. In news from Bangladesh, A. H. Jaffor Ullah begins, "[L]et us all agree that Jihad and Jihadism is not an innocuous term." He takes Yasin to task for not explaining that Jihad has a military aspect by, among other things, quoting from the "*fatwa*" issued by Osama bin Laden, saying, "the ruling is to kill the Americans and their allies is the individual duty for every Muslim who can do it, in order to liberate the Al Aqsa Mosque [Jerusalem] and the Holy Mosque [Mecca]." Ullah praises Yasin for calling for a fairer word, but castigates him for his use of Jihad. "[T]he likes of Zeyad Yasin should stick to the prevalent meaning of the word Jihad, which is well known to us."[53] Tashbih Sayyed, in *Pakistan Today*, is no less harsh in his criticism of Yasin. He, however, poses the argument in more subtle terms, arguing that there has been a long practice of Muslims misusing the concept. In his account "incrementally, and over centuries, the Islamist clergy and scholars brainwashed the unsuspecting Muslim main street into the belief that the true jihad is carried out only with the sword (Jihad-bis-Saif)."[54] This, he argues, has led to the use of force against civilians by various Muslim groups. He concludes:

Zeyad Yasin has to speak up against this tyranny of extremism and the Fascist manipulation of Islam, which has prevented the Muslims from learning about its noble principles. Let alone the rest of the world. He will have to condemn acts of terrorism carried out in the name of jihad in places like Palestine and Kashmir before any one can begin to believe him or his faith.[55]

The way in which our globalized media can carry the same story but with different narratives is a healthy indication that international culture is far from homogenized. In Pakistan, the ringing denunciation of the way Jihad is used for terrorism is neatly set against Americans' hearing that Jihad can be a peaceful form of struggle for justice. It would, of course, be far fetched to argue that fleeting images on television or column inches in newspapers necessarily become a permanent feature of public consciousness. However, the story of Zeyad Yasin's short speech reveals that the settled and stereotyped images of Muslims, Islamic culture, and Islamic law are now highly problematic in our post-9-11 world. Perhaps the most important discursive image that emerges from the media is that Islamic law—including Jihad—is not rigid and unchangeable but subject to multiple interpretations. Yasin's own Jihad to give his speech might not have been in vain.

Between Enemies and Traitors: Black Press Coverage of September 11 and the Predicaments of National "Others"

Roopali Mukherjee

I just thought of myself as black. But now I feel like I'm an American, more than ever.
> —Louis Johnson, Trinidadian American, 18,
> resident of Fort Greene, Brooklyn, New York

I'm sorry people died. But I can't get upset when someone hijacks a plane and someone has hijacked the goddamn government.
> —Mary, African American WPFW-FM radio listener

The "war on terror" is making war not on acts of terror, but on things that terrify us. In this war of the mind, the enemy is apt to become anybody who makes us afraid.
> —Patricia Williams, critical race theorist and Harvard law professor

The predicaments of those who are named "national others" and "state enemies" may be likened to a game of musical chairs, with each player making a run for inclusion into the coveted seated circle and collaborating in exclusionary tactics against those who are left standing. The game of musical chairs serves as an effective metonym for the politics of racial/ethnic difference in the United States for, as the game proceeds, the number of chairs available is reduced at each turn. Thus, the number of players who can find seats diminishes until the field is cleared to a single seated winner. If the events of September 11, 2001, have, however temporarily, offered black Americans a reprieve from racial profiling, and if, as some have suggested, the language of racial grievance has shifted overnight from cries about "driving while black" to "flying while brown,"[1] we may be witness to critical shifts in who finally manages to snag a seat in the national-racial game of musical chairs and who is left standing—the new losers against whom a variety of tactics of exclusion and elimination may now be deployed.

As is evinced in Louis Johnson's admission above, the events of September 11 have enabled some black Americans to "feel like Americans, more than ever." A series of questions emerge from such a declaration about the vicious plays of "belonging" and "othering" that have followed in the wake of the attacks. Furthermore, it is estimated that African Americans make up nearly one-third of the four million Muslims who live in the United States. Given these complex imbrications along ethnic, religious, and class lines—solidarities, antagonisms, and ambivalences—this essay seeks to understand the precarious politics of differences that characterize relations between African Americans and Muslim/Arab Americans as they are highlighted in the aftermath of September 11, 2001.

As is always the case, the black response to the attacks of September 11 is a complex and diverse one. By presenting themes and contradictions within black press coverage of the attacks, this essay seeks to understand shifting modes of complicity, contestation, and resistance revealed in "minority" responses to September 11. As hegemonic discourses of patriotism, national unity, and vengeful militarization create media spectacles of Arab and Muslim culpability for the "attack on America," this essay examines the complex positioning of black Americans within that national imaginary to highlight the ethno-racial valences of Americanness and embedded racial logics of the American nation.

I present a brief analysis of black press coverage over the course of the year following September 11, 2001. As scholars have argued, black newsweeklies and magazines remain key sites of hegemonic contestation, providing public spaces for dialogue, deliberation, and dissent among African Americans.[2] As Ronald Jacobs explains, "historically, the black press has served three important functions: providing a forum for debate and self-improvement, monitoring the mainstream press, and increasing black visibility in white civil society."[3] Given the paucity of diverse voices and viewpoints in the mainstream news, the black press serves as one of the few sites of vibrant exchange on questions of terrorism, patriotism, and war at the present time.

Focusing on a number of regional black newspapers,[4] I present an analysis of broad themes that emerge within news accounts from the post-9-11 period. Brief analyses of three themes are presented in the remainder of this essay, with careful attention to the ways in which they reconstitute familiar and resonant strains within black political discourse. They include first, super-patriots and their detractors; second, the black American as witness, conscience, and keeper; and finally, the promise and peril of interethnic solidarity.

"SUPER-PATRIOTS" AND THEIR DETRACTORS

Since the day of the 9-11 attacks, Americans have emerged in numbers sporting red, white, and blue flag T-shirts, baseball caps, designer purses, and jewelry, and claiming a newfound patriotism and spirit of unity. These public avowals, however, have celebrated a narrowly defined and hegemonic "super-patriotism,"[5] and have been accompanied by a series of vicious and violent attacks on "Arab-looking" people, as well as incidents of vengeful retribution against visible "others" perceived by untrained eyes to be suspect in the attack.

The most common among these retaliations are tactics of exclusion, "othering," and humiliation reported by scores of Muslim/Arab Americans since September 11, and include verbal assaults, vandalism, workplace harassment, and boycotts of Arab-owned shops and businesses. News sources have reported several instances of passenger panics where individuals with Middle Eastern names or appearances have been refused seats on airplanes because crew and passengers alike claim "they do not feel safe flying with them."[6] Thus, Ashraf Khan, a 32-year-old Pakistani-American in a first-class seat, was asked by a pilot to leave a Delta Airlines flight from San Antonio to Dallas during the first few weeks after September 11. Similarly, when four Jordanian men were barred from boarding a Delta Airlines flight from Cincinnati to Las Vegas, security officials explained it was because they had received "complaints from the crew and the captain."[7]

As Muslims and Arab Americans are left to make a myriad of self-conscious calculations to not speak in Arabic as they wait for their flights at airports nationwide, to not travel with their copies of the Quran or in groups of more than two or three, and to accept delays, humiliations, and targeted harassment as part of their travel experiences,[8] Hussein Ibish, spokesman for the American-Arab Anti-Discrimination Committee in Washington, explains that these passengers pass rigorous airport security checks "only to be taken off planes or prevented from boarding at the last minute."[9] Beyond the legal concerns, Ibish argues, such behavior toward Arab Americans raises moral questions, for nothing but racism can explain the targeted harassment described in these cases.

When three Utah residents of Middle Eastern descent were barred from boarding a Northwest Airlines flight to "reduce the effect of a situation on board where some passengers were so uncomfortable with their presence that the flight would have been delayed or canceled,"[10] Utah Attorney General Mark Shurtleff threatened to sue Northwest Airlines to send a message to the airlines and other businesses that his state would not tolerate such discrimination. In response, Shurtleff received "a flood of angry phone calls and blistering e-mail messages from across the country denouncing his defense of the passengers."[11] Claims to a newfound American unity since the 9-11 attacks, thus, turn on racist standards of "otherness," ensuring an uneasy tolerance and solidarity among those within the hegemonic circle, but various forms of violent retribution, ridicule, and suspicion against those outside it.[12]

The racialized anxieties spurring these passenger panics reappear in a recent incident involving Eunice Stone, who, while eating in a Shoney's restaurant in Calhoun, Georgia, reported that she overheard three men of Middle Eastern descent "making suspicious comments about the September 11 terrorist attacks." The three men turned out to be medical students, two of them American citizens, and the third a legal immigrant, who had not mentioned the 9-11 attacks once during their conversation at the restaurant. News reports revealed that they were on their way to study at the Larkin Community Hospital in Miami, Florida. But after their detainment by law enforcement personnel, they were informed by officials at the Miami hospital that, "they were no longer welcome there."[13]

When she learned the truth, Stone claimed her innocence stating: "I am not a racist, and I am not ignorant. I was just trying to do what's best [for America]."[14] The terms of super-patriotism, thus, tolerate racisms that would under other circumstances be cloaked and more subdued. For Michael Parenti, such "inverted moralities" typify the logics of super-patriotism, which he defines as "the tendency to place nationalistic pride and supremacy over every other public consideration, including a readiness to follow leaders uncritically in their dealings with other countries, especially confrontations involving the use of U.S. military force and violence."[15] Thus, the resurgent super-patriotisms of the moment condone an openness and acceptance of the racist terms of Americanness that otherwise typically circulate at a more subterranean level.

The terms and costs of such a reactionary super-patriotism are at their gravest in reports of deadly vigilantism, as in the case of Balbir Singh Sodhi, a 49-year-old gas station owner in Arizona. Sodhi, a South Asian Sikh American, wore a traditional turban and beard, and was shot to death outside his business in suburban Phoenix.[16] Frank Silva Roque, the 42-year-old aircraft machinist who was indicted for Sodhi's murder, shouted to reporters as he was being arrested, "I am a patriot, an American...I'm a damn American all the way. Arrest me and let those terrorists run wild."[17] Post-9-11 renewals of super-patriotic unity thus premise themselves on narrowly defined standards of patriotism and "love of country," demarcating in hyper-racial terms the difference between those who are American and those who are not.

Vicious plays of belonging and "othering" complicate this narrative of super-patriotism. Although news accounts have made little mention of it, Frank Silva Roque, the man indicted for the deadly attack on Sodhi, is a Mexican American. And similarly, some African Americans have been reported among angry mobs that have targeted Arab Americans in the days following September 11. As Richard Hatcher, attorney and former mayor of Gary, Indiana reported at a public forum organized by the Rainbow/PUSH Coalition: "Even though Gary's population is 85 percent Black, Arab Americans who live there have been victimized by hate crimes."[18]

There are numerous stories of black popular conformance with the mainstream super-patriotic response to September 11. Darnetta Lawson, a black resident of Oakland, California, for instance, was quoted in the *Sun Reporter* suggesting, "I think we need to start deporting all these Arabs. They are owning all the businesses in our community."[19] Similarly, Howard Baker urged, "We have to be Americans. Not Black Americans because when those planes hit those buildings in New York and Washington, those people who hijacked the planes didn't care if blacks were in those places and blacks were, because we are Americans."[20]

While Charles Muhammad of San Leandro, California, a black Muslim, urged African Americans not to overreact to media reports because "black people should know...better than anyone, given our history of dealing with racism and prejudice in this country," Philip Johnson, an African American truck driver from Oakland, California disagreed, announcing his allegiances as follows: "This is not going to put us on the side of the Arabs. I have a friend who works two blocks from the World Trade Center and another friend is a fireman in New York City."[21]

If, as scholars have noted, new immigrants seek, discursively and culturally, to gain entry into the coveted circle of Americanness by articulating their differences from African Americans, by learning the logics of American racism that locate black Americans perpetually and reliably "at the bottom of the well," as outsiders, others, and deviants,[22] the foregoing black responses to the events of September 11 serve precisely contrary ends. This time, African Americans are enabled a claim to Americanness by articulating discursive and cultural distance from Arabs, Arab Americans, and Muslim Americans. Thus, September 11 and its consequent demonization of Arabs/Arab Americans ironically enable African Americans, however temporarily, to a share in the dividends of the ethno-racial valences of Americanness.

As the resurgent super-patriotism of the moment reveals the racial logics of the lines between "real" Americans and those who are not, Ron Walters, writing for the *Indianapolis Recorder*, urged African Americans to be particularly vigilant of such zealous strains within public discourse for, as he argued, "these new super-patriots are also ultra-nationalists bent on using this moment of crisis to enhance their racial privilege."[23] Walters cautioned that the "Go back to Africa" taunts of the past directed at black Americans are analogous to the ethnic profiling and harassment of Arabs and Arab Americans at the present moment, and that the spurious message of "such hyper-Americanism has always been that 'real' Americans are white and that all others are suspect."[24]

Such critiques of the circulating super-patriotism of the moment have spurred debates among African Americans about national solidarity and black acquiescence. Robert Starks, Northeastern Illinois University professor, argued at a forum at the Harold Washington Institute that, "when the boat is rocking, they want us all to be patriotic and hug and love each other, but when the seas are calm and the boat is running well, they want to throw us overboard."[25] Black news accounts identify the pressure toward patriotic unanimity as particularly alarming because:

Suddenly, and perhaps for some time to come, guns will trump butter, security fears will trump civil liberties and civil rights concerns, American unity will trump dissenting critiques of how well America lives up to its own ideals, and the nation will rally around a president whom many black Americans, at least until September 11, considered unsympathetic and even illegitimate.[26]

The black press and black popular opinion polls both reflect a deep ambivalence on this point. One Gallup survey conducted in the immediate aftermath of the 9-11 attacks found that black respondents were more likely than whites to be suspicious of Arabs and believe that all Arabs—even those who are U.S. citizens—should be required to carry identification cards.[27] But another poll conducted in early October 2001 by the Pew Research Center for People and the Press reported that, "twenty percent of African Americans surveyed—compared with six percent of whites—did not support the President's military assault; another seventeen percent of blacks—but only eleven percent of whites—were undecided.[28] And more recent polls have revealed that while the overwhelming majority of Americans stand with George W. Bush on the question of the "war on terrorism," a large proportion of African Americans are considerably less enthusiastic in their response to White House proposals.

These divisions point to a deep and abiding "ambivalence about patriotism" among black Americans that is based on the nation's abysmal record on racial justice.[29] Quoting from the November/December 2001 issue of *Crisis*, Larry Aubry explains that historically, "wartime has been a source of patriotism and pragmatic idealism" for black Americans. "Blacks have fought for the ideals of the U.S. Constitution in the hope of winning the full citizenship they had long been denied, a kind of bartering of black blood for equality." And further, black patriotism "has always been a matter of balancing the perils of racism with a promise of America." As Harriet Lowery, a black resident of Unionville, Maryland suggested, "all the current flag-waving makes me uneasy and the talk of one America rings hollow... It's a bit hypocritical." Thus, Aubry concludes, "black Americans have filtered this national crisis through the terror of church bombings and lynching of our collective past and the problems of our present."[30]

Black press reportage of the events of September 11 falls in line with such a complicated and contested patriotism. Carefully balancing their critique of "monstrous, historic United States oppression" with condemnations of the "massive taking of lives, and destruction of family life" by al-Qaeda members, activist organizations like the Provisional Government of the Republic of New Afrika issued public statements arguing that in all their fights, African people in the United States had "never, never fought [their] oppression by killing great masses of people."[31] As Rotan Lee clarifies:

To suggest that black criticism of the president's response to the September 11 attack on America... reflects disloyalty even treason skirts the issue... That people of color always seem culpable... that many African Americans believe that the Palestinians have a raw deal and not much respect, that Israel's Ariel Sharon is a misguided demagogue, that the CIA and the FBI operate too covertly and abusively, that racism is alive and well, and that America's foreign policy is unenlightened does not equate to sedition.[32]

Urging a reasoned patriotism, as opposed to the fervent zeal that mainstream America has enunciated, black Muslims in particular navigate a precarious field. Recalling W.E.B. DuBois's caution that black Americans are characterized by a "twoness—an American and a Negro, two souls, two thoughts, two un-reconciled strivings; two warring ideals in one dark body, whose dogged strength alone keeps it from being torn asunder," Askia Muhammad admonishes al-Qaeda leader Osama bin Laden, stating, "Your fight is not in my name," and in the same breath, George W. Bush, saying, "This may very well be my country, but this is certainly not my war."[33]

As the super-patriotic fervor of the moment enlists Americans across racial, ethnic, and class lines in the service of retaliatory militarism and American supremacy, what Parenti refers to as the 'number one' syndrome,"[34] African American voices negotiate a precarious position between treason and collaboration, enemy and ally, variously proffering bold critiques of hegemonic patriotism and a racial opportunism that for once enables them, however temporarily, a coveted seat among the "real" Americans.

THE BLACK AMERICAN AS WITNESS, CONSCIENCE, AND KEEPER

As black news sources note a growing reticence among African Americans on the White House's escalating "war against terrorism," a significant number of these stories have focused on the unique position of black Americans to temper and illuminate the ethical questions at play in the debate over patriotism, war, and political dissent. These accounts locate African Americans as witnesses to the record of "homegrown terrorism" in America who are thus uniquely equipped to expose American hypocrisies, double standards, and deceptions. Similarly, these accounts have positioned black Americans as the mythic conscience of the nation and ethical keepers of American values and ideals who are uniquely capable of "press[ing] America to be what it professes to be."

Holding a mirror to domestic human rights policy, Vernon E. Jordan, Clinton confidante and high-power attorney, who drew media attention at the peak of the Monica Lewinsky scandal in 1998, argued in a much-publicized speech delivered at Howard University's Rankin Memorial Chapel that, "none of this is new to black people. War, hunger, disease, unemployment, deprivation, dehumanization, and terrorism define our existence. They are not new to us."[35] He continued:

Slavery was terrorism, segregation was terrorism, the bombing of four little girls in Sunday school in Birmingham was terrorism. The violent deaths of Medgar, Martin, Malcolm, Vernon Dahmer, Cheney, Schwerner, Goodman were terrorism.[36]

Such witnesses to the "homegrown terrorism of America" included former Illinois Appellate Court Justice R. Eugene Pincham, who argued that victims of racial hatred from American history deserved shrines to their memory, much like the victims of the terror attacks of September 11. Urging attention to the "terrorism against black Americans by white terrorists," Pincham declared that, "we are just as appalled at the destruction of the WTC and the loss of those lives as anybody else but we must bring to America's attention not only the WTC but the terrorism under which we've lived in this country for over 40 years."[37] Thus, the Black Radical Congress stated:

From the amputations, beatings, and rapes of chattel slavery, to the New York City Draft Riots of 1863, to the post-Reconstruction terrorism of the Ku Klux Klan, to the Tulsa Riots of 1921, to the government sponsored Counterintelligence Program of the 1960s, to the contemporary state-sanctioned murder and brutality we are fighting today, we as black people have lots of experience with the horrors of terrorism in the U.S., as it has too frequently been directed against us.[38]

Black news sources drew attention to "the many terrorist acts that our government has committed against many nations around the world and domestically,"[39] arguing that "there is no need to fight a war for democracy, if we do not fight for democracy at home."[40] As one writer for the *New York Voice* put it, "it is important to remember our own American brand of terrorism. More than 3,000 died in the World Trade Center and Pentagon attacks. But an estimated 4,742 black men and women died by lynching between 1882 and 1968."[41]

Tempering patriotic zeal, these reminders of American brutality serve as counter knowledges—what John Fiske refers to as "blackstream knowledge"—which is "produced by recovering facts, events, and bits of information the dominant knowledge has repressed or dismissed as insignificant."[42] Thus, the New Afrikan People's Organization placed full responsibility for American deaths in the 9-11 attacks on the U.S. government, suggesting that "this terrorist monster is one created by the United States government, which like the mythical Frankenstein's monster has turned on its own maker."[43] In step with the highly controversial poem, "Somebody blew up America," by Amiri Baraka, poet laureate of the state of New Jersey, which speculated that the U.S. government had prior knowledge of the 9-11 attacks and had deliberately done little to thwart them,[44] the New Afrikan People's Organization argued that:

It is the United States government that trained people like Manuel Noriega in Panama, Saddam Hussein in Iraq, Osama bin Laden and the Taliban in Afghanistan to murder and terrorize innocent civilians...American bombs have also murdered millions of innocent civilians in Hiroshima and Nagasaki, Libya, Vietnam, the Sudan...They, like us, have been "victims of Americanism"...And now the "chickens have come home to roost," as Malcolm X taught us.[45]

Along similar lines, William Raspberry argued in an article in the *Miami Times* that the current war on terrorism highlights key analogies between al-

Qaeda members and black Americans. Despite their differences,[46] Raspberry focused on critical analogies between the hijackers of September 11 and black Americans in terms of their relationship with the American nation. For instance, Raspberry explained, foreign terrorists and American blacks alike have sought to uncover the disjuncture between "America the ideal and America the hypocrite."[47] The main tactic of the American civil rights movement, Raspberry explained, was "to press America to be what it professed to be by demonstrating with telegenic clarity that it was not."

Black Americans during the sixties were faced with choosing between black militants and radicals demanding change on the one hand, and patriotic commitments to nation on the other. Raspberry recalled that the more white Americans resisted, the more black Americans were inclined to give tacit support and safe haven to the militants. Thus, much like the predicaments black Americans faced during the civil rights era, Islamic militants and Muslim and Arab citizens around the world may be faced with a similar, complicated choice between the hypocrisies of American foreign policy that has ravaged the Third World and the Islamic world in particular over the past two decades, and commitments to their country, religion, and each other. Given that black Americans did not waver in their demands for social change, and given that white recidivism during the sixties produced a generation of black radicals and revolutionaries, Raspberry wonders if we might expect a similar stance from Muslims and Arabs until major changes are instituted.

These critical and cautionary tales serve to expose the nation's domestic record of oppressions, brutalities, and terrorisms, and demand accountability from mainstream America for crimes it has committed and for which no retributions or compensations have been tendered. Several articles noted that the United States (along with Israel) had canceled its delegation to the World Conference Against Racism that had convened in Durban, South Africa a few weeks before the terror attacks of September 11. Among those who called in to express themselves on *Soul Beat TV* in Oakland, California, one stated, "Everyone is praying, but when America walked out of the [Durban] conference we were telling the world we didn't care what they thought, we can do what we want."[48]

Calling the United States out on its historical and continuing record of oppressions against African Americans and its disregard for widespread concerns over the twin legacies of racism and imperialism, black press accounts tempered self-righteous appeals by American political leaders for global unity against the "evil doers" of al-Qaeda. Thus, as Donald Jones argued, "We owe the many who have died something more than revenge, more than a gun fight, more than the Wyatt Earp like determination to get an outlaw 'dead or alive.' We owe those who have died, the creation of conditions for true broth-erhood between East and West."[49]

Recounting details from a past that might otherwise be eclipsed by the vengeful rush to condemn those responsible for the "unprovoked attack on America," these black American voices worked to construct an "oppositional knowledge" that stands apart from hegemonic discourses of super-patriotism currently in sway.[50] Recovering a record of racial profiling, discriminatory prison sentences, and threats of violence and intimidation by groups like the Ku Klux Klan and skinheads that is repressed in official knowledges, such black press accounts expose a "hypocritical, braggadocios attitude," as Libby Clark puts it, which "finds the United States trying to convince the rest of the world of the merits of its democracy, while denying vast segments of its minorities the rights and privileges indicative of liberty, justice, and free-dom."[51] As the Reverend Graylan Hagler, pastor of Plymouth Congregational Church in Washington, D.C., put it: "The dirt done at home is reflective of the dirt done abroad."[52]

Highlighting the consequences of the "war against terrorism" for Ameri-cans, and black Americans in particular, a significant number of black news stories voiced concerns about the impact of new federal policies that would "undercut protections that we fought so long to ensure."[53] As unrestrained computer and electronic surveillance, telephone interceptions, regular de-mands for personal identification, and limitations on travel and movement are instituted in the interests of counter-terrorism, these mechanisms, black voices argued, would exact a heavy price from Americans, and African Amer-icans in particular.

Thus, recalling the dangers of civil rights violations against black leaders like Martin Luther King, Jr. during the sixties, the Reverend Jesse L. Jackson urged action against "homegrown terrorism" embedded in U.S. Attorney General John Ashcroft's anti-terrorism measures. Jackson pleaded: "For civil rights, we marched so much, bled so profusely, and died so young. We can-not let Mr. Ashcroft take through fiat what so many martyrs died for."[54]

As state officials "busily lock down on America and institute more strenu-ous security procedures in areas that have no apparent relationship with ter-rorism," Howard University professor Ron Walters explained, they are being cheered on by Americans who believe that such measures would provide greater security, and enable authorities to react more effectively to potential threats.[55] But given American law-enforcement authorities' record of brutal-ity against black citizens in particular,[56] Donald Jones asked, "Would the power of law enforcement agents and agencies, extended after September 11 in the name of national security, facilitate worse forms of 'domestic terror'?"[57]

Opinion polls conducted since the attacks have shown that "attitudes of New Yorkers toward law enforcement officers" have changed significantly since September 11. While "sixty-six percent of blacks, and fifty-nine percent of Hispanics said that the police gave white New Yorkers preferential treatment compared to people of other races, over all, public approval for the job done by New York's police officers soared...Most strikingly, fifty percent of blacks and fifty-two percent of Hispanics credited the police with doing a good or excellent job."[58] By contrast, a poll taken in April 2000, about a month after four police officers were acquitted in the shooting death of nineteen-year-old African immigrant, Amadou Diallo, reported that "a mere twelve percent of blacks and twenty-six percent of Hispanics gave the police such high marks."[59]

Kevin Pough, an office manager at a Manhattan law firm, lucidly expressed the ambivalence of these new feelings, a wary comfort and confidence in law enforcement, as follows:

When I used to go home, it was nothing for me to be stopped, put against a wall, patted down. Since Diallo, they still stopped me—they stopped me last month—but it's no more of that attitude like I'm automatically a bad guy, like I'm a criminal. It's not, "Hey you, get against the damned fence." Maybe it's just an illusion...but when I talk to people, they're not looking at me as a black person anymore...But now we're singling out Arabs. They're coming under scrutiny, like we were. We're on the other side now, looking out and saying, 'That's the way we were treated,' and we're on the same side as the ones who treated us that way.[60]

Expressing concern that while they are intended at the present moment for monitoring Arabs and Arab Americans—the new enemies of the state—black voices argued further that new federal security measures would ultimately find their "resting place on the backs of those of us who are already victimized and suspect": black Americans.[61] In the same vein, a group of 19 African American Congressional representatives, voting against federal anti-terrorism legislation proposed by the White House, argued that, "our nation's tradition of civil liberties will be sacrificed at the altar of our war on terrorism."[62] They warned that the proposed policy changes would force the nation to "succumb to tyranny from within," and that "without checks and balances on the people in power, we black Americans, just because of our color, will be the first to feel the wrath of power-wielding government officials."[63]

Beyond the ways that these newly devised tactics of counter-terrorism would burden the lives of black Americans with increased surveillance, discipline, and control, black news accounts also appealed to the unique responsibility of African Americans to watch over the nation by serving as its mythic conscience. Positioning blacks as "the only ones who [have] held American values dearly," and as uniquely capable of shepherding the nation, psychically and spiritually, through a time of crisis, Vernon Jordan explained: "When this nation was in the grip of racism and segregation, it was black people who reminded America of its basic values of freedom and democracy. It was black Americans who helped America close the gap between its beliefs and its practices."[64]

Thus, for Jordan, "now that America is warring on terrorism, it is black people who remind America that we know terrorism well" and that the surest defense against terrorism is "affirmation of American basic values, the values we [African Americans] have learned in our churches, the values we have fought and died for in America's every war, even in segregated armies."[65] Thus, as witnesses to the nation's legacy of shameful violence, as the consciences of a nation as guilty as its foes, and as keepers of cherished national values, black Americans—and their efforts at producing oppositional knowledges of war, militarism, and patriotism—serve as muckrakers and whistle blowers of the present.

These efforts within black news accounts position the black American as mythic keeper and conscience with unique responsibilities to steer a "lost" and despairing America to act rationally and conscientiously, bearing a keen resemblance to Hollywood representations of the nineties that portray African Americans and "blackstream knowledge" as restoratives that nurture back to wholeness and innocence "lost" or fallen white protagonists. Thus, a young white hero who is fated to save the world from a post-apocalyptic stupor orchestrated by a malevolent cyber-intelligence relies upon the serene tutelage of a black caretaker in *The Matrix.* In *The Green Mile,* a white death-row guard, losing both faith and sanity, is miraculously restored after contact with a gentle black giant wrongly condemned for crimes he did not commit. And a disillusioned war veteran and golfer finds he is able to shed his psychic malaise and retrieve his "authentic swing" with help from a magical black caddy who enters his life in *The Legend of Baggar Vance.*[66]

This positioning of black characters as "caretakers" serving to rehabilitate white protagonists out of crisis and collapse is a familiar trope. As David Levering Lewis argues, "the role of the African American as surrogate for the troubles and malefactions of white people is as old as the Republic, a part carefully scripted in the antebellum South and archetypally acted out in American literature from Harriet Beecher Stowe to William Faulkner and beyond."[67] Cinematic representations of the nineties have followed in this tradition from *Ghost* (Jerry Zucker, 1990) and *Passion Fish* (John Sayles,

1992) onward through *Bulworth* (Warren Beatty, 1998), *Black & White* (James Toback, 1999), and *Save the Last Dance* (Thomas Carter, 2001), as black characters in mainstream films are placed repeatedly in the role of "counsel," "caretaker," and "spiritual guide."[68]

What this comparison to black news accounts of September 11 reveals, however, is that as long as cinematic texts locate the soulful black healer in heroic servitude, s/he is guaranteed success in her/his efforts to restore whiteness and, by extension, the American nation to spiritual, psychic, and mental health. But deployed by critical black voices toward oppositional and dissenting political ends, these repositories of lost insights and "blackstream" wisdom remain illegitimate and marginal, their counsel impractical and dangerous. Whistle blowers, after all, cannot be mistaken for caretakers, and the fantasy of racial codependence that has played out in cinematic texts of the nineties runs aground in the context of black dissonance with hegemonic militarisms of the moment.

The racial logic of the positions that African Americans occupy in the national imaginary tells a familiar story of the consequences of cultural and ideological non-conformance. When African Americans urge spiritual and psychic reform on the part of whites to restore the supremacist hierarchies of the American nation, to return white Americans to positions of leadership and control, their voices receive an ample hearing within mainstream cultural discourses. But, when they demand changes to the supremacist logics of the American nation—asking the United States to abandon imperialist foreign policies, racist trade agreements, and to correct its shameful domestic record on human rights—African American voices are, once again, repressed or dismissed as insignificant.

THE PROMISE AND PERIL OF INTERETHNIC SOLIDARITY

At the luncheon panel "The impact of foreign policy on Arab Americans," organized by the American-Arab Anti-Defamation Committee in July 2001, roughly one month *before* the attacks of September 11, African American Congresswoman Cynthia McKinney (D-GA) made a passionate speech urging African Americans and Arab Americans to develop the "special bonds" that existed between them. Providing historical detail on the U.S. government's efforts to "ensure that a potential alliance between these two minority groups did not develop," McKinney recounted how memos produced by the FBI's COINTELPRO program during the sixties expressed concern that "the emergence of an independent African American leadership would almost certainly side with the Arabs and not Israel."[69] McKinney quoted one such memo, which stated:

Taking into account the African descent of American blacks, it is reasonable to antic-ipate that their sympathies would lie with the Arabs who are closer to them in spirit and in some cases related to them by blood. Black involvement in lobbying to sup-port the Arabs may lead to serious dissension between American blacks and Jews.[70]

Offering historical detail on such state efforts to frustrate Arab-black coali-tions, McKinney urged Arab Americans and African Americans to "do more to connect and help each other since they share the same problems and his-tory."[71] Her speech, thus, presaged a number of key concerns about inter-ethnic solidarity among Arab and African Americans that would gain promi-nence after September 11.

Focusing on the developing practice of "terrorist profiling" or "country-of-origin profiling,"[72] as a result of which hundreds of young Arabs were rounded up by law enforcement and intelligence officials in the aftermath of the attacks, a number of black press accounts urged African Americans to stand opposed to such violations of Arab civil liberties. Recalling the Salem witch trials, the draconian blackballing and harassment of the McCarthy era, and the FBI's COINTELPRO operations during the sixties and seventies, the *Portland Skanner* reported that less than a month after the attacks, more than a thousand Arabs and Arab Americans were in police custody nationwide, without access to a lawyer, and many without any charges filed against them.[73] Similarly, Emily Whitfield, media relations director for the American Civil Liberties Union, reported that racial or ethnic profiling has become a de facto national security policy as Arabs and South Asians in the United States have been sought for questioning and often detained.[74]

For some black voices, the events of September 11 make it a necessary and effective deterrence to racially profile Arab Americans and Muslims.[75] Simi-larly, polls showed that right after September 11, African Americans were more likely than other racial and ethnic groups to support profiling and tighter air-port security checks for Arabs and Arab Americans.[76] A substantial chorus of black voices has urged caution against these views, however. Addressing the gravity of black apathy toward Arab detainment and recent increases in hate crimes against Arabs, Richard Hatcher, attorney and former mayor of Gary, Indiana, explained at a forum organized by the PUSH/Rainbow Coalition:

'Together' is not separation from another ethnic group...If I don't stand up for you when they come after you, then I cannot expect you to stand up for me when they come after me. Why is Ashcroft able to deny [people] fundamental, basic elements of our justice system? A lot of us have gone to sleep [and] forgotten where we came from [and what we had to] overcome to get where we are.[77]

Speaking at the public policy forum "America in transition: Rethinking national policy priorities," organized by the Joint Center for Political and Economic Studies in Washington, D.C., Eddie N. Williams, president of the Joint Center, argued that "black and Hispanic people have unique insights into racial and ethnic profiling, which has taken on new significance since September 11."[78] "The level of hate directed at people who appear to be Muslim, Middle-Eastern, South Asian ... gives bigotry a righteousness it does not deserve," argued Sanford Cloud, Jr., president and CEO of the National Conference for Community and Justice.

Others noted that the recent decision by the U.S. Supreme Court to not hear a case brought by a group of young African Americans from upstate New York, who claimed that they were rounded up by the police because of their race, was indicative of a shift in political and cultural attitudes about racial profiling.[79] For some critics, the Supreme Court's decision signals that "no federal law against racial profiling is in the works" and that September 11 will justify legislative and judicial authorizations of "profiling as a legitimate police practice." As Neal puts it, "this may be the first example of how the alleged fight against terrorism will be used to undermine key civil rights protections at home. Arab Americans and Muslims may well be the primary victims at the moment, but who can deny that African Americans are standing in line just behind them for the same treatment?"[80]

Thus, hopeful that the "new victims of profiling" would give proposed legislation in Congress the additional support it needed, Sanford Cloud argued, "we need racial profiling legislation now more than ever." As the moniker "public enemy number one" is temporarily wrested from young, black, inner-city males to indict young, bearded, Middle Eastern-looking males instead, the parallels between the treatment of African Americans and the violations of Arabs' and Arab Americans' civil rights offer the basis for interethnic empathy and the possibility of new alliances. Urging support for Palestinians who have become the "niggers of the Middle East," a number of black voices argued that, "the Palestinian fight is akin to the lost battle of native Americans, relegated to concentration camps called reservations. It is the Southern civil rights movement, the racism conference and the demand for reparations. There is no line of demarcation ... there is only one continuous cultural narrative written by poor and politically repressed people everywhere."[81]

Calling on such a broad coalition of "working and poor people" thus, the New Afrikan People's Organization urged all people of goodwill:

to oppose George W. Bush's so-called war on terrorism and all military adventures of the United States government. We believe that we are obliged to separate from and resist evil, brutal, and oppressive acts of any government or organization that perpetrates terrorism and the victimization of working and poor people. The blood of our people, the Native American peoples, the Mexican people and the peoples of Puerto Rico and the Hawaiian Islands soak the ground of America as a result of this type of American-sponsored terrorism.[82]

It remains to be seen just how productive a moment this one will turn out be for realizing the potential of interethnic solidarities to organize and marshal resistance against domestic and foreign injustices that the U.S. government is charged with in these accounts. Already, however, if mainstream news discourses are any indication, we are witness to subtle vilifications of these developing alliances. Within the one-year anniversary coverage, a number of mainstream news commentators claimed that the events of September 11 had jolted ordinary Americans out of their apathies into a renewed sense of unity with other Americans. Wolf Blitzer on CNN, Dan Rather on CBS, and Bill O'Reilly on Fox News flashed grateful smiles to the camera noting that September 11 had finally shown Americans that they were "mourning in shared grief," and that after decades of separating from each other, they were once again, finally, coming together.

These celebrations of American unity subtly reiterate a discursive opposition between the multicultural identity-based agendas of the sixties on the one hand, and the hegemonic patriotisms of the moment on the other. Mainstream media accounts took this opportunity to toast the demise of the American sixties while celebrating the ways in which the attacks had spurred Americans to move beyond the divisive politics of difference that had tragically balkanized them for decades. Thus, the theater of mourning that the major media orchestrated on the one-year anniversary of the 9-11 attacks raised its proverbial eyebrows at the potential for interethnic solidarities between African Americans and Arab Americans, which along with the multicultural malaise of the past few decades, they suggested, Americans now deserved to jettison.[83]

CONCLUSION

As mainstream news accounts and popular cultural texts in the wake of the 9-11 attacks have, in near unanimity, echoed dominant hegemonic agendas of super-patriotism and militarism, as they uncritically reiterate symbolic and material penalties for political dissent, and, consequently, reinforce the urgency of domestic acquiescence in the face of an unrelenting, foreign enemy,[84] black press accounts have provided a haven of dissent and debate on questions of war, patriotism, and national unity. Black Americans have articulated a range of responses to September 11 and the U.S. response to those attacks, occupying multiple, contested positions in the national imagination. Navigating precarious divisions between critics and traitors, enemies and allies, African Americans are in a critical position to denaturalize hegemonic and racialized characterizations of "evil doers," "cave-dwellers," and "barbarians." Similarly, black voices are likely to decisively interrupt the hegemony of the "us versus them" paradigm that has forcefully constructed the "war against terrorism" as an apocryphal "clash of civilizations."[85]

In the post-9-11 context, thus, African Americans have a substantially important role to play in tempering the super-patriotic excesses of the moment. Their rhetorical abilities and ethical responsibilities to demand accountability from politico-economic elites in the United States and their tenaciousness in pursuing alliances with Muslim/Arab Americans will play a critical role in influencing the course of war and peace in the coming years.

4

Commodifying September 11: Advertising, Myth, and Hegemony

Christopher P. Campbell

With 14 minutes and 54 seconds remaining in the first half of the 2002 Super Bowl, the Fox television network cut to a commercial break as the New England Patriots attended to an injured defensive back. The next image for the viewers—annually the largest global audience for any television program, which includes roughly 50 million homes in the United States[1]—is a pair of Clydesdale horses romping through the snow in a hilly pasture. Soft, orchestral music plays in the background. The audience then sees a series of close-up shots as a team of eight Clydesdales is harnessed to a Budweiser wagon. They pull the wagon down wintry country roads; close-up shots show their hooves plodding through the snow. Other than the music, the only sound in the commercial is of the clopping of hooves on pavement. They pass through the cobblestone streets of a small town, where the barber looks on in awe from inside his shop's window. They cross the venerable Brooklyn Bridge and come to a stop in a field from which the Manhattan skyline can be seen in the distance, the Statue of Liberty looming in the background. An extreme close-up focuses on the misty eye of one Clydesdale (the Anheuser-Busch eagle emblazoned in the horse's bridle is visible for only a second); its markings include a teardrop shape below the eye. The next shot is from a distance, and the audience sees the team of horses gracefully genuflect in unison, heads bowed toward the distant skyline. The music ends and the screen fades to black. The Budweiser logo—white letters on a red rectangle—appears for a few seconds to conclude the 60-second spot.

The commercial—designed to pay tribute to those who died in the 9-11 terrorist attack on New York's World Trade Center—drew a good deal of attention in advertising circles. Anheuser-Busch said the spot was "a message from the heart of the company. We hope people see it as we intended. That we're Americans. That we know what the cost of freedom is."[2] Even the most cynical of viewers might admit to being moved by the powerful image of the horses bowing to the skyline where the towers once stood. An *Adweek* critic called the ad a "tractor pull on the tear ducts."[3] The *St. Louis Post Dispatch* described the commercial as "lovely" and as Super Bowl advertising's "biggest lump-in-throat moment."[4] *Advertising Age* gave it a mixed review: "Truthfully, the sentiment and obviousness of seeing a Clydesdale team bow with respect toward lower Manhattan made us wince. But the film was beautiful and as understated as such a mournful paean can get, and we understand that most viewers will be touched. Unnecessary? In our view, yes. Cashing in on tragedy? No."[5]

The *Advertising Age* critique of Budweiser's Clydesdale commercial is reflective of a larger discussion that took place in the advertising industry after September 11. In the several months that followed the attacks, a number of companies and advertising agencies chose to make direct and indirect references to the tragedy in their advertising campaigns. The debate in the industry was over the invisible line that separated the shameless use of the tragedy to pitch products from more tasteful commercials that paid appropriate tribute to those who lost their lives. This chapter will examine that debate, a discussion that offers insight into the critical process that exists within the advertising industry. Through a textual analysis of the Clydesdale Super Bowl commercial, it will also examine the mythic significance of advertising and how the myths that television commercials reify can limit public debate and support status quo political ideology.

While the staging of the 2002 Super Bowl extravaganza was highly patriotic, with nationalistic pre-game and halftime shows that paid homage to American heroes and the American flag, the advertising industry largely backed away from September 11 on game day. Other than Budweiser's Clydesdale ad, only online job service Monster.com made direct reference to the tragedy, giving New York City Mayor Rudolph Giuliani 30 seconds to thank people for supporting the city. The most controversial ads that aired during the Super Bowl were sponsored by the White House Office of National Drug Control Policy, which used the game to launch an anti-drug campaign that equated illegal drug use with support of international terrorists. But well before the Super Bowl, beginning in late September 2001, television audiences in the United States were inundated with advertising that made reference to the terrorist attack and the country's political response. The auto and travel industries were especially aggressive in using September 11 to appeal to customers, but the tragedy was also used to pitch everything from investment banking to clothing to soft drinks to a New Orleans health-maintenance organization. My interest here is not so much in the actual commodification of September 11—how the event became a mechanism to sell products—but in how the myths that the commercials sustained contributed to a nationalistic political atmosphere that restricted discussion of U.S. foreign policy and the country's response to international terrorist activity.

MYTH AND MEDIA

Throughout history, people have created myths to help explain the world around them. The mythologies of ancient cultures told grand stories of good and evil through larger-than-life characters. Joseph Campbell argues that such myths were used to "validate a certain social order."[6] Contemporary myths may be less grand, but they can also work to sustain a dominant political ideology, and the "common sense" that lurks beneath the surface of a culture's myths has been examined by writers across disciplines.[7] French author Roland Barthes, who analyzed the mythic capacity of cultural artifacts such as professional wrestling, news photography, and soap advertising, among others, was concerned with the potential of modern myths to define acceptable behavior and *common* sense. In his seminal work, *Mythologies,* he said his interest in examining the myths of popular culture was in "track[ing] down, in the decorative display of *what-goes-without-saying,* the ideological abuse which, in my view, is hidden there."[8] Similarly, British cultural studies author Stuart Hall has described a process of "decoding" the myths embedded in media representations. He suggests three levels of analysis, beginning with the "preferred" meaning—that which was intended by the producer—and moving on to "negotiated" and "oppositional" readings of the same message. He writes:

The domains of "preferred readings" have the whole social order imbedded in them as a set of meanings, practices and beliefs; the everyday knowledge of social structures, of "how things work for all practical purposes in this culture," the rank order of power and interest and the structure of legitimations, limits and sanctions.[9]

Cultural anthropologist Clifford Geertz expressed similar concerns about the "common sense" imbedded in the myths of contemporary Western society:

As a frame for thought... common sense is as totalizing as any other: no religion is more dogmatic, no science more ambitious, no philosophy more general.... It pretends to reach past illusion to truth, to, as we say, things as they are.[10]

A number of media studies scholars have examined the role of myth in journalism, finding that the storytelling traditions of the news industry tend to subtly sustain dominant political ideologies.[11] S. Elizabeth Bird and Robert Dardenne describe recurrent myths that surface in news coverage "that are derived from culture and feed back into it." They argue that the mythical qualities of news "offer reassurance and familiarity in shared community experiences; it provides credible answers to baffling questions, and ready explanations of complex phenomena such as unemployment and inflation."[12] Coverage of September 11 in the U.S. news media certainly exhibited such mythical qualities. Jack Lule's analysis of *New York Times* editorials that followed the 9-11 attacks found:

The New York Times responded to the catastrophic events of September 11 by drawing upon stories and structures of myth. *The Times* lamented the loss of innocence and grieved over a world in which everything had changed. It offered the myth of the Victim, called out for vengeance, and built support for survivors. It constructed and celebrated heroes and bolstered leaders as they responded to the crisis. It mobilized for war and warned of a foreboding future, of suffering and sacrifice to come. Taken together...these myths offer a formidable array of strategies for dealing with the enormity of September 11.[13]

Like journalism, the advertising industry has a similar capacity for myth-making; indeed, it may be the form of popular culture that relies most heavily on cultural myths as it endeavors to sell products, ideas, and lifestyles. Martin Esslin argues that "the TV commercial, exactly as the oldest known types of theatre, is essentially a religious form of drama which shows us human beings as living in a world controlled by a multitude of powerful forces that shape our lives."[14] He continues: "If the winds and waters, the trees and brooks of ancient Greece were inhabited by a vast host of nymphs, dryads, satyrs, and other local and specific deities, so is the universe of the television commercial." Similarly, Himmelstein argues that "many interesting parallels can be drawn [between television advertising] and traditional myth recitation." He explains:

The commercial jingles and the background musical scores of television may substitute for traditional chanting. Jingles and chants are both mnemonic and diachronic devices. They etch, in individual and collective consciousness, the rhythms of the public imagery with which they become forever associated; and they produce a common memory of traditions within the culture. The television icons are pictorial representations that, like traditional ritual masks and sacred religious icons, are drawn from the world of everyday lived experience and at the same time transcend the world. Television's internally structured visual and aural time signature is analogous to the rules for a traditional ritual; the segments, and particularly the commercials, "announce" themselves and demand our attention.[15]

Sut Jhally argues that the television commercial serves contemporary society in the same way myths served ancient cultures:

In advertising are the universal problems of life (good and evil, life and death, happiness and misery), as well as their promised resolution. Advertising is an anxiety-reducing institution, serving a function assigned to other institutions in premodern societies.[16]

In his video *Advertising and the End of the World,* Jhally argues that the advertising industry is the chief purveyor of myth in the United States:

Culture is the place and space where a society tells stories about itself, where values are articulated and expressed, where notions of good and evil, of morality and values, are defined. Every culture has a cultural field that talks about these things. In [U.S.] culture, it's the stories of advertising that dominate the cultural field. Advertising, in fact, is the main storyteller of our society.[17]

After September 11, the advertising industry relied on a shared mythology of American strength and unity as it went about selling various products and encouraging audiences to return to their pre-9-11 consumer habits. Television commercials reflected a *common sense* of compassion for the tragedy's victims that was coupled with support for a wrathful military response in which good would triumph over evil. The debate within the advertising industry, however, did not acknowledge the possible role that advertising played in influencing the country's political response to September 11; rather, the discussion was largely limited to the issue of whether specific 9-11 advertisements were appropriately patriotic or shamelessly tactless.

POST-9-11 ADVERTISING: "HELP AMERICA TURN THE TABLES"

The automobile industry was the most aggressive in referring to September 11 in the commercials it created following the attacks. Both General Motors and Ford launched campaigns before the end of September that announced interest-free financing and equated car-buying with patriotism. The theme of the General Motors campaign was "Keep America Rolling." Ford's slogan: "Ford Drives America." Both campaigns implied that the companies were offering zero-percent financing as their contribution to the country's political response to the terrorist attacks. Among the General Motors commercials created by the McCann-Erickson Advertising Agency was one that referred to the "American Dream" and GM's refusal "to let anyone take it away."[18] Another showed a rising sun as an announcer says, "The flags are back up. They're playing football again. And people are once again experiencing the simple joy of buying a new car."[19] A Ford ad announced: "In light of these challenging times, we at Ford want to do our part to help move America forward."[20]

The ads worked. Although the industry was slumping before September 11, by the year's end it had completed the second-best sales year in its history. In October, car sales jumped by 24 percent compared to October 2000.[21] The advertising industry, however, did not entirely embrace the ad campaigns. In an *Advertising Age* front-page critique that provoked a larger debate in the advertising world, columnist Bob Garfield described the ads as "simply repulsive. While it is true that our political leaders have encouraged us to get back out into the economy, to pervert that message into a self serving sales promotion is a cynical exploitation of the terrorists' victims and an unforgivable insult to those who grieve for them." Garfield described the "invocation of national interest" as:

[A] pretext, a transparent gimmick to convert a nation's inchoate emotions into sales. Furthermore, it is utterly unnecessary. Announce zero-interest financing. Sing its praises to the heavens. Offer it and they will come. But in the name of decency, leave the sacred burial grounds of Sept. 11 alone.[22]

Like the auto industry, the travel industry demonstrated significant patriotic zeal in its post-9-11 advertising. The Travel Industry Association of America created a newspaper advertising campaign that described travel as "a cherished right," adding:

America's travel industry has pledged its support to the U.S. Congress and other federal agencies to ensure that travel is safe and secure. After all, America was founded, expanded and made great by travelers. And nobody can take that away from us. Not now. Not ever.[23]

A television commercial produced by the same association used video from a speech made by President Bush shortly after September 11 in which he urged the country to "return to normalcy."[24] Fallon Worldwide Travel Agency developed a series of documentary-styled commercials for United Airlines that made direct reference to the tragedy.[25] In one spot, a United pilot tells the audience, "We took a blow, but we're gonna get up." In another, United workers praise the "freedom" of flying anywhere, anytime in the United States. One says, "We're not gonna let anyone take that away from us." Another worker adds, "We're Americans, and this is not gonna beat us down." The ad industry's critique of the commercial did not accuse United of capitalizing on the tragedy, but focused on whether or not the approach was strategically wise. One ad executive questioned United for "reminding people of what they wanted to forget."[26] A Harvard business professor offered another view: "Normally, an airline wouldn't want to be out there advertising after a major accident. But in this instance, the impact of September 11 is so massive in terms of the traveling public's minds, you can't hide."[27]

The auto and travel industries were not the only ones to rely on patriotism in their post-9-11 advertising. Soon after the attack, the windows in Ralph Lauren's retail stores in New York were adorned with American flags.[28] Breathe Right Nasal Strips introduced a Stars and Stripes version of its product.[29] The National Restaurant Association adopted the slogan "Help America Turn the Tables," and a New York fitness club urged potential customers to "Keep America Strong."[30] New Orleans agency Trumpet Advertising created an overtly nationalistic 60-second commercial for The Oath, a health-maintenance organization. As a child sings "God Bless America," a string of words in red type scrolls across a white screen: "Mom. Dad. Ray Charles. We, The People. Foot-long Dogs. The Girl Next Door. D-Day.... "[31] An executive for the HMO explained: "In light of the recent tragedies, we didn't really want to go with our original advertising campaign. Instead we wanted to do something to honor the day-to-day life of our country."[32]

Using patriotism to sell products and ideas certainly did not begin with September 11, and members of an earlier generation will recall similar approaches used during World War II. An ad for Plymouth that ran in the *Tampa Tribune* December 8, 1941 included this copy: "A strong automobile industry is the backbone of defense."[33] The current generation of advertisers, however, utilizes sophisticated research tools to determine how audiences will respond to their messages. After September 11, the ad industry went to considerable lengths to determine what audiences might consider appropriate references to the tragedy. Knowledge Networks and Statistical Research conducted surveys to find out if respondents would pay attention to television ads that "mourn the loss of individuals/groups" (29 percent said they would), "pay tribute to heroes" (40 percent), "all for people to stand united" (45 percent), "identify products as made in America" (23 percent), or "remind citizens of the country's strengths" (36 percent).[34] Cone Communications released results of a poll two weeks after September 11 that found 75 percent of its respondents thought it was appropriate for advertisers to return to their routines.[35] The company recommended that advertisers adopt "thoughtful patriotism" in their commercials.[36] Euro RSCG Worldwide's Strategic Trendspotting and Research Team found that half the people it surveyed over the age of 55 were more likely to "buy American" after September 11.[37]

While advertising agencies generally interpreted the research to justify their use of the tragedy to pitch products and ideas, discussion within the industry reflected a mixed reaction to the research. The president and CEO of a Hollywood ad firm offered this advice in a letter to the editor of *Advertising Age*:

So what's it going to take to get the marketing machinery moving? People want to feel good again! Indicating how your products and services will help them feel good is the most important concept to communicate.... We must stop talking about how bad things are. This is simply a self-fulfilling prophecy. It's time to move forward and start making some noise on the Western front of marketing.[38]

The managing partner of a St. Louis ad agency suggested, "It's a good time for a company to communicate the values it and its employees stand for. It's time to go back to some common values. It's not a time to be silly or frivolous. It's a time to be honest and real."[39] Many of the advertisers who commented on post-9-11 advertising recommended a cautious approach, like the St. Louis ad executive who counseled, "Attempts to tap into patriotism need to be done very carefully. They should not be seen as exploiting the situation."[40] The chief creative officer for an office of Ogilvy & Mather Worldwide agency in New York said making references to the tragedy was "a very hard line to walk,"[41] adding that his agency's approach was to "get a message out, a sign of solidarity, and not [trying to sell specific products]."[42] He said his company's patriotic ads—for AT&T Wireless, American Express, Cotton Inc., and Miller beer—were not an effort to capitalize on September 11 but were simply a reflection of the country's collective nationalistic attitude: "We're holding up a mirror to what we're seeing."[43] The dominant sense among members of the advertising industry was that the ads that most overtly commodified September 11 were probably not effective. As the president of a Milwaukee ad firm cautioned, "It all depends on how shamelessly it is done. If [an ad] looks exploitative, it won't work; if it looks sincere, it will work."[44]

Perhaps the most controversial use of September 11 was the previously mentioned anti-drug campaign backed by the federal government launched during the Super Bowl. The White House Office of National Drug Control Policy paid Fox $3.5 million to air the ads, directed by British filmmaker Tony Kaye, which suggested that young people who buy illegal drugs are financing international terrorism.[45] The first commercial—a takeoff on a

MasterCard campaign—featured a series of shots of terrorist-related items and their prices, including items designed to bring September 11 to mind: "Safehouse $7,200." "Fake I.D. $3,000." "Box cutters $2." Shot in black and white with a hand-held camera, the images appear to show two men packing a car's trunk with automatic weapons and explosives and heading to an airport. It concludes with the announcer saying, "Where do terrorists get their money? If you buy drugs, some of it might come from you." The second commercial featured a series of headshots of culturally diverse, drug-using teenagers saying things like, "I helped a bomber get a fake passport" and "I helped blow up buildings" interspersed with comments like, "It was just innocent fun" and "It was not like I was hurting anybody else." In its final seconds, the screen reads: "Drug money supports terror. If you buy drugs, you might too."

The campaign inspired some fairly vicious comments about its blatant use of September 11 to try to stop young people from using illicit drugs. New York *Daily News* critic-at-large David Hinckley wrote that his immediate response to the ads was to "burst out laughing."[46] The problem, he said, was:

[t]hat the message is silly, and kids know it. Do some drug sales fund reprehensible activities? Of course. So do some oil profits. Osama bin Laden is a billionaire because his family builds things for Saudi Arabian rulers who make so much money from our love of gas-guzzling motor cars. But our government isn't buying ads on the Super Bowl to warn us that every time we fill 'er up, we finance terrorism—and while obviously there are larger and more complex issues with oil, that's also true with drugs.[47]

The assistant director to New York's Drug Policy Alliance agreed: "It's a cynical, cheap shot to take in the current political environment. To make it sound like a kid who smokes pot is responsible for putting cash in the hands of Osama bin Laden is ludicrous."[48] However, the Office of National Drug Control Policy said that 60 percent of the teenagers who participated in focus-group testing said they would be less likely to use drugs if they knew about the connection between drugs and terrorism.[49] A government spokesperson admitted that September 11 inspired its decision to aggressively associate drug use in the United States with international politics and economics: "I think now people care a whole lot more."[50] The *Tampa Tribune* lauded the campaign in an editorial, saying, "If the message resonates with thousands of adolescents under peer pressure to experiment, then those commercials did their job."[51] But, by far, the reaction on American newspaper opinion pages viewed the campaign as a cynical and misleading attempt by the federal government to capitalize on the country's anti-terrorist sentiment.

As The *Washington Post*'s Abigail Trafford wrote:

Mixing the old war on drugs with the new war on terrorism is a stretch. It's hard to see any link, say, between American teenagers trying Ecstasy and foreign terrorists attacking the World Trade Center. To put them under the same patriotic umbrella diminishes the hard realities of both kinds of tragedy.[52]

The decision of the Office of National Drug Control Policy to use September 11 as part of its war against illegal drugs was an overtly political decision designed to influence support for its drug policies. In this case, September 11 was used to influence specific behavior and attitudes about a specific issue. That was not the case for the ad agencies, corporations, and businesses that used the terrorist attacks as part of their efforts to sell products and to encourage consumer activity. Taken as a group, the 9-11 ads did more than that. They contributed to a larger, mythic sense of a country that was unified in its reaction to the tragedy. Himmelstein describes the collective sense produced by advertising as a dream world, and he argues that the mythology that is imbedded in television commercials works in the same way the myths of ancient societies provided a citizenry with an ideology in which to believe:

"Dreams" in the mythic world of television advertising are no less "real" than those of traditional mythology, with its emphasis on cosmogony (the origin or creation of the world or the universe); both speak to us of entire ways of life and canonize patterns of organization of society that regulate behavior, ensuring a continuity of values and beliefs.[53]

The mythical world of post-9-11 advertising encouraged consumerism as the appropriate counterpart to stepped-up military action. As President Bush attempted to convince the country that the United States needed to wage war against Osama bin Laden and international terrorism (eventually including Saddam Hussein and Iraq), the advertising industry had helped build a common sense of political unity that defied any other response to the tragedy.

A "NEGOTIATED" READING: "THIS BUD'S FOR YOU"

The Clydesdale commercial that Anheuser-Busch aired during the 2002 Super Bowl was rife with mythical significance. The majestic Clydesdales romping together in the snowy pasture reflect an idyllic life of pastoral beauty. The attention of the audience is drawn to the simple elegance of the process of harnessing the horses as they are prepared for their trip across the country-side. Close-up shots of the horses' hooves reveal the wood-floored quaintness of the red barn that is their home. The small town they pass through looks to be a utopian community: "Main Street" is lined with two-story, turn-of-the-century brick buildings; the streets are paved with cobblestones; the white smock worn by the town barber is reminiscent of simpler times. Himmelstein has described a series of myths that television engenders, including the "myth of the rural middle landscape," which contrasts the "chaos" of urban life with the simplicity of country living, "the strong mature rural citizen coping with the evil world crashing all around him by maintaining pure country values, including the sanctity of the extended family and the value of hard work not for achievement, but for a higher moral purpose."[54] But as the horses approach New York City, the audience is presented with an equally romantic notion of the United States' largest urban center. A high angle shot of the Clydesdales crossing Brooklyn Bridge reveals its structural magnificence. The camera pans across the Statue of Liberty and the Manhattan skyline, high-lighting the city's history, majesty, and splendor. Of course, the image of the skyline intentionally brings to mind the missing World Trade Center towers and the tragedy of September 11. The horses bow, as if they are magically aware of the event and the terror and heroism that it spawned. The Clydes-dales become a mythical symbol of a grieving country that has roots in a sim-ple, agrarian culture and that mourns its tragic conflict with the world beyond it.

Their trip is filled with enchantment, shown entirely in slow motion. A win-try gray sky in one shot becomes a spectacular sunset in the next, a bright blue sky in the next. Their travels seem to transcend the concept of time: The sleepy town that the horses pass through appears to be from an earlier era; it evokes memories of the mythical Mayberry from television's classic *The Andy Griffith Show*, where the barber shop on Main Street served as a hub for community activity. The commercial's geography also relies on magic. After crossing the Brooklyn Bridge, presumably into Manhattan, the horses end up in a field from which the borough's skyline is visible in panorama, the Statue of Liberty just off to the side. The high-quality, film-style production was designed to elicit a powerful reaction. Anheuser-Busch hired a new advertising agency, Hill Holliday, to create the commercial, described later as a "super-secret assign-ment."[55] The commercial's producer, veteran adman Bryan Sweeney, was praised by Anheuser-Busch for his creative ingenuity and "taking impossible tasks and getting them done."[56] Sweeney apparently arranged to have the Brooklyn Bridge shut down one Saturday morning to shoot footage for the commercial.[57] The company's intention to emotionally engage the audience—

what Hall would describe as the commercial's "preferred" reading[58]—was largely successful. *USA Today's* review of Budweiser's Super Bowl commercials praised the ad (though in remarkably sexist terms), saying that it "scored especially high among women who wanted their heartstrings plucked more than they wanted their funny bones tickled."[59] This reading of the commercial works only at the denotative level; that is, Anheuser-Busch created an ad designed to evoke sympathy for 9-11 victims and demonstrate its patriotism: "That we're Americans. That we know what the cost of freedom is."[60]

What Hall would describe as a "negotiated" reading of the ad, however, allows for analysis beyond the meaning intended by the commercial's producer. According to Hall, such a reading requires a recognition of the "dominant ideology" that is at work and how that ideology is "shot through with contradictions."[61] Hall writes, "Negotiated codes operate through what we might call particular or situated logics: and these logics are sustained by their differential and unequal relation to the discourses and logics of power."[62] For Hall, the denotative, commonsense meaning of the Clydesdale commercial—Anheuser-Busch is a good, compassionate corporate citizen that grieves about September 11 along with the rest of the United States—is less significant than an interpretive reading of the commercial. Similarly, in *Reading Television,* John Fiske and John Hartley rely on Barthes's semiotic notion of myth to describe three levels of "signification" to be found in television messages.[63] Like Hall's "preferred reading," the first order is the denotative message and "the sign is self contained."[64] Like Hall's "negotiated reading," the second order calls for the connotative reading of the message, including its potential for myth-making. In this analysis, Fiske and Hartley include the impact of television production techniques to connote meanings: "Camera angle, lighting and background music, frequency of cutting are examples. Music in particular is used to clarify and sometime create the connotative meaning of a shot."[65]

Anheuser-Busch went to substantial effort to create and air the Clydesdale commercial, which aired only once—during the 2002 Super Bowl. The production cost alone likely exceeded over $1 million. Jhally has pointed out that the per-second production costs for television advertising far exceed the per-second costs of producing a high-action, blockbuster film.[66] The new agency Anheuser-Busch hired to produce the commercial managed to shut down the Brooklyn Bridge for a morning shoot. It ventured to Norwich, Vermont, to shoot footage of the farm that would represent rural America. The high-caliber production relied on spectacular slow motion images, soothing music, and the sound effects of plodding hooves to create a powerful, unmistakably patriotic tribute to a mythical understanding of American life. Of course, the commercial ends with a full-screen shot of the Budweiser logo to remind the audience just what it is that is tugging at its heartstrings. Given the symbolic stature of the Clydesdale horses—as recognizable as McDonald's Golden Arches as a mainstay corporate symbol—such a reminder of the corporate world that is behind Super Bowl advertising was probably not necessary. Anheuser-Busch, perpetually the biggest Super Bowl advertiser, paid Fox approximately $3.9 million to air the ad, bringing its total cost to roughly $5 million. That's a lot of money to pay for a company to establish itself as a good corporate citizen.

Few television commercials these days attempt to convince audiences that one product brand is better than another; advertising is much more about a product's image: Kids wear Nike sneakers not because they believe the shoes are better than Adidas or Converse, but because of Nike's association with superstars like Michael Jordan and Tiger Woods. The advertising industry uses the Super Bowl as a stage on which to build a company's image, and Budweiser has been the most aggressive player on that stage. William Leiss, Stephen Kline, and Sut Jhally correctly point out that advertising has "become an accepted part of every day life."[67] They explain:

The symbolic attributes of goods, as well as the characters, situations, imagery, and jokes of advertising discourse, are now ingredients of our cultural repertoire. Some spectacularly successful advertising campaigns...themselves became media events and were reported as news.[68]

Anheuser-Busch carefully considered its decision to spend $5 million to produce and air its Clydesdale Super Bowl ad, which did become a media event. A "negotiated" reading of the ad demonstrates that Anheuser-Busch, the world's largest brewer, was looking to do more than pay tribute to September 11 and establish itself as a compassionate, patriotic corporation. It was also selling beer. While the advertising industry may have deemed the approach to be appropriate, the brewer was—at best—using the tragedy to raise its corporate profile, and—at worst—exploiting September 11 to sell a product. This reading of the commercial allows us to consider the economic stature of Anheuser-Busch and its longtime commitment to incredibly expensive and aggressive marketing campaigns; in such a reading, the brewer may have just as well ended the high-priced Super Bowl commercial with its trademark tagline: "This Bud's For You."

AN "OPPOSITIONAL" READING: BUDWEISER AND HEGEMONY

Discussion within the advertising industry of the use of September 11 to sell products was largely limited to matters of taste. Many of the commercials that made reference to the terrorist attack were deemed acceptable. ("It all depends on how shamelessly it is done."[69]) For ad industry executives, the debate did not include the possibility that patriotic advertising could have an impact on larger issues of public policy. While the commercials may have been designed to sell products or encourage consumerism (the "preferred" reading), there was a larger recognition within the advertising industry and among its critics that 9-11 advertising could be seen as exploiting the tragedy (a "negotiated" view). What's missing in that discussion of 9-11 advertising is any recognition of the industry's complicity with a dominant political ideology and the public policy interests of the U.S. government. Such a discussion would call for what Hall has described as an "oppositional" reading of media messages in which a viewer "detotalizes the message in the preferred code in order to retotalize the message within some alternative framework of reference."[70] Hall says, "One of the most significant political moments...is the point when events which are normally signified and decoded in a negotiated way begin to be given an oppositional reading. Here the 'politics of signification'—the struggle in discourse—is joined."[71] Similarly, Fiske and Hartley describe the highest level of analysis of television messages as that which recognizes the "mythology" or "ideology" that hides beneath the surface of media messages: "This, the third order of signification, reflects the broad principles by which a culture organizes and interprets the reality with which it has to cope."[72]

Contemporary cultural studies critics often rely on Italian political theorist Antonio Gramsci's notion of ideological hegemony in describing the way in which a dominant political ideology subtly finds its way into a culture's artifacts and common sense.[73] Such an analysis recognizes the role of advertising and the mass media in contributing to a dominant political and economic order. As sociologist Todd Gitlin explains:

Commercial culture does not *manufacture* ideology; it *relays* and *reproduces* and *processes* and *packages* and *focuses* ideology that is constantly arising both from social elites and from active social groups and movements throughout the society (as well as within media organizations and practices).[74]

Similarly, Jhally points out the need to see advertising in a larger political and social context:

We should treat advertising as a cultural system, as a system that impacts how human beings make sense of the world, how we understand its meanings. The images, the values, the ideas of advertising are lodged inside us because that's the way culture works.[75]

Budweiser's Super Bowl commercial, when viewed from the larger, "oppositional" point of view, can be seen in the context of advertising's place in consumer culture. Fiske and Hartley recommend that such analyses consider television's "syntagms," or sign sequences.[76] Syntagmatic analysis allows for a reading of the commercial as part of television advertising's sequential, meaning-making chain. That is, the Budweiser commercial was one of about 60 that aired during the Super Bowl, and one of thousands that air during television broadcasts throughout the United States on a daily basis. Additionally, the commercial was just one of many that made reference to September 11 in the months that followed the attack. Television audiences are adept at reading advertising's denotative messages; in the case of the Clydesdale commercial, it was easy to understand the emotion that Anheuser-Busch had intended to elicit. Many audience members are wary enough to realize there are also messages just beneath a commercial's surface; for instance, some viewers likely realized they were also being sold a sense of Anheuser-Busch's compassion and good will. Few audience members, however, see commercial messages in the syntagmatic context of a vast consumer culture that contributes to a dominant political ideology; the hegemonic nature of the advertising industry makes such a reading unlikely. Judith Williamson argues that advertisements sell products as well as the mythical world that shapes a culture's political and social beliefs:

Ideology is the meaning made necessary by the condition of society while helping to *perpetuate* those conditions. We feel a need to belong, to have a social place; it can be hard to find. Instead we may be given an imaginary one.[77]

According to Williamson, advertisers "are selling us ourselves."[78] That audiences might not recognize this process is because the advertising industry is not a societal institution designed by manifest to shape education and values. Leiss, Kline, and Jhally explain that advertising "is a major factor in socialization, [b]ut...the danger is that, while advertising wields great social power, there is little social accountability for its operations. In this respect, it differs from institutions such as churches and schools."[79] Because of the advertising industry's covert role in shaping societal attitudes, it is likely that most members of the audience will not recognize corporate and political interests and values in a commercial designed to evoke sympathy for 9-11 victims.

The commercial included only a few brief, apparent images that specifically represented Budweiser: "Anheuser-Busch, Inc., Budweiser Beer, St. Louis, Mo." is superimposed on the bottom of the screen for the first few seconds of the commercial; the corporation's eagle logo is briefly identifiable just above the eye of the "crying" Clydesdale; the commercial ends with a full frame of the Budweiser logo. The Clydesdales alone are perhaps the commercial's most potent symbolic representation of Anheuser-Busch. Indeed, the commercial is not much different from the company's annual Christmas advertisement that features the horses pulling the Budweiser wagon through the snow. When the horses bow down to the New York skyline in tribute to September 11, they do not suddenly become just any horses. They are conspicuous symbols of the world's largest brewery. In this reading, the Clydesdales no longer represent a mythical America in mourning; they are symbols of a prominent, international corporation; they represent the interests of Anheuser-Busch, a major player in a global economic structure that allows giant Western corporations to dominate the world's resources. The symbolic nature of the Manhattan skyline to which the horses bow is also worthy of consideration. The magical Clydesdales are actually paying tribute to a significant absence from that skyline—the World Trade Center towers. The enormous towers did not solely represent American engineering ingenuity; they were an international symbol of global economics, symbolism that was not lost on the attackers. The 9-11 attack on the World Trade Center was not the first. In 1993, terrorists detonated a bomb that heavily damaged one of the towers (an event that did not generate the same response in political or advertising circles). The terrorists' selection of the World Trade Center as a target was very likely intended to send a message about global economics. Considering the symbolic magnitude of the fallen towers, the Clydesdales' homage is no longer just about those who lost their lives; it is also about the damage to the global economic system that the World Trade Center represented.

In *Manufacturing Consent: The Political Economy of the Mass Media,* Herman and Chomsky describe the symbiotic nature of the relationship between American commercial media, global corporations, and the U.S. government. They explain:

The dominant media firms are quite large businesses; they are controlled by very wealthy people or by managers who are subject to sharp constraints by owners and other market-profit-oriented forces; and they are closely interlocked, and have important common interests with other major corporations, banks, and government.[80]

Anheuser-Busch is a significant player in the global economy, as is the Fox television network, which is owned by one of the world's largest media conglomerates, Rupert Murdoch's News Corporation. In 1993, the corporation paid the National Football League $1.58 billion in a deal that included the rights to air the Super Bowl (outbidding CBS by $540 million).[81] That Fox chose to frame the 2002 Super Bowl as a highly patriotic event was consistent with the American corporations and advertising agencies that chose to use September 11 as an opportunity to sell a product and to endorse a united, nationalistic response to the tragedy.

That was also the case with Budweiser's Clydesdale ad. The implicit endorsement of the government's response to the tragedy—to wage war in Afghanistan, to seek out Osama bin Laden, to pursue Iraq's Saddam Hussein—was not just a matter of patriotism. The endorsement of U.S. foreign policy also served the interests of the global corporate economy, in which Anheuser-Busch and Fox are significant players. In this context, a Super Bowl commercial showing the Clydesdales bowing to the Manhattan skyline is hardly an appropriate tribute to those who died on September 11, but rather a cynical attempt by corporate giants to elicit public support for policies that they believe will ultimately prove economically beneficial for them. In an "oppositional" reading of the commercial, the horses do not just represent a country unified in mourning, and the Manhattan skyline does not just represent the country's sense of loss; the horses' tribute to the fallen towers can also be viewed as a response to an attack on a global political and economic system that serves the interests of major corporations (including Anheuser-Busch and Fox). In this reading, the commercial is not just about the incredible loss of life that occurred on September 11, but also about the conflicting views of world economics and politics that were apparently at the heart of the attacks. Such a reading allows for consideration of issues that seemed to be overlooked in the United States' political response to the attacks, which was marked by quick and extreme military action. In an "oppositional" reading of the commercial's symbolic value, the ultimate tragedy of September 11 is not just in the lives that were lost that day, but in the acts of violence and terrorism that will continue until serious discussions of differences commence and a truce is declared among those who hold disparate and conflicting world views.

CONCLUSION

I have attempted in this chapter to provide an overview of the advertising industry's response to September 11 and to analyze at three different levels the Clydesdale commercial that Anheuser-Busch aired during the 2002 Super Bowl. I have argued that 9-11-related advertising contributed to a nationalistic political atmosphere that supported the U.S. government's foreign-policy response to the tragedy. My primary concern is that American media institutions—advertising, journalism, primetime television, and the film industry—offer audiences a fairly limited worldview, one that tends to support a

dominant political ideology. As part of a global economic system, these institutions have a lot to lose if world events were to cause that system to collapse.
In the wake of September 11, the U.S. government asked its citizens to be
united in a stand against international terrorism. In a speech to a joint session
of Congress nine days after the tragedy, President Bush announced to the
world that the United States would use its military might to avenge the
attacks. He said of the attackers, "They hate our freedoms: our freedom of
religion, our freedom of speech, our freedom to vote and assemble and disagree with each other."[82] He cautioned the country and world leaders that
opposition to a military retaliation was unacceptable: "Either you are with us,
or you are with the terrorists."[83] The full force of the country's commercial
media system reflected the unity the president was seeking. Dissent was not
tolerated. When talk show host Bill Maher suggested that America's military
response was "cowardly," Sears and FedEx pulled their commercials off of
Politically Incorrect, and his program was ultimately canceled.[84]

In interviews with European journalists in the two weeks after September
11, political activist, author, and MIT linguistics professor Noam Chomsky
cautioned the world against a response to the tragedy that did not include a
discussion of world politics and economics. When President Bush told the
world that the people behind the attacks "hated freedom," the American
media system—especially the advertising industry—provided a mythology
that demonstrated the country's love of freedom. Chomsky suggested that a
long-term solution to world terrorism would require:

[A] willingness to examine what lies behind the atrocities. One often hears that we
must not consider these matters, because that would be justification for terrorism, a
position so foolish and destructive as scarcely to merit comment, but unfortunately
common. But if we do not wish to contribute to escalating the cycle of violence, with
targets among the rich and powerful as well, that is exactly what we must do.[85]

By contributing to a mythology of national unity and military might that
limited discussion of global politics and economics ("what lies behind the
atrocities"), the advertising industry was complicit in confining the country's
political discourse to anything other than support for a full-scale military
response to September 11. Because television commercials are not perceived
as inherently political or as a means of providing citizens with information
about public policy, their messages can pack powerful implicit meanings.

Certainly, one could argue that analysis of a single Budweiser commercial
is hardly enough to make a case that the U.S. advertising industry is a complicit partner in a political system that is dominated by the economic inter-

ests of global corporations. I admit that by selecting just one commercial for analysis, I run the risk of reading too much into too little. But my purpose here is not to offer empirical proof that Anheuser-Busch and corporate America are part of a worldwide conspiracy to control political ideology; I do not believe that such a conspiracy exists. Rather, my purpose is to contribute to an ongoing dialogue about the role of the media in times of global crisis. My efforts here have been to examine the mythical weight of a single television commercial and to do what cultural critic James Carey has described as "interpret[ing] the interpretations."[86] That is, by "reading" Budweiser's Clydesdale commercial while considering a variety of points of view—the Super Bowl audience, the advertising industry, Anheuser-Busch, global corporations, the federal government, the enemies of the United States—I have attempted to demonstrate that even a 60-second beer commercial can be a vehicle for understanding what happened to the world on September 11.

Rituals of Trauma: How the Media Fabricated September 11

Fritz Breithaupt

Already a quick glimpse of the media's reaction to the terrorist attacks of September 11, 2001, reveals a puzzling unanimity and even monotony among these responses.[1] The media have met their audience with a monolithic "September 11" that channels not only information about the attacks but also the emotional responses of audiences according to a "therapeutic arc...from shock...toward...resolve."[2] The purpose of this paper is to analyze this song in unison of the media by focusing on the fabrication and ritualization of "trauma" in September 11. This will lead us to ask what is *not* expressed by the media, and to which degree "trauma" polices a taboo.

In speaking of the fabrication of "trauma," I do not mean to imply that there has not been an enormous amount of suffering among relatives and friends of the victims and people all over the world. However, I do want to draw attention to how the media's staging of trauma does not so much record the human suffering that has taken place but instead serves as the central axis of organizing the diverse information material in such a way to bring about the said response in the audience. In short, the media themselves responded to the attack by creating that which they perceived as the outcome of the attacks: "a trauma." At the same time, the media recommend themselves as therapist, as the agent of national healing. Obviously, the impulse behind this staging of therapy is something other than therapy, and I propose to explain it as a ritualistic practice with its specific mandate, totem, and taboo. I will need to apologize in advance for the generalizations that will be relied upon for the demarcation of this pattern. Perhaps the most conspicuous generalization here is the usage of the simple notion "the media," as if I were referring to a single, unified entity.

TRAUMA

The idea of "trauma" only emerged in the last hundred-some years. Ruth Leys, who studies the history of trauma as an idea, describes its modern application:

Post-traumatic stress disorder is fundamentally a disorder of memory. The idea is that, owing to the emotions of terror and surprise caused by certain events, the mind is split or dissociated: it is unable to register the wound to the psyche because the ordinary mechanisms of awareness and cognition are destroyed. As a result, the victim is unable to recollect and integrate the hurtful experience in normal consciousness; instead she is haunted or possessed by intrusive traumatic memories. The experience of the trauma, fixed or frozen in time, refuses to be represented *as* past, but is perpetually reexperienced in a painful, dissociated, traumatic present. All the symptoms characteristic of PTSD—flashbacks, nightmares and other reexperiences, emotional numbing, depression, guilt, autonomic arousal, explosive violence or tendency to hyper vigilance—are thought to be the result of this fundamental mental dissociation.[3]

Curiously, that which "trauma" maps out in negative terms matches the positive description of the media. The media are the apparatus that make possible the repetition of events, that amplify the magnitude of events, that offer events as an experience to those who were not present, and that bridge spatial and temporal orders (such as the past and present). From another perspective, one could reformulate the above definition of "trauma" to observe that the media force replays on their audience, that they overwhelm the audience, that it becomes unclear who experiences and who does not, and that the temporal order of then and now is confused. Thus, there is a functional similarity between the concept of "trauma" and the modern mass media. "Trauma" is a memory disorder that prevents an individual from processing events in such a way that they become "past" events. Similarly, the media bring about a heightened present in which the storing of the past *as past* does not and cannot take place.

While this functional affinity between the mass media and "trauma" can be observed in general, the media's fabrication of September 11 emphasizes the formal elements that correspond to the therapists' notion of "trauma." "Trauma," it turns out, provides an effective way of arranging material and assembling narratives. In short, "trauma" is very much like a recipe for cooking a story.

For the media, "trauma" is an organizing device, that is, a concept. This is why the word "trauma" appears in quotation marks in this text. Concepts "grasp" reality by offering a clear vision of otherwise complex situations. As a concept, "trauma" is not a diagnosis of existing medical conditions, but rather a prescription for arranging the scenario of an event. Concepts guide the perception of reality: We see (perceive) what we already (conceptually) know; concepts prepare for future situations. In the world of concepts, there are always competing concepts. Indeed, instead of "trauma," there are numerous other concepts that could have guided the media: "anxiety," "anger," "vengeance," "tragedy," "sobriety," "mourning," "disbelief," "dialogue"—all of which do structure some responses to September 11, whether they are named or not. Choosing between concepts always involves making decisions that are not guided by the actual material. This is why concepts imply ideologies: concepts are applied to situations rather than derived from them. For reasons to be examined, "trauma" seems to have been *the* prime concept (or at least one of the prime concepts) governing the organization of the information involving the attacks on the Twin Towers.

To indicate how curious it is that media by and large picked "trauma" to organize these events, it helps to pick a (non-idealistic) alternative, such as "sobriety," to organize the stories. The plot of "sobriety" would (and has) follow(ed) a pattern of before-and-after, with the attacks serving as the welcome-to-reality call. The sobriety narrative emphasizes the idealistic beliefs of the post-cold-war 1990s that have come to an abrupt end. These narratives, one would imagine, are not self-righteous in assigning positions of good and evil, but instead focus on the misguided beliefs and the wishful thinking of all sides, including of "the West." One could even ask whether the "sober" response involves more mourning than the "trauma" scheme.

The most prominent and, so to say, appealing aspect of the ideology of "trauma" is, of course, the innocence of the victim. It seems likely that the formation of "trauma" as a cultural concept has been motivated and propelled by the attribute of innocence. Especially in the past three decades, "trauma" has taken its place as one of the key modes of explanation for human behavior. Not so long ago, for example, legal practices were shaken by the idea of "trauma" and subsequently re-evaluated the sentences of penal law: On the one hand, certain ("traumatic") crimes, such as rape and domestic violence, advanced to major crimes; on the other hand, the behavior of certain offenders suddenly found a potentially exculpatory factor in their own ("traumatic") pasts. And, of course, the recent interest in the Holocaust and slavery would probably not have reached its current dimensions— and would not have been that appealing to Hollywood—without the category of "trauma." In the four

key instances of "trauma"—rape, domestic violence, genocide, and slavery—
the innocence of the victims is beyond question. Legal experts, psychologists,
and activists have worked hard to establish that the victims of a rape have not
provoked the rape, and that whatever a victim of these crimes may have done
cannot be used to justify the behavior of the perpetrator.

However, this idea of innocence can be manipulated. Once one manages to
position oneself as a "trauma" victim, one seems absolved from possible
involvement. Yet, this line is blurred: victims of a second attack may have
been the aggressors of a first. In the case of September 11, it is clear that from
the perspective of those who were killed, the attack was an unprovoked act of
hatred. But the same cannot be said on the political level, as past U.S. actions
and policies have taken many lives in the Middle East. To be sure, previous
U.S. activities do not justify the recent mass murder. Still, it is striking to see
how little the media discussed the earlier activities and policies of the United
States in the larger region. Only a few critics, such as Noam Chomsky, have
sketched the prehistory of the attacks (he puts the number of U.S.-caused
deaths during the last decade in the area tenfold higher than the deaths of
September 11).[4] A discussion of the U.S. military activities and strikes would
not have conformed to the ideology of "trauma" and thus had to be ignored.
Or conversely: Precisely because the U.S. involvement is not convenient,
choosing a concept of "trauma" is a good choice to whitewash this involvement, since the innocence of the victim also tints the U.S. government as a
whole. Still, one should ask—and we will do so below—which taboos
guarded the U.S. loss of innocence.

The consequence of the ideology of "trauma" is clear: By presenting America as the victim of a "traumatic" event, the victim can legitimately claim
innocence and does not have to question her actions that might have led to
the attack. Rather, the victim can focus on planning counter-attacks. Obviously, as a conceptual tool, "trauma" is quite welcome to political leaders, and
they played their part well.

In order to organize the events of September 11 according to the basic plot
of "trauma," one would have to stress the following elements:

• shock
• repetition
• emphasis on experience
• involuntary memories
• states of confusion
• afterlife of the event
• attributing the shock to some external source ("the villain")

• focus on healing
• attempts to memorialize and put memory back into place

Indeed, one can find this basic plot of "trauma" mirrored everywhere in the media, including in many of the beautiful (if one can say that) picture books published by leading news organizations and photographers soon after the attacks. One of the first of these is Reuters' *September 11: A Testimony.*[5] In this photo catalogue, it is both the selection and the arrangement of pictures that confirm the "trauma" plot. While the book shows typically one picture per page and is not divided by headlines or chapters, there is a clear progression informing its organization:

I. World Trade Center attack
    a. Explosions of planes, collapse of the World Trade Center (pages 2–27)
    b. Pain on the faces of people watching the collapsing Towers (29–37)
      • the U.S. flag (39)
    c. Ruins (41–49)
      • the U.S. flag (51)
II. The other two airliners, Pentagon & Pennsylvania (53–61)
III. Airports closed all around the country (63–67)
    a. the U.S. flag (69)
IV. Firefighters and other officials (71–105)
V. The U.S. president, close-up and teary-eyed, etc. (109–23)
VI. Memorials
    a. Candles, flowers, improvised shrines (125–49)
    b. Funerals (151–59)
    c. Guests of funerals, close up (161–73)
VII. Normalization: cleaning up, stock market reopening, police (175–91)
    a. Osama bin Laden on a wanted poster (193)
    b. the U.S. flag (195)
VIII. Paying tribute
    a. Sport stadium, the Yankees (197–217)
    b. Others (219–21)
    c. International heads-of-state (223–49)
IX. Manhattan skyline (251–59)
X. Closure: a single firefighter with flag at a mini-memorial on top of gravel (261)

Next to the fact that this and similar books are marketable commodities, what is perhaps most remarkable is that the book portrays a proper closure of how to deal with this attack. From the initial shock to its repetitions, from tears to paying tribute, and from memorializing to normalizing, the coffee-table book maps out the steps to recovery. In general, what might be the most unique and notable aspect of the media's response to the terrorist attacks is the therapeutic mission the media seem to have assigned to their reporting: to further the healing and reconcile the loss. This is not limited to a few exceptional productions, but includes standard reporting. The new role of the news media is to be a friend and therapist.

In the media, this therapy and healing is intimately linked to memory and its derivatives, such as experience and memorials. Insofar as "trauma" is a memory disorder, the proper memory will end the pain. Still, what does this have to do with the media? How is an aestheticized, commodified memory in a coffee-table book going to help?

Works of memory promise to heal "trauma." Once one remembers, memorializes, the event is truly over. By memorializing September 11, so goes the logic of "trauma" therapy, it is put into place so that a "healthy" relationship can be had with it. Thus, finding a proper memorial is not simply a matter of remembering and honoring what will otherwise be forgotten, but its mission is healing. This explains the rush with which officials and the media threw themselves on the search for proper memorials of September 11 while the fires were still burning. Hardly a newspaper did not report daily about possible monuments. Most remarkably, the media responded by themselves becoming memorials. From *The Portraits of Grief* by the *New York Times* to the anniversary documentaries, the assumption seems to have been that memorializing is a form of healing.

But this logic of a healing by memory is a shortcut, driven not by therapy or the needs of an actual patient, who tries to come to terms with her past, but merely by the expectations raised by the ideology of "trauma." "Trauma" mandates memory, hence the media deliver. Therapy is reduced to a formalized practice from an assembly line: If all elements are there, healing ought to be the result; if there is a memorial, we are supposedly healed. To be sure, I do not argue that there is some authentic healing of "trauma" that is somehow betrayed by the media or public leaders after September 11. Instead, I argue that to the degree that "trauma" therapy is a formalized and prescribed practice, it is more correctly described as a voodoo that implants healing, rather than brings it about. In other words, the therapy the media invoke is a ritualized practice. At this point, this consideration helps us to be skeptical about the emphatic and optimistic notion of healing frequently used by political leaders and put to work by the media. One should suspect that the chanting of "trauma" and "healing" has other implications and purposes than healing.

In short, monuments are not a means of therapy. Rather, they are institutions that master and rule over memories in such a way that the institution echoes the violence that accompanied the initial shock.[6] This does not disqualify memorials and monuments—quite the contrary—but it forbids placing them as the destination of healing to replace the actual work of mourning. Instead, monuments alert us to the fact that the very passage to the past that they open is simultaneously blocked by them (and others).

The declared "national healing" requires that "trauma" be presented as "trauma." According to the basic theory of "trauma," the repetition of the shocking event is an element of dealing with it. In short, the re-traumatization—or, in fact, traumatization itself—by the media can be presented as a necessity for "national healing."

The irony is clear: the media have to become "traumatic," produce "trauma," and then pose as the cure. Or conversely: in order for the media to pose as friend and therapist, they have to bring about "trauma." Indeed, the aforementioned functional affinity between mass media and that which psychologists describe as "trauma" has become heightened after September 11. While these structural similarities between "trauma" and the media are usually balanced by certain elements—such as the narrative voice, the numbing effect of media, and the possibility for individuals to choose to stop participating, i.e., to switch off the television—it was precisely these elements that were suspended when the media took up the hijacking of four airplanes. It was difficult to avoid the media and the repetitions of the same shocking film clips in the very days after the attacks. No strong narrative and neutral voice accompanied the images to give order to the chaotic material and to present opinions that one could agree or disagree with. Instead, the televised events were in a flow, uninterrupted by analysis, thought, and commentary. The media's case of September 11 was not a matter of opinion. Instead, it was mostly about shock, immediacy, intensity, experience, repetition, and memory. In this sense, the media themselves became "traumatic." Or to put it less dramatically: the media offered the experience (not analysis) to everyone.

The picture books and the filmed documentaries are first-hand experiences and eyewitness accounts of September 11. These promise to make everyone feel as if they were there, in the Twin Towers. But why? What is the special need to be at the site of this catastrophe? Not just the visual media provide ample first-hand material; there is also the absolutely astonishing flood of publications that offer individual "oral history" descriptions of the events. These individual accounts are not limited to the most involved witnesses (rescue workers and escapees) or experts, but rather reach out to anyone who has seen some "debris" (one of the top ten words of September 11), in New York or on television.[7]

What is so remarkable about these reports of individual experiences is that they have actually been collected and published, even though they tend to be completely homogenous in their basic story of a normal day interrupted, and they rarely offer anything surprising. (Yes, there are some stunning accounts, too, but they are in a slim minority and do not explain the high number of edited volumes.) The question then is, how one can account for the necessity of recording the firsthand or secondhand experiences of many thousands of individuals. The answer seems to be that we have been persuaded that September 11 is a matter of experience, rather than of opinions, considerations for the future, or informed expert discussions. And again, it is a matter of experience, because it seems that there is some promise within the experiences. This promise is apparently so strong that it overcomes the boredom of these thousands of redundant experiences. Since the actual experiences are so lacking, it seems likely that the promise does not originate from within the realm of experiences, but rather from some expectation, namely the expectation that something is yet to be resolved, experienced, or revealed. One might suspect that the very idea of a yet-unresolved experience derives from the media's employment of the "trauma" narrative, since the idea of a failed experience is the minimal structure of "trauma."

The media's September 11 is all about experience. To understand how the media construe the "trauma" experience, it is useful to distinguish between the overwhelmingly shocking experience of the past that haunts the present and the not-yet-experience that promises a future. It seems that the media have successfully molded the former into the latter. They have presented a truly terrible and traumatizing shock of the past as something yet to come, but still to be experienced. Thereby, the terrible event that gives nightmares to many victims becomes a strangely appealing promise for the masses who witness it through the media. It is the experience not of an overwhelming shock, but an experience precisely because it seems to hold something back that is not (yet) experienced. In this holding back, in this promise or expectation of more, the clinical "trauma" is turned into a commodity that sells news. In the media, "trauma" is generated as the promise for a true and absolute experience, precisely because such an experience is not offered. The media thereby recommend themselves as the place where the "forgotten" experience can be picked up. (One might even wonder whether this conflation of past and future experience is the underlying structure that has made experience into one of the key categories of life in the past two centuries. However, this claim goes way beyond the task at hand.)

Still, it should be pointed out that this fabrication of "trauma" as an appealing not-yet-experience does not always work. According to several studies, it is especially the children all over the country who reacted to the media coverage by actually being traumatized.[8]

It seems that for many, September 11 is the first experience of history. This may account for the over-emphasis of stories that focus on the questions, Where was I when I learned the news? What did I think? What did I do? History now has the face of "trauma."

How does the actual healing from "trauma" take place? It helps to recall Sigmund Freud's paradigms, which are still the underlying pattern of most current theories of "trauma." In *Beyond the Pleasure Principle* (1919), Freud offers two narratives of "trauma" that he collapses into a third, psychological story. The first is of a wounding, a story set in the register of biology; the second is of a healing that takes place in the register of theatre. The biological story goes as follows: Every life form can be affected and wounded. Against the possible wounding, each creature produces a protective skin *(Reizschutz)* to deflect the external stimuli. However, when a stimulus is too strong, it will simply break through the protective skin and enter the being. The energy of the attack remains within the being, cannot be processed, and does much harm inside. At this point, Freud switches his account from the register of biology to that of theatre. To heal the wounded being from the wounding energy within its hidden center, the individual has to transpose (imagine) the energy of the attack as once again coming from the outside, and thus reexperience it. This (imaginary) replay of the scenario of the wounding is likely to lead to an opening of the wound again and again. However, in replaying the scenario over and over again, the protective skin will be strengthened in such a way that it will at some point be able to deflect such an attack. This strengthening of the skin will at that point not only prevent future attacks but heal the original one as well.

For Freud, the very switching of registers from biology to theatre constitutes, here and elsewhere, the sphere of the psychological. At least, this is what we must conclude when Freud adopts names for the faculties involved: The protective skin is "consciousness"; the energy within the being enters the "unconscious." The only reason that consciousness exists is to protect from outside stimuli. It does so by deflecting the energy. Apparently, Freud has in mind a process of rapid thought associations that help the individual to understand and cope with the situation and thus to not find it shocking, overwhelming, and hence "traumatic." A strong consciousness prevents an external stimulus from leaving its wounding trace within the unconscious. Freud draws the often-quoted conclusion that consciousness and leaving a (unconscious) memory trace exclude each other.

The relevance of Freud to current "trauma" debates is certainly not undisputed (although it can be said that his "trauma" theory is perhaps the only part of his thought that still shapes the debates by most major schools of psychology). However, a key Freudian assumption remains largely in, namely that the repetition compulsion *(Wiederholungszwang)* to reexperience the event involuntarily is both the problem and the path to a solution, since the repetition may serve the healing by allowing the creation of a proper response to the event and by producing a proper memory. The repetition is necessary because of the failure of the first experience.

If one uses the Freudian model to describe the media's reaction to September 11, one must face the question, What do the media propose as the protective skin, that is, the Freudian consciousness?

The answer: emblems, frozen images, the flag, totems, and pictures of Osama bin Laden. It seems appropriate to resort to a specific case. Anniversary documentaries serve as a good starting point, since they indicate the afterlife of the attack. Most of the documentaries are constructed around the same quasi-chronological narrative as the picture books. However, film adds the possibility of repetition, and most documentaries make ample use of repeating the shocking sequences of the plane attacks and the crumbling towers. "Trauma" writes the script. One of these documentaries, the HBO special *In Memoriam: New York City 9–11/01, With the Honorable Rudolph W. Giuliani* (September 2002), intersperses the chronology with Mayor Giuliani reflecting about the Twin Towers, terrorism, and the future. "I realized," we hear him say, "that we are in something different than anyone of us had ever prepared for, any of us had thought we'd live through. I realized that I was in some kind of a horrible, awful, horrific experience." Giuliani's clear voice and controlled appearance sets a stark contrast to the scenes taken on the road, with people running, the camera shaking, powerful acoustics of screaming and crying people, explosions, and pictures of dust-covered people that seem to borrow from the iconography of the Holocaust. Fast- and slow-paced sequences alternate, producing the effect that each new plane-crash sequence hits the spectator with new intensity, new surprise. Finally, after several of these mini-shocks, the replaying of the attacks—with much dust, tears, and noise—there is the turning point. Here the flag comes in, whether at funerals or lifted by firefighters. The final shots have the camera resting on the flag filmed against the sun in such a way that the picture turns black and white. Similarly, the turning point of CNN's *America Remembers: The Events of Sep-*

tember 11 and America's Response (September 2002) consists of a stunning shot of the American flag that is out of focus at first, and as the image becomes clearer, it reminds one of sunlight reflecting off ocean waves. Other focal points follow, such as shots of firefighters, on which the camera lingers, and an image of the president. After the initial shock and the repetition of the shock, reassuring static images or totems emerge.

The "trauma" therapy of September 11 is one of finding not just images, but the Image. In addition to the flag, this includes giving faces to good and evil. News programs airing on the very day of the attack saw the emergence of the other two key images: the firefighter and Osama bin Laden. This is the visual return of the hero, as well as the surfacing of absolute, mythical evil.

Obviously, images are not therapy. In precisely the position where we would have expected to find a dynamic therapeutic consciousness, there is what seems to be the opposite of consciousness: a surface, a mere static image, a reflecting shield. Whereas therapy requires a verbal trauma narrative, as Judith Herman, in a medical standard book on the stages of trauma recovery, asserts,[9] September 11 presents static images. At this point, it becomes clear that the therapeutic mission of the media loses its target to instead take a simpler path of confirmation and comfort. This is a regression from understanding to believing and from word to a totem image. The medium of September 11 is not one of communication and exchange but of communality and devotion.

At this point, we have to conclude that the media's employment of "trauma" only formally mimics therapy to set up a ritual instead. According to the fundamental studies on ritual by Emile Durkheim in *Les Formes Élémentaires de la Vie Religieuse,* a ritual is that which unites a people by bringing about the consciousness of society as such. In key rituals such as sacrifice, this happens in a two-step process. The first, negative step consists of acknowledging the absolute power of the higher being by giving (sacrificing) the gift of the totem. Then, in the second, positive step, the people elevate themselves to the same level as the higher being by sharing (eating) the totem and thus identifying with it. First, there is loss (sacrificial animal, the loss of lives, the firefighters, and Americans who died), then there is the higher unity of identifying with the totem (the flag), the higher being (America), and thus the generation of society. The totem images of the flag and the American firefighter are first seen in the ashes, lost in debris, and then they become the means by which one can achieve the union with this higher being: America. The flag on top of the ruins is the totem that solidifies "trauma" as a ritual.[10]

We are now in the position to describe how the media fabricated September 11 by transforming the concept of "trauma" into a ritualistic sequence (for this, we can leave aside the actual rituals that people performed, ranging from candlelight marches to funerals and from money donations to pilgrimages to Ground Zero). The media rites begin by recalling the attack on the Twin Towers. This recall can best be invoked by a physical presence on the sacred space of Ground Zero. The story of suffering is told next. Instead of giving factual information, a mimetic presentation offers the event: the story is to be told in the first person by a witness—what he or she saw, did, and thought. This is the moment of crisis that the ritual has to both bring about by repeated recalls of the shock and the vulnerability of the clan, and to master by showing how the totem overcomes the pain. Indeed, the next step is to depict the totem being reborn from the ashes like a phoenix: the flag is raised in the midst of the dust of destruction. It is now time for the purification to begin. Since the ritual serves the function of adding the deceased to the strength of the totem, it is vital to stress the strengths of the dead. Today, this means to depict them in their individuality (or rather, what figures for individuality today, such as certain memberships or cracking certain kinds of jokes). Indeed, this seems to be the agenda of many stories of the dead, most notably *The Portraits of Grief* by the *New York Times.* The result has to be that the victims are recalled by their proper names and are sanctioned as innocent heroes or saints. Along with these acts of purification through memory comes a second set of purifying rites that are meant to end the contamination by the aggressors. The aggressors are named and exposed, but in a very different way from the victims: instead of portraying their individual lives, the reports focus on where they have been and whom they have met. The perpetrators are contagious and hence the purification needs to curse certain places (Mohammed Atta's Hamburg, Germany; Florida flight schools; the Taliban's Afghanistan). The endpoint of the ritual is—following the script of Durkheim's peoples of Australia to the letter—the spreading of the totem ashes to secure a stronger totem than ever before.

In what is probably the strongest recent theory of rituals, the German system theorist Niklas Luhmann suggests that rituals are "communication that avoids communication."[11] The idea is that rituals offer a way to deal with those things that cannot or should not be communicated (we might think of holy matters, death, sexuality, matters of science that are not understood, perhaps unwanted opposition, etc.). Rituals take place to get around asking and answering questions of these taboos (e.g. the funeral rites make it possible that we can avoid the troubling questions surrounding death). Again, we can see the contrast between "trauma" and ritual: Whereas "trauma" requires communication, rituals replace communication.

If the media's September 11 is indeed a ritualistic practice, one needs to ask what is off-limits for communication. If September 11 is ritualized, then there must be a taboo in connection with the totem image. What is to be avoided in communicating September 11?

The taboo of September 11 is empathizing with the hijackers. Empathizing with the terrorists is not limited to actual (military, political, financial, logistical, propagandistic) support, but also includes anything from admiration of their radical act, or identification with their imagined motives, to applauding opposition to the world's only superpower. Whereas actual support risks triggering "actual" responses, it is the latter that seem to be targeted by the taboo. The implicit purpose of ritualization, then, can be described as the elimination of human empathy with the terrorists.

The considerations of a taboo may seem far fetched, both in terms of the likelihood of anyone actually empathizing with terrorists and in the success of not empathizing by means of ritual. However, statistics from around the world quickly established that a significant percentage of the (Western) public were willing to sympathize with the attackers (several sources gave numbers as high as 25% of the population), while still mostly condemning the act. Apparently, the possibility of sympathizers was also taken seriously by the White House. At least it seems that this was the aim of the president's declaration that the attackers were "cowards." These words caused a bizarre and intense public semantic debate about what a "coward" is—sparked by objections from Susan Sontag, David "Davey D" Cook, and others that suicide bombers are not cowards—that can best illustrate the underlying taboo. Ari Fleischer, the White House press secretary, at one point said that people such as Bill Maher of *Politically Incorrect* "should watch what they say, watch what they do."[12] Generally speaking, only in the first days after the attacks were there words about the terrorists that gave any indication of respect such as, "How did they pull this off?" A few days after the mass murder, this rhetoric of respect and secret sympathy disappeared entirely.[13]

One might wonder about the necessity of this ritualization and its taboo. Two readings seem plausible. The weak reading would be to say that any empathy with the enemy seems to exclude the harsh and strong reaction mandated in response to the attacks. This is a weak reading because there is no logical necessity that empathy excludes a powerful policing or judicial reaction: one can relate to a criminal and still demand the strongest punishment, strongest pursuit, and uncompromised cooperation of one's allies. To understand is not to tolerate. The strong reading is to suspect that the taboo externalizes an internal ambiguity. Perhaps people harbor the secret, inner desire for this kind of event which, however, they cannot admit to themselves, so that the wish needs to be condemned and then purified by the ritual. The attackers have to be off-limits precisely because they are also within us. The reason for such a desire does not have to be that we have some envy of the former inhabitants of the World Trade Center.[14] Rather, it seems that the structure of the sensationalist media partly induces such a desire for the absolute extraordinary in us. And the absolute extraordinary would be the fall of the most powerful paradigm of our modern world: the economy, as symbolized by the World Trade Center. In short, the inability to admit this part of ourselves may lead to a ritualization. A Ritualized Nation is thus a nation victimized by its own shame.

One of the effects of these rituals is the creation of a specific reality that is distinct from other realities. Notably, the ritually induced reality differs from most Hollywood products since Hollywood clings to the pattern that those individuals who rebel against the big institution are heroes. In September 11, these few individuals are the criminals. One could argue that breaking this Hollywood pattern of sympathy with the minority requires strong measures, such as a ritualistic attitude toward "trauma" and a taboo.

Another positive effect of the ritualization is patience. In the critical period right after September 11, some called for immediate action and revenge. However, "trauma" and ritualized "trauma" offered a wider time frame than "an eye for an eye" would have so that military actions could be delayed.

Still, there is a price tag to rituals. In this case, it is the rift between "the West" and "Islam." By placing a taboo on empathizing with the attackers, their mission, and the background of their acts, they are placed "outside" of "our" world. By means of the synecdoche of part and whole, this draws the line between the religious worlds. And this is as counterproductive as it is misleading. The rise of hate crimes against Muslims in 2002—up by 1,600 percent, according to the FBI's annual report on hate crimes—is only an indication of the lasting effects of the resulting rift. These hate crimes are not some form of scapegoating, but rather an attack on the enemy one cannot have empathy for.

To conclude, the crossover between ritual and "trauma" therapy in the media's September 11 is not to the advantage of either of the two practices.

The crossover causes "trauma" to borrow from ritual in such a way that which should be therapy ends in the fabrication of sacred and thus untouchable objects that are beyond the reach of question and thus therapy. Conversely, the crossover causes ritual to be grounded in therapy in such a way that ritual must constantly justify itself by means of its therapeutic effect. But this can take place only by constantly confirming the malady of those in need of ritualistic cure. This includes the right and even mandate of the media to (re)traumatize its audience. Thus, the rituals of community after September 11 require the constant performance of "traumatic" behavior and victimization or at least infantilization of the public. This has a further consequence: since one cannot entrust "traumatized" people with making decisions, it is clear that others (the government, the military) should have unrestricted freedom of operation, undisturbed by democratic processes.

In short, it would be unfair to say that the media "failed" after September 11. By and large, the media acted quite responsibly. There has rarely been so much self-censorship by the media, so much careful wording, and consideration of the affected people. However, it is this very self-censorship and the very therapeutic mission the media implicitly assigned to their reporting that has fabricated September 11 as a ritualistic practice that deepens the divide between "us and them." The media's attempt to educate and cure has backfired by infantilizing and addicting the public to a cult. "Trauma" has become a means of molding stories and connecting individual healing with unreflected collective nationalism. Ironically, the media's focus on therapy has made therapy harder—for there is indeed the necessity for therapy which, ironically, the media by large have not proven. It leaves A Ritualized Nation without agency and without access to its wishes and thus imprisoned by shame.

II

News Texts and
Cultural Resonance

6

"America under Attack": CNN's Verbal and Visual Framing of September 11

Amy Reynolds and Brooke Barnett

It's one of the most heinous acts, certainly in world history.
—New York City Mayor Rudy Giuliani, September 11, 2001

We're at war. We're absolutely at war.
—U.S. Rep. Curt Weldon (Pa.), September 11, 2001

Horrific. Extraordinary. Unprecedented. These are words that government officials, journalists, and eyewitnesses used frequently to describe the events of September 11, 2001, during breaking live coverage. As news of the terrorist attacks started to reach most Americans, government officials such as Giuliani and Weldon wasted no time making strong declarations that might help people understand exactly what had happened.

As CNN and other broadcast media outlets reported these words, viewers repeatedly watched images of commercial airplanes crash into the World Trade Center towers. Many people saw the towers collapse "live" on television. They saw images of panic-stricken people fleeing massive debris clouds in lower Manhattan, running for their lives. They saw fire at the Pentagon. They saw the charred earth scattered with the small, twisted-metal remains that used to be a commercial airplane in rural Pennsylvania. They would see journalists reacting like human beings rather than detached observers, sometimes in nearly stunned silence: "Good Lord. There are no words....This is just a horrific scene and a horrific moment."[1]

The above examples are only small snapshots from the live televised coverage of September 11. A more complete look provides some insight into how broadcast media framed the events of September 11 both verbally and visually. This chapter qualitatively deconstructs CNN's verbal and visual "breaking news" coverage. We suggest that CNN created a powerful visual and verbal frame with its coverage by arguing to viewers that the events of September 11 comprised an act of war so horrific that immediate military retaliation was not only justified but necessary.

CNN was selected for this analysis because viewers consistently considered it their primary news outlet. Surveys by the Pew Research Center report that 90 percent of Americans received news about the 9-11 terrorism attacks from television; of those, 53 percent turned to cable, led notably by CNN.[2] Further, a previous analysis of 9-11 breaking news coverage on ABC, CBS, NBC, and CNN showed strong similarities in coverage among the four media outlets.[3]

FRAMING DEFINED

For this study, we conducted a verbal (audio) and visual frame analysis of the first 12 hours of "breaking" live news broadcast by CNN. Noted sociologist William Gamson has suggested that a complete frame analysis has three components: an examination of the production process that "alerts us to issues of power and resources;"[4] an examination of texts, which can occur on different levels of analysis; and an attempt to address the "complex interaction of texts with an audience engaged in negotiating the meaning."[5] According to Entman, "to frame is to select some aspects of a perceived reality and make them more salient in a communicating text, in such a way as to promote a particular problem, definition, causal interpretation, moral evaluation, and/or treatment recommendation for the item described."[6] Entman argued that the social power of journalism is reflected in the ways that journalists designate what is most salient through, among other things, the sources they select and the ways in which they provide order and context to stories.

Communicators make conscious or unconscious decisions in deciding what to say, guided by frames...that organize their belief systems. The text contains the frames, which are manifested by the presence or absence of certain keywords, stock phrases, stereotyped images, sources of information, and sentences that provide thematically reinforcing clusters of facts or judgments.[7]

After an extensive review of the literature on framing, James Tankard conceptually defined a frame as "a central organizing idea for news content that supplies a context and suggests what the issue is through the use of selection, emphasis, exclusion and elaboration."[8] This fits Entman's notion of framing and is consistent with the way that many other scholars have defined framing in studies that have addressed a variety of issues related to the mass media.[9] Tankard and Entman's definitions of framing are used here as guiding principles for both the verbal and visual analyses.

The Production Process

As Gamson noted, identifying and explaining the production process is a necessary first step in any framing analysis. He suggested that this process look at the ways in which "carriers of particular frames engage in activities to produce and reproduce them."[10] Gamson also suggested that studying the production process involves identifying issues of power. We begin this section with a look at the media as our frame "carriers" and end this section with a brief examination of the issues of power in the context of media, politics, and public opinion.

Media Function

The study of the social structural context of press practices is often called "media sociology" and is one theoretical area that informs our research, especially in terms of the production of media messages.[11] The study of media content is important because it is the basis for determining media impact and predicting media effects.[12] Studying content also serves as an indicator of other underlying forces in communication content, allowing scholars to learn about the people and organizations that produce media content.[13]

Previous media sociology studies have suggested that factors intrinsic to an individual journalist (such as gender, race, age, education, or political affiliation) do not substantially impact or influence media content. Personal and professional notions of objectivity tend to render these influences moot.[14] These studies suggest that greater influence on media content comes from macro-level influences—cultural and social ideological influences and extra-media influences (the sources journalists interview, for example).[15]

This chapter will examine CNN's content in the context of a significant breaking news event. Significant breaking news is different from planned daily "live" news or even routine "breaking news," such as police chases or serious fires, because it subsumes all other news. All of a news organization's resources are devoted to coverage of the significant event. Commercial breaks are suspended. The duration of coverage is counted by hours, perhaps even days, rather than minutes. Efforts between national news organizations and local and/or international news organizations are coordinated. Prior to September 11, some well-known significant breaking news stories included the start of the U.S. air attacks in Iraq during the Persian Gulf War, the O.J. Simpson Bronco chase in Southern California, and the Oklahoma City federal building bombing.

In previous research, we have suggested that breaking news fundamentally alters the traditional process of reporting by changing the routines that journalists follow. Rather than relying on the routine of objectivity, which often means striving for accuracy, balance, and fairness, journalists covering significant breaking news events restructure their environment to work around speed to become the first to break a story or provide new information.[16] We argue that this shift in routine allows a journalist's individual ideological frames to show more clearly than in more traditional reporting situations. These personal ideological frames frequently reflect the dominant ideological frames of a given culture.

Visual Framing

This study will examine media content in terms of both audio and video. The definitions of framing noted earlier apply to both audio and video (either can be considered "text"), but it is useful to add information here about visual framing and the message production process as it relates to creating images. Messaris and Abraham have suggested that visual framing is different than verbal framing because of three distinct properties of visual images—analogical quality, indexical quality, and "lack of an explicit prepositional syntax."[17] Analogical quality refers to the idea that the relationship between most visual images and their meanings is based on analogy or similarity to the objects that they represent.[18] Similarly, indexical quality suggests that visual images contain direct pointers to objects that give them a "true-to-life" quality that causes people to believe visual images are more accurate than other forms of communication.[19] In the context of framing, this could "diminish the likelihood that viewers would question what they see."[20]

The third distinct property of images is that they lack "explicit prepositional syntax." This refers to the relationship between images and suggests that the connections are "loose, imprecise and unsystematic," which is opposite of the properties of verbal language.[21] That is, when we use verbal language to communicate we use certain types of syntactic devices to make propositions or connections, whether we are asserting causality or making generalizations. Since images lack this "explicit prepositional syntax," a viewer's ability to make sense of a series of images is based on other cues. In the context of video, this means that the ways in which individual shots are edited together can convey different kinds of meanings to viewers. One example of this is the phenomenon of associational juxtaposition, an editing device that, in essence, allows the qualities of an object or a person in one image to be transferred to an object or person in the next image.[22]

Issues of Power

Noted scholars have argued for decades that the media influence public opinion. In the 1920s, Walter Lippmann wrote that the media are our windows to the world beyond our direct experience and that they determine our cognitive maps of that world.[23] Agenda-setting theory suggests that over time the agenda of the news media influences the agenda of the public.[24] This is one way to consider the power issue in the context of mass media. Decades of research in the "effects" tradition of the mass media suggest at a minimum some limited effect of mass-media content on the formation of public opinion.

Another way to look at power within the context of mass media involves questions of access and ideology. Whose voices are heard? What ideas dominate? In *Manufacturing Consent,* Herman and Chomsky sketch out a propaganda model and apply it to the U.S. media. They write: "It is a 'guided market system' that we describe here, with the guidance provided by government, the leaders of the corporate community, the top media owners and executives, and the assorted individuals and groups who are assigned or allowed to take constructive initiatives."[25] Political scientist Michael Parenti uses coverage of the Sandinista rebellion in Nicaragua as one example of how a propaganda theme works in U.S. media. For decades the United States gave military aid to Nicaraguan dictator Somoza, and in return he opened the country to U.S. corporate investors. The Sandinista popular rebellion, which wanted to end Nicaragua's client-state status, brought them into conflict with the United States.[26] Parenti notes that most of what was written about Nicaragua in the mainstream American press neglected to reflect the reality of the situation. He uses a William Shannon-penned *Boston Globe* column to illustrate this:

(Shannon) explained it this way: "[The Sandinistas] hate America. This is understandable given their limited education and their years spent in exile, in prison, or in the hills battling what they perceived as an American-backed dictatorship." Shannon rules out the possibility that "what they perceived" might have had a basis in reality. By leaving unmentioned the role the U.S. played in supporting the Somoza regime, he can reduce the Sandinistas' anti-imperialist policy to an anti-Americanism.... Why else would anyone feel unfriendly toward U.S. policy?[27]

Altschull has suggested that "it is important for leaders in all nation-states to see to it their press behaves in an acceptable fashion.... The press in all instances is an agent of political and economic power."[28] He notes that sociologist Max Weber recognized this agency role of the press early in the twentieth century; however, it was fellow German sociologist Ferdinand Tonnies who expanded this conception of press vulnerability to manipulation by the elite. Tonnies's analysis of opinion formation concluded that public opinion was actually the expression of the elite and not of the masses, so when the press gave voice to public opinion it was actually giving voice to the viewpoints of the elite.[29]

Communication scholar Robert McChesney laments a similar problem, but puts it in the context of the corporatism of modern media:

The corporate media cement a system whereby the wealthy and powerful few make the most important decisions with virtually no informed public participation. Crucial political issues are barely covered by the corporate media or else are warped to fit the confines of an elite debate, stripping ordinary citizens of the tolls they need to be informed, active participants in a democracy.[30]

Many of the points raised by these scholars are supported qualitatively in this chapter. CNN's breaking news coverage of September 11 strongly suggests that the parameters of the debate about terrorism were confined to narrowly defined categories.

METHOD

To verbally and visually analyze CNN's "breaking news" coverage of September 11, we obtained the first 12 hours of video of CNN's coverage, which began at 8:48 A.M. The tapes came from personal recordings, CNN's videotape service, and the Federal Document Clearing House (www.fdhc.com). We developed a master transcript by downloading breaking-news and special-event transcripts from CNN's Web site and from Lexis. The complete 12-hour transcript was compared to the video prior to analysis to ensure accuracy. Some of the downloaded transcripts from the CNN Web site were incomplete. When we discovered these information gaps, we transcribed text from the videotape. Once the final transcript was complete and we were certain no text was missing, we did a final accuracy review. The entire printed transcript was compared to the 12 hours of video and no errors were discovered. The transcript was then printed and we worked to create a video log to match the audio transcript for analysis.

To create the video log we matched the details of every single video shot (defined as visual material with no break in continuity of action) with the transcript.[31] Every text graphic that appeared on screen was transcribed and then matched to the audio and video so that for analysis we had a complete picture of what was seen on screen as we read or evaluated any word or phrase. Each author individually logged six hours of video. Prior to this we spent two hours in the same geographic location logging material together to ensure reliability. Both authors have professional broadcast journalism backgrounds and teach broadcast journalism courses.

We analyzed these media texts using qualitative frame analysis for two reasons. First, we believe it's important to connect the audio and visual aspects of the breaking news coverage to provide a more complete understanding of the frames CNN presented. To do this quantitatively would require two distinctly separate analyses (verbal and visual) that would be difficult to puzzle together in a meaningful and coherent way. Second, as Hertog and McLeod have observed, one of the shortcomings of quantitative text analysis is that "very powerful concepts, central to frames, need not be repeated often to have great impact."[32] In practice, the qualitative framing approach we used was guided by Gamson, Entman, and Tankard's definitions of framing and combined with a qualitative framing analysis process suggested by Hertog and McLeod. They suggest developing lists of symbols, language, usage, categories, themes, and concepts identified from the texts. Then, general analysis is guided by exploring the relationship between culture, ideology, frames, issues, and narrative structure.[33]

CNN'S VERBAL AND VISUAL FRAMING OF SEPTEMBER 11

CNN's breaking coverage of September 11 contained a plethora of keywords, images, sources of information, sentences, and thematic elements that, in the end, created a powerful, dominant frame—that a U.S. military-led international war would be the only meaningful solution to prevent more terrorist attacks. Perhaps one of the most striking and significant elements of CNN's early coverage of September 11 was its reliance on government sources to try to make sense of the terrorist attacks. Eyewitnesses, journalists, and news producers were the primary sources used to describe events and add verbal detail to the images. But CNN relied almost exclusively on current and former government officials to provide interpretation of the day's events and to effectively frame what had happened and what would happen as a result.

When we combine the keywords, sentences, images, and sources from the first 12 hours of CNN's coverage, several thematically reinforcing clusters of judgments emerge. These thematic clusters, when taken together, result in the creation of the aforementioned dominant frame for CNN's breaking news coverage. In essence, CNN's early framing of the events of September 11 created the impression that war was inevitable and necessary to combat the horror and devastation that Americans had just witnessed. These three thematic clusters involve war and military response, American unity, and justification. Each is discussed separately below.

War and Military Response

Anchor Carol Linn began CNN's breaking news coverage with these words: "You are looking at obviously a very disturbing live shot there. That is the World Trade Center, and we have unconfirmed reports this morning that a plane has crashed into one of the towers." Words like "disturbing" and "extraordinary" were heard from the very beginning of coverage and frequently throughout as general descriptors. The most common descriptive keywords included "horrible," "horror," "horrific," "horrendous," "disturbing," "unbelievable," "extraordinary," and "terrible."

In a brief statement at 9:30 A.M., President George W. Bush confirmed that the two plane crashes were terrorist attacks. After the president confirmed the terrorism connection, CNN journalists and their sources used symbolic keywords to contextualize the events. These keywords included referring to the United States more frequently as "America" instead of "the U.S." or "the United States"; using the word "war," which was heard 234 times in 12 hours; using the words "cowards" and "madmen" to describe the terrorists; making atypical references to "God" and the need to "pray" or for "prayer" (the three words were mentioned 61 times, often by journalists); and using words like "freedom," "justice," and "liberty" as simple descriptors of America and its ideals. Viewers also started to hear a shift in the context in which the descriptive keywords were used because they were frequently accompanied by a strongly worded personal reaction statement from journalists. An example comes from anchor Judy Woodruff after discussing with a reporter the terrorists' use of the airplanes as bombs:

Absolutely chilling to hear you say that, David, that there are people in these organizations—and we now know it—who could fly commercial jetliners to do what, these horrible, unspeakable acts that have been committed today in the United States.

The word "war" was used in a number of ways to express different ideas. Frequently when sources were asked to make sense of the attacks most answered like U.S. Senator John McCain of Arizona: "This is obviously an act of war." Once journalists had sources suggesting an "act of war," they began to incorporate that into their questions and their own interpretations of the events. For example, early in the day when CNN's senior White House correspondent, John King, was asked what the White House was doing to address the attacks, he answered, "Well, I don't want to guess at all, but from the White House situation room, a president or a vice president can direct a war, can direct a full scale war."

The war theme arose in other contexts. Just before 2:00 P.M., Judy Woodruff was interviewing U.S. Senator Christopher Dodd of Connecticut, who observed, "in a day like this, which rivals if not exceeds the attack on Pearl Harbor almost 60 years ago...we stand totally united behind our president and our government." Once Dodd offered a Pearl Harbor analogy journalists brought this into their questions and discussions with other sources more than a dozen times. A local New York City journalist interviewing an eyewitness to the collapse offered: "A lot of people equated this to something like Pearl Harbor. You were there (today). Nothing has ever happened like this." Sources also used it to underscore the war point. James Kallstrom, former FBI assistant director, said, "I think (this is) clearly an act of war.... it's a different time, but it's everything that Pearl Harbor was and more."

As sources more frequently labeled the terrorist attacks "an act of war" and made symbolic comparisons to Pearl Harbor, the notion of an American-led military response started to surface. For example, at a press conference, New York Governor George Pataki observed, "Clearly this is an attack upon America, it's an attack upon our freedom and our way of life and we must retaliate and go after those who perpetuated this heinous crime against the people of America." In an unrelated press conference several hours later, Bush advisor Karen Hughes delivered a prepared statement that provided a much more subtle example of the use of the keyword America in connection with retaliation predicated by an assault on American values: "Our fellow citizens and our freedom came under attack today, and no one should doubt America's resolve."

Some CNN sources were direct in their advocation of a strong military response; others were subtle and often spoke through the reporters. Here are two different examples:

Former Secretary of Defense Lawrence Eagleburger: What you do is you strike at them militarily. I mean, I know this is going to sound awful, but my point is there is only one way to begin to deal with people like this, and that is you have to kill some of them even if they are not immediately directly involved in this thing.

David Ensor, CNN's National Security Correspondent: There's a certain amount of black humor also now setting in...when I asked (intelligence officials) whether there were considerations being given to some sort of retaliation against targets in Afghanistan, one official said, "I wouldn't be planning your vacation there if I were you."

Some of CNN's sources discussed the military response against an international backdrop. It seems quite possible that, given the incredible number of references to the need for international support, many government sources were using CNN to send messages to other world leaders and vice-versa. For example, Israel's foreign minister, Shimon Peres, told CNN:

And I am sure that as bitter and painful the event is, the only one that can save humanity from this terrible danger is the United States of America. It was not an attack only upon America, but an attack upon civilization, an attempt to introduce the wolves of the jungle in our life, not to permit people to fly freely, to walk safely, to be assured at the places they live. It is like a declaration of war, or an introduction of a terrible arm, and we have to draw all the conclusions fully, uncompromisingly and right away.

In an example of a more general appeal to an international effort, former U.N. ambassador Richard Holbrooke said, "To find the people responsible is going to take a unified international effort. No one nation, not even the United States, can do it on its own." This kind of comment was heard often during the first 12 hours of coverage.

American Unity

The second thematic cluster that contributes to the dominant frame involves the significance and importance of American unity. One underlying assumption in the choice and language of CNN's official sources and reporters was that Democrats and Republicans made up the spectrum of all available viewpoints. Once this was established, clear-cut agreement by the two parties suggested that the entire country would be unified and in agreement regarding all issues related to terrorism. Not once during the first 12 hours of coverage did CNN interview any official source with a political affiliation other than Democrat or Republican. Not once did anyone, source or journalist, suggest that an option other than supporting the president would exist.

New York's democratic senator, Hillary Clinton, typically at odds with the Bush administration's agenda, clearly stated her support for him in the context of the need for American unity during times of crisis: "We're all united behind the President... the legislative leadership of our country, from both Houses of Congress, on both sides of the aisle, saying just as clearly as we can that this was an *attack on America* (emphasis added). And the President of the United States is our President. And we will support him in whatever steps he deems necessary to take...."

CNN anchor Wolf Blitzer noticed the power of the image of unity when he referenced video from later in the evening that showed members of Congress at the end of a press conference singing "God Bless America." He observed that it was "a pointed display of bipartisan unity at this critical moment in U.S. history. It seemed like a spontaneous singing of 'God Bless America' by scores of members of (Congress) seriously trying to send a message of unity during this difficult moment."

Other examples of unity that again came from this narrow parameter include:

Illinois Republican Rep. Dennis Hastert (Speaker of the House): Senators and House members, Democrats and Republicans, will stand shoulder to shoulder to fight this evil that's been perpetrated on this nation. We will stand together to make sure that those who have brought forth this evil deed will pay the price.

Virginia Republican Senator John Warner: I can assure you that the Congress stands behind our president, and the president speaks with one voice for this entire nation.

CNN correspondent Jamie McIntyre: (General Hugh Shelton, Chairman of the Joint Chiefs of Staff) was flanked with bipartisan support from Capitol Hill. The leading Democrat and Republicans from the Senate Armed Services Committee there to show support that the United States, when attacked, has no divisions in its political will.

It is noteworthy that unity was defined in such a narrow way. CNN gave viewers the perception that because government leaders from the two dominant American political parties were unified, the entire country was unified. While this most likely accurately reflected a majority view, it discounted many other available viewpoints that in theory might have altered, or at least encouraged, some substantive debate. CNN's sources repeatedly connected the keyword "America" with freedom and other American ideals, which included the implied notion that it would be un-American to voice political dissent given the magnitude of the day's events. This, of course, runs contrary to First Amendment values and ideals, yet it was clearly tied to notions of what it means to be a "good" American. By this definition, good Americans stand united and always support the views of the president in times of crisis. Two statements by former government officials illustrate this and help to build on the theme of American unity:

Former FBI assistant director James Kallstrom: People that hate us and hate what we stand for and hate our way of life have demonstrated that over and over again.... and today they've brought that terrible hatred to the United States of America and we, as a country, as a nation, need to stand together.

Former Georgia Senator Sam Nunn: I think it's very important we remain steadfast in this country—we always rise to the occasion and work together when we are in crisis, and I think this qualifies for mustering the American will to remain calm and collected and determined and firm, but most of all solidarity here at home with the president....

Once it was established that the country's leadership was unified and would support the president's response, the next logical question CNN journalists started to ask was, What is the response? This takes us back to the first thematic cluster, which told viewers that military retaliation was the only meaningful option in the face of an "act of war."

Justification

The third thematic cluster provided justification for a U. S. military response. America and notions of American values were used in sentences to justify an immediate response to the terrorist attacks, reinforcing what other sources were emphasizing in the context of war. The unified support for a military, retaliatory response was clearly reinforced visually by the repeated arousing images of the devastation and "horror" of the terrorist attacks, which will be discussed below. Justification themes also played out verbally. First, they did so in the ways that officials gave the terrorist attacks historical meaning and context. The most powerful example of this came when New York City Mayor Rudy Giuliani said the attacks were "one of the most heinous acts, certainly in world history." In the words of U.S. Attorney General John Ashcroft:

Today, America has experienced one of the greatest tragedies ever witnessed on our soil. These heinous acts of violence are an assault on the security of our nation. They are an assault on the security and freedom of every American citizen.

Ashcroft and Giuliani's words (and similar comments from many, many others) not only tried to provide historical context, but also gave support to the images that had showed Americans the magnitude and devastation of the events. Some other verbal examples that get to this issue of magnitude came from journalists. CNN analyst Jeff Greenfield remarked, "Whoever is behind this, this is of a dimension that literally dwarfs even fantasy." Judy Woodruff said several times during the day: "I have to say in my 30 years as a journalist I have never seen anything like this. Never covered a story of the dimensions of this."

Journalists and sources also gave viewers strong verbal clues about the magnitude of the events by making frequent references to God and the need for prayer and salvation. Judy Woodruff's comments are particularly striking given the fact that journalists rarely make such strong personally defining references in the context of religion:

We want to say God bless the souls of those who have lost their lives today or who are dying or are dying as we speak in hospitals and in places where they cannot be reached. I think that even those out there who may not believe that there is a God at a time like this, we all reach out for a higher being and we want to believe that there is someone who can bring us salvation.

This third thematic cluster of justification incorporated many of the descriptive keywords discussed earlier, such as "horrific" and "unbelievable," and those keywords were reinforced by the arousing imagery of the first 12 hours of coverage. Additional influence came from the strength of the emotional language offered by many of the journalists, considered by viewers generally to be detached and unaffected by the news that they cover. A detailed look at the images CNN presented in its breaking coverage will show a significant amount of support for the theme of justification, and provide reinforcement for the idea that a unified military response would be the only real alternative to combat future devastation and terror.

Images

CNN's first 50 minutes of coverage showed only live images of the World Trade Center towers burning and smoking from a variety of angles and distances, as well as both live and recorded images of the second plane flying into the south tower. Between 9:03 A.M., when the second crash occurred, and 9:30 A.M., CNN replayed the crash video 11 times. Of those 11 times, twice they showed the images in slow motion with some freeze frames (particularly the frame that showed the impact with the tower). One of the times they showed the images with a digitally added bright spotlight around the plane. A journalist did not appear on air until Aaron Brown began broadcasting from a rooftop in New York City with the smoking towers in the background, at about 9:35 A.M.

After the first hour of coverage, CNN used two different split-screen techniques to show viewers images simultaneously. CNN's initial split-screen technique involved showing a smaller box for video on the left and a larger box for video on the right. The trend throughout the first 12 hours of coverage was to use this type of split screen to show a press conference, live reporter shot, or interview "sound bite" in the smaller box on the left side of the screen, while watching either live or replayed edited images in the larger box on the right side.

A second standard split-screen technique appeared about two hours into the breaking news coverage when CNN was trying to broadcast live from New York and Washington simultaneously as the Pentagon crash occurred. This second technique would also appear later in coverage, when longer, more extensive interviews became a focus of coverage. This second standard split-screen technique used two boxes of equal proportion. When used to show two breaking news scenes at once, CNN typically aired "live" video from New York on the left side of the screen and "live" video from Washington on the right. When this equally proportioned split-screen technique was used for longer interviews, typically the journalist would appear on the left and the interview subject on the right. This equally proportioned split screen was usually replaced by the initial split screen as interviews progressed. When this happened, the interviewee (or "sound bite") appeared in the smaller left box and edited or live video continued to appear in the larger right box.

Throughout the day, the images on the right side of the screen were predominantly of the plane crashing into the tower (from a variety of angles), the towers smoking and burning, the towers collapsing, and shot after shot of terrified and often injured people fleeing the debris clouds created from the collapses. CNN also repeatedly aired shots of rescue workers in the haze. These shots were designed to take viewers to what later was called "Ground Zero," to give them a stronger sense of place. These images from New York, which dominated the afternoon coverage, were intermixed with "live" shots as well as edited video from Washington during much of the late morning hours as the Pentagon crash story began to emerge.

Likely because of the incredible difficulty in managing and producing such an enormous "live" event for television, CNN producers made no apparent effort to connect the information the viewers were hearing from sources on the left side of the screen to the images they were watching on the right. The one exception to this came at 3:00 P.M., when at the beginning of each hour an anchor in Atlanta would recap the day's events to fairly well-timed and matched edited video. This was also a time when afternoon viewers saw images from the Pentagon fire and the Pennsylvania crash site. Otherwise, the general shots of the World Trade Center mentioned above dominated coverage after about 1:00 P.M. Given the graphic nature of these images, they effectively showed the devastation and "horror" of the attacks and likely caused a heightened response to what viewers were hearing. Although the images seemed unrelated to the audio in a literal sense, they created a strong sense of urgency that also could have potentially invoked greater fear. CNN almost certainly was not intentionally trying to frighten people, but given the nature of the images that end result seems apparent. This magnification effect was even illustrated in some of the comments that CNN journalists made. For example, at one point, CNN analyst Jeff Greenfield suggested that the number of fatalities could approach 20,000. He said his figure was based on both factual information and his impressions from the images he watched throughout the day.

The video that CNN aired during this first 12 hours was powerful because the reality of the images was so arousing and overwhelming. It is extremely rare to see footage of an airplane crashing into a skyscraper. Add to that footage slow-motion or freeze-frame effects and you get a heightened viewer response.[34] It is not as unusual or arousing to see footage of a building collapse, because old buildings are often imploded in front of news and movie cameras. But, the context of this footage, coupled with the edited series of shots that often followed the shots of the dramatic collapse, is what was striking here. CNN continuously "looped," or replayed multiple times, a series of edited shots that began with a tower collapse, was followed by a shot of the massive debris cloud rolling into the streets as people frantically tried to escape, continued with shots of the ensuing darkness, and ended with shots of debris-covered and injured people seeking help from emergency workers. This edited series of shots and several others like it took the less personal but dramatic and frightening images of the towers collapsing and personalized them for an even more fear-invoking and arousing effect.

It was in this context that we heard journalists trying to help viewers understand what they were seeing, sometimes using the keywords discussed earlier. Even the president acknowledged the incredible impact of the day's images.

CNN anchor Aaron Brown (After a replay of the second place crash): You know, we have seen this now, we have seen this honestly dozens of times. And it's no less powerful and no less sickening to see it again. Again, let's just look at this scene. This is amateur video. The plane coming and now—*no words, no reason.*

CNN anchor Paula Zahn: As I stand here on this balcony tonight and look back at the smoke continuing to billow from the wreckage of the towers, it makes you sick.

President George W. Bush: The pictures of airplanes flying into buildings, fires burning, huge structures collapsing have filled us with disbelief, terrible sadness, and a quiet, unyielding anger.

One additionally powerful and arousing series of images was shown during the first 12 hours of coverage on CNN—Palestinians celebrating in the streets of East Jerusalem. This video appeared three times between about 3:35 P.M. and 3:45 P.M. Although the appearance of these images without the context of the terrorist attacks would not seem to provoke an emotional viewer response, their juxtaposition with the images of the death and destruction in the United States were further examples of ways that seemingly disconnected video could reinforce the general themes offered in the audio, creating strong arousal within viewers. This fits the notion of associational juxtaposition discussed earlier.

The culminating effect of these images provides additional support for the three themes that emerged to create the dominant frame in CNN's breaking news coverage. Seeing Americans coming together to rescue and help each other showed unity. Seeing the devastation and magnitude of the attacks in such arousing ways would support an emotional response to the notion that when one is attacked, one retaliates. Finally, on a different level, seeing the devastation and "horror" of the attacks gave unspoken justification to the retaliatory response. Perhaps CNN anchor Aaron Brown noted this most strongly when he said, while looking at a shot of the smoking New York City skyline in the evening hours, "just take a moment and try and absorb, not with the facts, not with the pieces of information, but just look at that scene and think about what happened today. There were 50,000 or so people who came to work on a beautiful, late summer morning here in New York in those two towers that are now gone. These are people with families, with children, people who had offices and have them no more, people whose lives are forever changed."

Finally, we believe that CNN's graphic theme also served as strong indication of the frame CNN presented in early coverage. At 10:57 A.M., CNN named its coverage "America Under Attack." They did so by adding a bold graphic in red, white, and blue to the bottom third of the screen and by incorporating that phrase into their verbal summaries of the day's events. For example, nine hours after the attacks, anchor Bill Hemmer introduced himself into the coverage by telling early evening viewers, "I'm Bill Hemmer live in Atlanta, continuing CNN's coverage of America Under Attack." Consistent with the keywords, sentences, images, and themes we've discussed in this chapter, the phrase "America Under Attack" suggests both unification and the potential validity of an aggressive response in light of "attack." The use of the word "under" also suggests ongoing conflict and continued vulnerability.

CONCLUSION

Our qualitative framing analysis of CNN's breaking news coverage of September 11 shows that CNN created a powerful visual and verbal frame. This verbal and visual frame told and showed viewers that the events of September 11 comprised an act of war so horrific that immediate military retaliation was not only justified but necessary.

We do not mean to suggest that CNN was conspiring with officials to create this frame. Rather, we believe this frame came about because several forces were in operation. First, macro-level ideological influences on content showed themselves. The frame that CNN presented was consistent with dominant American ideology. Second, journalists' individual ideological frames of reference, which fit the dominant ideology of American political culture, reinforced this. Journalists' comments throughout this chapter showed less objectivity and more interpretation and commentary. Third, extra-media influences such as CNN's sources and even CNN's function as part of a media conglomerate[35] impacted the network's perspective. This fits McChesney's idea that "crucial political issues" are "warped to fit the confines of an elite debate, stripping ordinary citizens of the tolls they need to be informed, active participants in a democracy."[36] This does not occur because of evil corporate intent—at least, we do not want to make that argument. Rather, this comes about because of a fundamental flaw in the corporate conglomerate culture within which American mass media operate today.

Gamson writes that the last stage of a framing analysis should attempt to address the "complex interaction of texts with an audience engaged in negotiating the meaning."[37] Obviously it is beyond the scope of this analysis to show how CNN's framing of the first 12 hours of 9-11 coverage impacted viewers. We can, however, suggest that by creating a frame of unified, justified military retaliation in response to the 9-11 terrorist attacks, CNN notably contributed to the confinement of the parameters of meaningful citizen debate. If advocates for pacifism or critics of American foreign policy were given some meaningful voice in the public debate, then at least we could conclude that the American system of democracy and First Amendment ideals were put into play.

Historian Howard Zinn has said that it is easy to protect free speech rights, expand debate, and hear many voices when the stakes are small; but when the issues are life and death, America's democratic government has a history of choking the debate.[38] In this case, CNN provided an example of how the media was complicit in narrowing, rather than broadening, meaningful discourse about America's response to the events of September 11, events that had real human consequences then, now, and likely into the future.

Internet News Representations of September 11: Archival Impulse in the Age of Information

*Michelle Brown, Leia Fuzesi,
Kara Kitch, and Crystal Spivey*

The events of September 11 are now routinely described as the most widely documented tragedies of all time.[1] Such assertions imply an authenticity and totality in capturing the day's events that potentially raise the standard of the historical record and provide for a greater comprehensibility of the terms of September 11. And yet, amidst the pervasive images of September 11, sheer documentation by various forms of technology and media has done little to clarify why the attacks occurred, the nature of change and transformation in the United States and across the world since those events, nor even ensure a "total" picture of the occurrences of that day. Such is the nature of trauma in representation, where tragedy and its impact can only be partially and situationally expressed. But this limitation is also a product of culture, ideology, and specific technological forms, conventions, and accumulation in media presentation, where, as Walter Benjamin asserts, "even the most perfect reproduction ... is lacking in one element: its presence in time and space, its unique existence at the place where it happens to be."[2] In fact, many theorists of visual culture argue that "the unceasing flow of images" that characterizes a globalizing world has begun to expose the uncertainty and ambiguity at the center of both reality and interpretation, where no single meaning is possible.[3]

This chapter engages one specific kind of media culture, Internet news services, whose technological basis and sponsorship in many ways promises the seductive possibility of a plurality of perspectives and accounts culminating in a more deeply objective, total, and absolute inscription of September 11 in public memory. This promise is manifest in the imagining of cyberspace as a medium that is distinguished first and foremost by its seemingly unlimited spatial configurations and infinite networks of information. But, as Brown and Duguid write:

Today, it's the myth of information that is overpowering richer explanations. To say this is not to belittle information and its technologies. These are making critical and unprecedented contributions to the changes society is experiencing. But it is clear that the causes of those changes include much more than information itself. So the myth significantly blinds society to the character of and forces behind those changes.[4]

This chapter contends that, among various forms of technology and media, Internet news services function to archive September 11 in a way that both mimics more popular and accessible news media, but also provides the illusion of a space where September 11 can be remembered in a manner approximating totality, potentially forever—ready to access and relive with a single click. In outlining this archival function, a number of interesting discursive intersections and disjunctures appear that have perhaps useful implications for understanding the relationship between mainstream news, Internet design, and cultural tendencies.

In the aftermath of September 11, all major U.S. news agencies (and many international ones) organized exclusive Web sites, separate from institutional home pages, around coverage of September 11.[5] These sites were very similar in design and content from the start, sharing similar elements, images, and interactive features, and modeled after mainstream television and print news. As news sites, their content was primarily descriptive and informational, chronicling in detail the trajectory of events on September 11. Based upon accessibility and specialization of coverage, a number of news media outlets were selected for analysis, some for their diverse political orientations, others for their mainstream news appeal, and even others for the purposes of foreign perspectives, all in the hopes of identifying a range of representations.[6] This chapter will focus specifically upon the Internet coverage of mainstream U.S. news agencies as a preliminary exercise, with other studies to follow from these data. In order to classify the specific components of representation employed by these sites, the authors employed a qualitative content analysis, directed at the systematic identification and description of all components of the Web site interface with attention to emergent themes and discourses.[7] Our research design was structured methodologically with a consideration of the ways in which particular elements are configured by Internet news media agencies into recognizable "interpretive packages,"[8] media frames that attempt to "make sense of and give meaning to issues,"[9] as well as discursive engagements with these events.[10] We treated Internet news as a viable source for understanding the manner in which public attitudes and cultural logics converge as Americans attempted to make sense of the events of September 11 through the processes of social construction.[11] In the course of examining these sites, careful attention was given to the manner in which dominant frames developed though key "signature elements," such as metaphors, exemplars, catchphrases, depictions, roots, consequences, and appeals to principles, as well as through a discursive decoding of emergent ideologies by way of a survey and application of various kinds of analytical readings.[12] As a foundation for this analysis, the essential structure of each Web site's interface was systematically coded with attention to Web design, including such elements as site headlines and banners, mission statements, sponsorship, pop-up windows, advertisements, visual images, interactive components, feature content, and all available links. Each research team member was assigned a particular group of Web sites and then coded content through the use of a shared instrument. All sources were coded at least twice and often multiple times by different team members for reliability purposes. Our guiding questions included: How is each Web site presented? What are its central elements? How does Web-site configuration shape interpretations and meanings of September 11? And finally, how does the interface of Internet news shape the consumer's role in the construction of meaning?

WEB THEORY

The basic properties of Web sites, their interrelationships in design, and the functions and goals of Web configuration are essential to understanding the Internet as a particular media form. Originally imagined as a space that would incorporate all other media, the Internet was visualized as a place to incorporate print, computer, and broadcasting technology[13] through information technology that would be shared and freely exchanged.[14] In cyberspace, seemingly everything could and would "be recorded, transcribed, digitized, and shipped in packets."[15] Consequently, cyberspace offers itself, by design, as a systematic, factual space—an "information highway" where consumers browse, select, interact, schedule, process, store, and consume. World consumers pay bills, purchase material goods, reserve flights and hotels, check movie times, access checking accounts, communicate with friends, conduct business, and organize acts of terror. In this respect, in a manner unlike other forms of media, the interactivity of the user is built into the construction of narrative and knowledge with what, at first glance, appears to be an unusually high level of shaping power. This is why agency, identity, commodification, globalization, and the changing nature of the public and private spheres are central parameters of cyberspace debates. In the particular structure of mainstream news on the Internet, we find, not surprisingly, that there is a particularly static quality to this interactivity.

Internet news sites, as singular units within the Web, still mimic the larger scope and vision of Internet functions as they are primarily designed through hypertext. Unlike text, hypertext (or hypermedia) is multidimensional[16] and nonsequential: "There is no single order that determines the sequence in which the text is to be read."[17] It incorporates digitized sound, imagery, graphics, animation, and text in a manner where there are potentially always alternative pathways for organizing a user's browsing. Nodes of text are aligned together through links that permit interactive navigation from an anchor to a destination, and there is usually a backtracking command that will return the user to previously visited sites. Frequently there are annotations that appear (often acting as footnotes) via pop-up windows, brief definitions, or friendly user guides. There is generally an engine at the site's center—a way of searching by keyword, a function that is performed exclusive of considerations of context. The structure of the site and its internal code are always hidden behind a user interface. Thus the user imagines the full network structure whose termination points remain vague. The interface design is predicated, within the professional culture of Web construction, upon usability, efficiency, and attractiveness. These spaces, centered upon hypertext, are imagined as deeply interactive, with "both the structure and content of this type of information technology . . . constructed partly by writers . . . and partly by readers," thus implying the alluring promise of the possibility to allow users "to make their own connections, to incorporate their own links and to produce their own meanings."[18] However, the promise of the Internet must also be reconciled with the rapid manner in which it materialized as a commercial enterprise, through a language that is acutely market-oriented, prioritizing and privileging such economic terms as efficiency, surplus, profit, and subscription.[19] Although this chapter cannot speak directly to those processes, it attempts to map the contours of an intense homogeneity in the distribution and reproduction of news agency portrayals of September 11 and how this uniformity emerges from the complex interaction of specific media conventions, commercial sponsorship, cultural drives, and archival impulses in the face of a national tragedy with no precedence.

A FORMULA FOR DISASTER

In cyberspace, the mechanics of Web-site construction—the essential components of any site and their arrangement—ultimately create the context out of which meaning will be derived. Across the surveyed Web sites, a number of essential elements emerged as analogous, culminating in a formula for the representation of September 11. This formula ultimately provided the frame of reference from which to distinguish what potential elements, contests, and narratives were omitted in these designs. For instance, each site centered upon a colorful title banner: "America on Alert," "A Nation United," "War Against Terror," "America Attacked," "America at War"—which, like news headlines, declared the essential parameters of public understandings and reactions to September 11 that, while consistent with commercial enterprises, simultane-ously attempted to catch the attention of a Web-surfing audience through moral appeals and visual attractiveness. Each banner was generally anchored by a photograph, most typically of the crashes at the World Trade Center or its collapse into ruins, and feature text that summarized the day's events. The structure of the main page consequently worked immediately to bring together the tragic events of September 11 and a discourse of war. Operating within this axis of organization, the following key elements appeared rou-tinely and consistently across the surveyed Web sites as navigational links in the periphery of the page.

Timelines and Summaries: Each site offered a tight timeline (often down to the minute) of the day's events, accompanied by descriptive text. These timelines followed a strict chronology, beginning with organizational and planning efforts by the terrorists, the seemingly normal departure of the unsuspecting flights and the beginning of the workday, the attacks, and official and public reaction. This description often consti-tuted the bulk of featured content and, with its singular focus upon September 11 as a discrete unit, offered little context with which to historically ground the tragedy.

Continuing War Coverage: Typically, each page offered links to a war page, dedicated to a description of the ongoing war on terror by the United States.

Threats and Risks: This was an often rapidly changing set of news coverage links cen-tered upon speculation of emergent issues related specifically to terrorism and Sep-tember 11: anthrax and other potential biological warfare, nuclear weapons, drug trafficking, the escalating crisis in the Middle East, Iraq, and other terrorist "hotspots" and strategies.

Bin Laden: Coverage of al-Qaeda and terrorism was predominantly centered upon the "hunt" for Osama bin Laden and accompanying biographies, interviews, and pursuit updates.

Recovery: Specific links to individual and national grief therapy (for citizens, families, and children) as well as coping mechanisms, suggestions, and advice on how to deal with psychological trauma, stress, and anxiety were regularly provided across the sites. These links persistently employed a language grounded in the experience of September 11 as a national trauma to be dealt with through a developing notion of national recovery.

Chat Rooms: Most sites arranged online discussion centers open to the general public for engagement with news staff and security and terrorism experts.

Emergency Information and Victims Links: These links included missing persons hotlines and lists, as well as information about volunteer organizations and ways to help.

Photo Essays and Slide Shows: The visual aspects of September 11 were presented through images of the World Trade Center collapse, the rubble of Ground Zero, the destruction at the Pentagon, as well as numerous action photos of rescuers, political officials, and citizens engaged first in dismay and horror and then in rescue and recovery efforts. Images of the U.S. military at war in Afghanistan were often presented, as was American iconography, such as the firefighters raising the American flag at Ground Zero, or similar images of solidarity across the United States.

Audio/Video Coverage: Often main features of the site, most pages included video footage and audio accounts of the fall of the towers by way of eyewitness reports, journalistic coverage, as well as official political reaction (e.g., President Bush's emergency national address; New York Mayor Rudolph Giuliani's official reaction).

Interactives: Many of the sites contained extensive collections of images, maps, and informational graphics animated to represent the attacks (flight trajectories, points of impact, structural collapse), the war on terror (battle guides, military weaponry), international alliances, terrorism hotspots globally, and al-Qaeda organization.

Advertisements: Across these sites, advertising banners and pop-up windows routinely appeared, including subscriptions to the print news source, various magazines (*Forbes, Sports Illustrated,* etc.), and ads for security systems, cell phones, computer technology, and investment firms and financial quotes—commodities, ironically, that all played strangely haunting roles in the day's events.

Most news sources routinely included an archive of select articles and commentaries preceding and continuing through September 11, which could be printed, downloaded, or e-mailed to friends. Within each of these components, there were often other sets of links directed elsewhere in a network of coverage. Print news sites and alternative political sites, both of which offered longer, more complex commentaries and articles, were never as visual nor as explicitly interactive as television news sites.

The top stories and features of these sites tended to work, like news production in general, to provide a sense of direction in the developing narrative of September 11. This story-building centered upon the conception of September 11 as a national turning point initiating a seemingly natural chronology of social reaction and cultural psychology. This discourse of the transformative and traumatic is most evident in the detailed recreation of the events of the day in fastidious fashion through the recurring main feature of the timeline—a mechanism for ordering the tragedy into an explanatory framework. As elements of the timeline were regularly hyperlinked to other sources, it is through this process that we find September 11 narrativized as we witness the attacks themselves (footage of the jets crashing into the World Trade Center and its consequent collapse), the shock and confusion of Americans (eyewitness testimony and on-the-scene photos), official reaction (archived speeches, statements, and images), and an emergent sense of a nation working together in solidarity through the process of rescue, then recovery, and finally war. This patterning of September 11 marks the general layout of the these sites whose links to survivor and eyewitness accounts, victims pages, grief and trauma counseling, al-Qaeda and bin Laden, and an expanding world of risk and threat, gradually hardens into a kind of "total" narrative that, regardless of the order of its pathways in browsing, moves naturally, without contestation, toward a justification of war.

This narrative is deeply intensified through what proved, in many ways, to be the distinguishing features of Web news from other forms of news media: the incorporation of a wide array of technologies and media forms dedicated to the preservation and reproduction of September 11 in a manner that is perpetually and immediately available. For instance, CNN's site included several photo "galleries" arranged for screening under such titles as the "Unimaginable," "The White House Reacts," a time-lapse record of the World Trade Center collapse, and an external link to the widely circulated photo essay "Shattered" by *Time* magazine (which shares the same ownership as CNN). This particular site also included a three-dimensional animation of the attacks accompanied by an "infographic interactive attacks explainer," which seeks to reveal precisely how the strategic actions of the terrorists produced the moment(s) of impact—and a specific cultural trauma. Although these Web sites are clearly driven by multiple kinds and forms of media representation, their incorporation within mainstream Internet news remains centered upon the preservation of the singularly specific incidents, images, and individual experiences of the day—culminating in an intense focus upon the compulsive recreation of the tragedies themselves. Within this framework, explanatory accounts were predominantly missing, with an origin most generally grounded in the digitized imagining of the specific moment of aircraft impact into the World Trade Center, with no explicit connection to events that precede that moment or that day. We feel there are many reasons for this tendency toward a unified discourse within mainstream news representation on the Internet and that they are always bound up with not only the presiding conventions of news production and cyberspace design, but also specific kinds of cultural logics, historical drives, and inherent contradictions from which these conventions derive.

ARCHIVING SEPTEMBER 11: THE INFO-MEMORIAL

> The archive is first the law of what can be said, the system that governs
> the appearance of statements as unique events.... [20]

Mainstream Internet news agency sites serve many functions, but perhaps most clearly, in this context, they attempt to create a particular historical order out of the chaos of September 11. The multiple accounts (visual, audio, and textual) that mix personal and national tragedies and reactions serve to preserve the memory of September 11 as the single most shocking and tragic day in American history, but one which Americans rapidly overcome through the deep mythographic reserves of cultural heritage and a unified impulse toward war. As Stuart Hall describes discursive formations, "the event must become a 'story' before it can become a communicative event."[21] A recognizable discourse, familiar and comprehensible, must emerge in order for the event to be adequately decoded, contextualized, and, in short, made sense of. The primary effect of these sites, consequently, given both their content, thematics, and technology, is one centered in the construction of public memory—a kind of memory that is culturally recognizable, acceptable, and, through the basis of its medium, cyberspace, stored electronically through data collection and, thus, subject to instant retrieval. Interestingly, one of the earliest conceptualizations of the Internet is routinely located in a system planned by Vannevar Bush in the 1930s that would record books, records, and communications on microfiche. The system was known as the Memex, short for memory extender.[22] In its contemporary manifestation, the Internet serves a similar purpose and end—an archive of the essential elements of cultural experience and identity. But, as recent elaborations of archival theory have outlined, no archive is without its distinct limits.

In Jacques Derrida's version, the archive is an institution that always acts simultaneously to preserve and guard against the very thing it seeks to process in a movement that is directed theoretically toward massive replication and infinite expansion.[23] As archives generally exist in both material and abstract terms, we can imagine them as any permanent dwelling or shelter that serves as a site of and for the inscription of knowledge. For instance, in their most material forms, archives, like museums and libraries, are places designed for long-term conservation, a function similar to news Web sites dedicated to September 11. But archives also mimic canons as sites where particular forms of knowledge, a culture's most valued and highly prized ideas and texts, receive protection. Thus, the archive permits the material and abstract dimensions of a discussion of September 11 to intersect, bringing together the empirical reality of tragedy and a discussion of the knowledges and ideologies bound up in the clash of the day's events. In this way, as Foucault insists above, the nature of "what can be said" and what cannot will be settled in the incorporation of fact, event, and knowledge into the archive. Certain perspectives will be selected for commemoration. Others will not. Thus at the center of the archive, beyond simple preservation, is also a defensive act, guarding against the very thing it seeks to process—in the case of September 11, perspectives and accounts that do not mesh culturally with dominant American understandings of themselves or their own identities. Consequently, the archive is inevitably selective, both assertive and repressive, and the outcome is a historical record replete with gaps and structuring absences. For instance, news agency Web sites, in their deep attention to specific facts and descriptions of September 11, serve theoretically to "guard against" or omit particular kinds of explanations and understandings of the attacks of September 11. Because the archive subscribes immediately to the historicizing impulse, it permits the conceptualization and inscription of one's own experience into the canon of historical registry. In this respect, the frequent invocations of Pearl Harbor and the assassination of John F. Kennedy in the context of the loss of American innocence post-September 11 demonstrate how the archive serves to sustain the unifying drive of history. The conventions of Internet news documentation and the pathways of user interactions then are mapped through American myth and habit.

Derrida's extrapolation of the archive alerts us to the principle of subscription (or selection) that informs the accumulation of knowledge and memory. The very cornerstone of social construction rests upon the notion that knowledge is subject to change through social interaction—that "truth" is always mediated through various kinds of experiences and institutions, most specifically in late modernity, the mass media. Through the processes of selection and a variety of filtering mechanisms, media agencies act as knowledge distributors, choosing among competing interpretations of the world and their respective claims to center finally upon a dominant construction, an "accepted view" of reality, which in turn shapes social action.[24] The elements of the Web and the configuration of news sites are ultimately, as with all media, value-laden choices about what kinds of knowledge are worthy of preservation. And in this selection, they shape the course of social action. In the particular case of September 11, the act of preservation is guided by the cultural habits and mythologies that inform traditionally appropriate understandings of American identity at a particularly intense moment when these very categories are under direct assault. This paradox is not lost within the archiving of the event, but is instead distinctly apparent in particular contradictions that structure the appearance of Internet news.

In this manner, the archive is not built simply through the conventions of Internet news documentation nor the sheer dominance of a single ideology. Rather, it emerges through cultural practice. The discourse of September 11 and its trajectory toward war are cultivated through the most powerful and engaging of American metaphors—*the individual narrative*—of survivors, workers, victims' families, leaders, and "ordinary heroes." The insistent focus upon September 11 as a singular event and national turning point, the identification of Osama bin Laden as the outstanding target, the prevalence of President Bush as the primary voice of official authority, and the networking and organization of discrete links profiling the personal and the individual (survivor, witness, authority, enemy) as the national—these are all mobilized through the discourse of individualism, which often obscures the intensely social dimensions of democratic practice and the alternative possibilities of collective social action.[25] Instead, citizens are directed through carefully preserved cultural habits toward single points of blame, a process in which the *only* sources of vast social problems and the *only* necessary solutions/reactions become single acts and/or individuals.[26] This national narrative is clearly facilitated and legitimated by existing cultural vocabularies that not only push citizens away from an analysis of the global impacts and social causes of such tragedies, but expose the limits of these languages and discourses through the emergence of particular kinds of cultural contradictions.

Nowhere is this more apparent than in the most crucial point of disjuncture in the otherwise fairly homogenous discourse of Internet news coverage of September 11: the use of advertising. In the midst of a uniform narrative and ideological trajectory, each site was accompanied by numerous commercial ads, which in placement, appearance, and themes emerged as specific points of paradox, precisely marking the limits of dominant cultural vocabularies. For instance, one advertising banner that ran just above the headline on CNN.com asks: "Need to stay on top of the market?" Then, the rolling banner asserts, subscribe to CNN's *Money Magazine*. The banner is perfectly aligned, running from left to right, with the photo that anchors the page: the collapse of the World Trade Center. These kinds of strange, ironic moments are not unusual across these sites, with their frequent pop-up advertisements and strong commercial sponsorship. A sample rotation of banners included a cycle with ads for such things as Fantasy Basketball, vacation getaways, luxury automobiles, print magazine subscriptions, and a far-ranging series of investment portfolios and financial quote services. We witness the distortions and misunderstandings that emerge inevitably from the production of the discursive—those key analytical moments that are "shot through with contradiction" and "only on certain occasions brought to full visibility."[27] In this manner, what the archive represses inevitably surges to the surface at particular key cultural conjunctures *as* disjunctures. The missing explanatory frameworks for September 11—the globalization of American-style free markets, the impact of consumerism in the far regions of the world, the widening gap between the increasingly rich and expanding poor—collide head on into one another in the configuration of mainstream news Web sites whose commercial sponsorship ultimately undercuts the legitimacy of the dominant narrative of September 11. Yet this is a disjuncture, regardless of its surprising prevalence across media outlets, that goes largely unnoticed, encoded rather than decoded, an immediately striking instance of cultural aphasia.

We point out these contextualizations not as simple critique, but rather to emphasize the role of cultural vocabularies in mapping and navigating Internet news media coverage—and of capturing the discursive act in motion. The events of September 11 are acts with no clearly apparent limits or senses of boundaries—events that inevitably exceed the limits of representation and as such the borders of what ordinarily can be imagined. Beyond these ruptures are fundamental questions about the social order and its ideological sustainability—fear of the incomprehensible. The frames in which we develop our explanations and accounts of understanding consequently mark the contours of our cultural vocabulary and our ability to articulate the nature of crime, disaster, suffering, and trauma. In limiting our perspectives, they also safely shield us from troubling disruptions to the social order and fundamental questions about the nature of American national identity. Perhaps most importantly, such narratives often push citizens away from an analysis of the complex social causes of cultural problems and tragedies—limiting rather than refining our critical vocabulary for understanding such events, which are left suspended, largely unexplained and unaccounted for, only apparent in the emergence of strange repressions and disjunctures within existing cultural vocabularies. In our analysis of Internet news depictions of September 11, we witnessed this complicated process of cultural articulation in action, shaping primary news narratives and interpretations of September 11.

IMPLICATIONS FOR THE USER

"All major newspapers now have Web sites. Certainly, newspapers have a strong institutional identity and a well-honed sense of audience. And to their experience with immediacy (which the Web favors) they can add experience with archiving and access to deep archives (which the Web has tended to ignore) to position themselves."[28] "Information should not be a value in and of itself. Our society, seemingly afflicted with a new kind of information-age amnesia, seems to be forgetting to ask the important questions. What is the nature of the information? What is its source? How reliable is that source? What will the information be used for? Who validates it? Who disagrees with its validity? What is its level of quality?[29]

In our analysis, we often found ourselves asking what alternative representations of September 11 might look like on news Web sites. In such a consideration, we came to conclude that the most usable forms of representation are those which illuminate their subject through the most essential properties of their medium. In this respect, cyberspace, as technology, is dizzyingly promising. With its potential incorporation of all forms of media, its infinite networks of knowledge and explanation, its ultimate storage capacity in housing unlimited banks of information, and its original vision as an interactive, shared space encompassing the world, the Internet remains an archive with unimaginable potential and impact. Yet in its most mainstream and commercial configurations, this possibility remains deferred. Amidst our research, we came to question the possibility of any "total" archive and the dangers that surround a medium which suggests such a reality. We also were concerned with realities ignored. As Michael Heim argues, "Cyberspace is more than a breakthrough in electronic media or in computer interface design. With its virtual environments and simulated worlds, cyberspace is a metaphysical laboratory, a tool for examining our very sense of reality."[30] What is perhaps most glaringly apparent across these sites is the manner in which Americans have come to understand September 11 and how these interpretations are culturally based through frames that news media invoke in a sophisticated, yet strangely homogenized manner. In the case of September 11, what is primarily absent from cyber-information is strikingly essential—meaning and context. Brown and Duguid write, "Ignoring the clues that lie beyond information doesn't only lead to a narrow world of deception. It leads to a world of what we think of as tunnel design—a kind of purblind design of which, in the end, we are all victims," culminating in a "neglected periphery" of not just the visual, but also the social workings of human activity.[31] All the information, all the specific facts and descriptions surrounding any event, cannot create meaningfulness without an open discussion of context and perspectives. This can be particularly problematic in a space that advertises itself as having all the "solutions" and "answers" we may ever need at our fingertips.[32] In such a context, one must ask, What does it mean to "browse" through September 11? And, also, What sorts of public and civic debates about the proper and just response to such a complex, and ultimately, global event are overlooked in this browsing?

The implication of interactivity in the understanding and constructing of these narratives is not highly sustainable as interactivity is commonly understood across these sites solely as a click. Rarely did the central explanatory frameworks for September 11 emerge through editorial comments or opinion, but rather they were constituted primarily within the framework of an emphasis upon factual, objective description. The use of such a descriptive register for presentation is theorized to distance the consumer from the construction and selection processes of media agencies,[33] particularly in cyberspace, where authorship and sponsorship is conducted through teams of technical personnel or anonymous Webmasters. Here, more so than any other medium, we are potentially confronted with the dissolution of the author-subject relationship and its possibilities.[34] This raises the question of what precisely constitutes meaningful interactivity at a time when many argue the space between public and private is often problematically blurred. As Edward Linenthal writes of the Oklahoma City bombing, such acts often culminate via the media into "a social spectacle of suffering," where there are "no boundaries separating appropriate expressions of human concern from shockingly inappropriate intrusions into the intimate world of people dealing with the mysteries of violent death," where we come to treat such sites as an "experiential tourist destination."[35] In cyberspace, such risks seem particularly acute. In late modernity, in the midst of global technologies and media focal points that change momentarily, there is also the question of what is to become of the 9-11 archive (and memory) in the transient, digital space of the Internet. Where will these sites—and the memory of September 11—be not next year, but next month?

CONCLUSION

As spaces that were imagined as non-hierarchical, open, dissonant (in a productive manner), and user-centered, mainstream news Web sites do surprisingly very little to accentuate these elements of cyberspace. Hypermedia was conceived originally to disrupt the canons and conventions of representation—to open up a space for a more honest image of an uncertain, destabilized late-modern (or postmodern) world. Mainstream sites, in their importation of homogenous categories similar to print and television media conventions, challenge such assertions and utopian spaces. Internet news links do provide a fluidity missing in other forms of media, an interactivity that opens up the possibility of movement beyond narrative, but these links are surprisingly static and circular, culminating in similar, familiar stories and unified ideological orientations. Of course, the luxury of the Internet is that one is free to search for alternative viewpoints and other kinds of information, history, and memory. Nonetheless, at some of the most frequently visited sites on the Internet, the notion of cyberspace (with respect to mainstream Internet news) as boundless and of hypertext as having "no beginning, no immutable order in which the information is set out, and no ending," remains illusory.[36] In its mainstream manifestations, there are distinct centers, abrupt ends, and a distinctly superficial surface depth to networks and accounts of news events. As large and seemingly complex as these sites may be, one rarely finds oneself in the forking pathways of the labyrinth through which one may be lost or found—a space that demands work and thoughtful ingenuity in building accounts and unraveling explanations.[37] On the contrary, in these spaces, meaning and explanation are so assumed as to be solely descriptions (rather than debates or engagements) of what occurred. It would seem then that in cyberspace, there is still much work to be done in the archive, particularly in creating spaces that might definitively alter and challenge the role of the reader, viewer, user, consumer, especially as we are perpetually reminded that September 11 has irrevocably changed our world. In such an application, the lines between author and reader would grow more blurred and a certain assessment of one's own place in the events of September 11 would become preeminent. Rather than the use of the cyber-memorial in order to perhaps forget (safely through the traumatic repetitions of media convention and cultural myth), such a space would remind us of the perpetual personal and social work involved in cultural remembering.

8

Reporting, Remembering,
and Reconstructing
September 11, 2001

Maggie Wykes

In August 2002 a British national newspaper, the *Guardian,* published an article in its review section entitled "After the Fall." The piece, by arts critic Mark Lawson, considered the lasting effect on "cinema, music, theatre and literature" of the attacks on the World Trade Center on September 11, 2001. He said, "Even as the dust was settling on Ground Zero, songs, movies and books were hastily being tweaked to take account of the attack."[1] In his highly critical account of early efforts in the world of the arts to portray September 11, Lawson commented that "mawkish hindsight and fear of offense" have largely inhibited and made "sickly" ensuing art forms. He concluded that "The best works of creative imagination surprise, explain and provoke. It will be many days before it is possible to do any of those things about that day."[2]

The best of journalism should also perhaps "surprise, explain and provoke," especially if it is in any sense radical, campaigning, and serving the public interest, rather than the mere mouthpiece for power it was in Britain before the changes forced by the unstamped and illegal presses of the early nineteenth century. The drama, negativity, symbolism, globalism, and all-round newsworthiness of September 11 led to a huge volume of news coverage. The event's ongoing significance in many discourses has led to the generation of many ensuing theories and stories. But have the factual media managed a more valuable development of accounts than the fictional media in Britain? This chapter compares British newspaper accounts of September 11 (published on September 12, 2001) with those published on its one-year anniversary, September 11, 2002, in order to look for similarities and differences in the immediate reportage and retrospective reflection, and considers what these might reveal about journalism in the United Kingdom, both at the time and in relation to lasting effects.

THE BRITISH PRESS: PROVIDING NEWS IN THE NEW MILLENNIUM

The United Kingdom retains a significant national press, spawned by the tradition of Fleet Street and still mostly produced in London, with minor variations to the editions printed by some newspaper businesses for the regions.[3] Bromley and Cushion argued that Britain is unusual as a country, in that the national press dominates readership, rather than regional or urban publications, that "60 percent of the U.K. population still reads a daily national newspaper," and "nearly 13 million people bought a national newspaper each day" in September 2001.[4]

The British press is widely bought and read but narrowly owned and controlled.[5] In fact, ownership is highly centralized, with owners often enjoying close, if not symbiotic, relationships with political power to the extent that Rupert Murdoch's the *Sun* even claimed responsibility for the current Labour government's victory in the 1997 British general election. The editor was told by the proprietor to switch allegiance from the Conservative party in the spring and did so with the headline "THE SUN BACKS BLAIR: Give change a chance."[6] The explanation for this was that a Labour victory appeared increasingly inevitable—and Murdoch wanted to be seen to be backing a winner—but also that the New Labour party was no longer perceived as a "threat to Murdoch's news Corporation's commercial interest," as its older, more socialist version had been.[7]

Narrowness of ownership and control and volume of readership has tended to underwrite two critical academic models of the British press: First, that the interests of those who own, control, and practice journalism are culturally and economically middle class and so provide a diet of information that serves to legitimate and reproduce middle-class ideologies alongside profit; and second, that the domination of commercial interests seeks to entice, excite, and exploit a mass audience, leading to a tendency toward uniformity and populism. The first model has informed a constant critique of the news in terms of its perceived bias: bias toward conserving the characteristics and authority of Britain's most powerful—white, patriotic, middle-class, and male.

Racism in the news has been well researched and documented.[8] Even at the millennium, and after the 1986 Public Order Act prohibited incitement to racial hatred or the possession of racially inflammatory material, there has been evidence of racism in British culture. In 1999, the Stephen Lawrence Inquiry was conducted by Sir William Mcpherson. Four years previously, 18-year-old Stephen Lawrence had been knifed to death as he waited at a bus stop in London. Stephen's parents set up a campaign for justice after Metropolitan police were slow in making arrests of three white teenagers, against whom charges were dropped in September 1995, for the murder of their son. Mcpherson made 70 recommendations, including applying the Race Relations Act to the police. Yet, the Commission for Racial Equality received many "hate" letters and phone calls in the wake of the Lawrence case—including one stating: "This nigger got what he deserved."[9] In the same article, Chris Myant, their press officer, commented, "despite thirty years of effort, there are still people who hold these ideas. You can't talk about British society without recognizing there is this undercurrent within it and it has not gone away."[10]

The stereotype linking black skin to crime may not be as obvious in contemporary news accounts as it was in the early 1980s, but "The discourses of nationalism, chauvinism, patriotism and racism are still there and sometimes bubble to the surface or appear in sanitized or reformist guise."[11] Racism in the contemporary press is never more evident than in accounts of war, when patriotism (or rather, nationalism) is most rife. Most recently the "enemy" has been Arab. Beginning in 1991, when accounts of the Gulf War established funds of "sometimes benign but never inoffensive stereotypes of Arabs were toughened and sharpened to describe Saddam Hussein and the Iraqi forces."[12] The "East," or at least Middle East, had been thoroughly made "other" and negatively labeled well before September 11. In the wake of September 11, those Arabic labels were honed to imply not just race but also religion; not just Afghanistan or Iraq as a country but Islam as a nation; and not war but terror.

Class as an ideological component of news has been most profoundly and clearly analyzed by Noam Chomsky in his work on the economic orientation of the American media. His critique applies well to the British press. Money and power are able to filter out the news fit to print, marginalize dissent, and allow the government and other dominant interests to get their message across. The operation of these news filters occurs so naturally that media news people, frequently operating with complete integrity and good will, are able to convince themselves that they choose and interpret the news "objectively" and on the basis of professional news values.[13]

Chomsky identifies close alignments between the interests of those who own and control media corporations and those who govern the nations in which they operate. In the United Kingdom, those alignments appear to be confirmed by research on the profile of influential journalists. They are mainly male, middle class, and university educated—often at Oxbridge—and they work and live in London. They mix with politicians, lawyers, and businessmen for work (relying on them as sources) and leisure; they live in the same inner-city enclaves of good taste and send their children to the same schools.[14] That uniformity/conformity of interests, both cultural and economic, would suggest a likely closing of mutual ranks in defense against any perceived external threat.

Other work has confirmed the masculinity of the profession of journalism noted by Tunstall and the implications of that for the content and format of news.[15] The male profile of journalism supports a macho work culture that "maps onto the implied reader a hierarchical configuration of 'newsworthiness.'"[16] Hard news—politics, crime, business—is perceived to be attractive to male readers; soft news—health, education, relationships—to women. For Allan, hard news is deemed more important, as it lies in the public sphere and so is dealt with by "objectively factual reporting," or at least the effort to present the "truth of the matter" within the boundaries of patriarchal experience and attitudes prevalent in journalism.[17] The harder the news, the more likely that a "hard news man" will report on it, especially in the newspapers. So, ironically, the effort at offering a truth about reality is greater the more serious the news. Yet this may give rise not to objective accounts from multicultural, multi-gender, and multi-class perspectives, but to a reinforcement of the perceived truth of the journalist assigned the task of reporting, still likely to be white, male, and middle class.

The second academic critique focuses less on the industrial and professional profile and practices of journalism and more on the commercial pressures that work on the constitution of a newspaper by constraining reporting according to time, space, journalistic experience, the need for advertising, and the consequent search for audiences. As a result, there has been much concern about and many studies of a supposed "dumbing down" of the British press in order to generate the mass sales required by the pressure to profit.[18] News values have been theorized as shifting more and more toward the easy, amusing, and ephemeral. "Newspapers seek to entertain and divert rather than inform and engage readers with the affairs of their communities,"[19] and news content may be less than 20 percent of the whole, especially in the tabloid press. Such populism would not seem well equipped to deal with a crisis of the magnitude and complexity of September 11, and certainly there have been claims of a return to serious journalism in the immediate aftermath: "Most papers reported the events, both in words and pictures, with a breadth and depth that, in recent years, have been all too often conspicuously lacking from their shrinking foreign affairs coverage."[20] Examining whether this was evident at the time and why and whether there was any "lasting effect" on British journalism, which might inform academic critique, is of course the aim of this chapter.

Not only are there broad external constraints on the nature of British news—profit, ideology, and popularity—but there are also more precise, internal controls, not always far removed from the external, that act to select and shape a story as newsworthy. In order to make the news, an event has to have certain constituents. Galtung and Ruge identified these as frequency, drama, unambiguity, cultural relevance/consonance, rarity, continuity, elite-ness, personifiability, and negativity.[21] A recent example conforming to many of these criteria in the United Kingdom was the saturation news coverage of the death by drowning of a young man in the swimming pool of a homosexual television personality. After a late night drinking and drugs party, the body was found in the pool belonging to Michael Barrymore. Anal injuries, discovered at the post-mortem, led to a furor of speculation in the press. It was newsworthy because it was rare, negative (someone died), personifiable, culturally familiar (Barrymore's shows had large audiences), dramatic, elite (Barrymore was a star), and could be unambiguously interpreted as "bad" on many levels.[22]

Crime satisfies many of these news value criteria and the more extreme the crime the better "fit" to journalists' professional imperatives. Chibnall focused on the reporting of violent crime and added to these criteria five further aspects of a crime story that make it essential news: high visibility, political or sexual connotation, graphic presentation, individual pathology, and a deterrent potential.[23] News about extreme violence also allows for the narrative playing out of familiar cultural myths of good versus evil: such news thrills because it threatens—but only symbolically. It "evokes threats to but also re-affirms the consensual morality of the society."[24] And how violent crime is reported matters, because for most people, most of the time, news is our only experience with and means of constructing an opinion about violence. Yet that news is necessarily selected and represented within very particular sets of value criteria allied to external and internal ideological and practical controls on the practice of news-making.

So the news about September 11 was generated by a British media industry deeply entrenched in delineating economic, cultural, and professional conditions. It was news about suicidal and murderous assaults using jetliners as a weapon, on the symbol of the most powerful nation's global dominance, the World Trade Center; on "the heart of America's military machine,"[25] the Pentagon, and included a foiled attempt on the presidential base at Camp David. They were deliberate and planned assaults that not only destroyed two huge buildings, damaged the Pentagon, and killed over two thousand people, but also destroyed the United States' very sense of itself and its security—and the rest of the world's sense of American power and autonomy. It was an "act of callous ferocity…crimes against humanity…mutant, predatory 'final solution' politics."[26] September 11 demanded journalism: it epitomized, totally, everything that constitutes news. It was relentlessly a threat to Western/white power so fitted to the theorized meta-political agenda of the British press; it required little more than mere description to tell the story in clear, simple, populist, saleable terms—hence the heavy use of images; and it complied with many of the specified news values in relation to knowledge about news values.[27]

SEPTEMBER 11, 2001: READING/RESEARCHING NEWS

So unsurprisingly, the British press produced volumes on September 12, 2001, and again in memoriam on September 11, 2002. That press is notably politically and intellectually partisan, alongside the other constraints of commerce, ideology, and professional practices. It divides roughly into the conservative/right wing, liberal/left wing, broadsheet/quality press, and tabloid/popular press. Two tabloid papers, the *Daily Mail* and *Daily Express,* hover slightly above the populist base. In this analysis four nationals were selected to cover each of the above characteristics. The conservative papers are the tabloid *Daily Mail* and the broadsheet *Daily Telegraph;* the liberal papers are the newly converted (but not always politically steadfast) *Sun* and the broadsheet *Guardian.* What it printed on both occasions are data: history about the world we live in, but do not personally experience, evidence of the nature of British journalism, and a portrait of national culture and sensibilities. So is it possible to be more positive about the factual media accounts than Lawson was about the fictional media? What were we told in Britain about September 11 and after? How? Why and with what possible implications for understanding both journalism and the world it reports?

Focusing closely on the text—visual and verbal—of newspapers avoids the generalized assumptions often present in analyses of journalism that examine the commercial, political, or professional contexts of the press and extrapolate from that theories about content and meaning. Discourse analysis offers a more substantive means of exploring ideology, which is so often the goal of work on the mass media, than ethnographic, politico-economic, or audience research, because it deals with the vehicle of ideas, language in its many forms. However, although language was the "material" or data for analysis, the object of analysis here was meaning, and methods of arriving at meaning through discourse work are diverse. For example, syntactic analysis might focus on quantifying the occurrence of action clauses in texts that link to the attribution of blame and associated value judgments.[28] Content analysis might undertake a large-volume statistical approach, as in Gunter, Harrison and Wykes.[29] This study's aim was to map, label, and count the incidences of violence per time period and channel in televised texts to try and relate the resulting data to actual violence trends and the debate on media effects. Such quantitative approaches have much to offer in identifying dominant themes from a base of no preconception.

But my interest in September 11 was to use it as way of interrogating British journalism, both in the terms of the two dominant theoretical frameworks of the industry—political and commercial—and also in relation to the act of reportage (apparently so dominated by newsworthiness yet claiming to seek truth objectively), which was inspired precisely because of the criticism of post-9-11 arts media posed by critic Mark Lawson. My focus was not the media or press per se, or even whole editions of a paper, but the coverage of one story only—immediately and a year on. The analysis, in no way random, was informed and specifically geared to a search for evidence of powerful political ideologies (racism, middle-class values, masculinity, and nationalism), "dumbing down" and "mawkish hindsight and fear of offense."

Such a thematic approach derives from Foucault's work on power.[30] He argued that in "Western societies since the middle-ages the exercise of power has always been formulated in terms of law."[31] For monarchs, law offered a means of maintaining order not through direct physical coercion, but through the construction of cultural consent to a value-system. Consent was required to the rule of law, or punishment was (and still is) applied. So the interests of the powerful became conventionalized as the interests of all through legislation/legal discourse.

Discourse for Foucault is the mechanism of hegemony. Emanating from powerful knowledge sources—ultimately the law, but also other authoritative institutions like religion, medicine, psychiatry, education, and the media— discourse permeates social practice and subjective identity with meanings and values. Inevitably those meanings and values will be linked to the perspectives and interests of those who have control and access to the construction of institutional discourses. Discourses are not discreet, fixed, or impermeable.

Rather, they leak and bleed into one another, and the most powerful discourse, law, does this most efficiently, both shaping and absorbing from other socio-cultural discursive sites.

So, for example, a newspaper headline "Blonde kills married lover with rat poison" clearly relates to the law and cannot be positively value-laden in the legal discourse, but it also has other meanings. It cannot mean "man accidentally causes death of wife" (though technically, lexically, and syntactically it could). Rather, in the Western world in 2002, it means "woman of dubious sexual and intellectual reputation deliberately and calculatedly murders man with whom she has an illegitimate sexual relationship." So this is a legal story, but it is also one about sexuality, gender, religious morality, and social status. Yet each is colored negatively by the legal discourse before and during this event. So by reading carefully, behind and around the denoted meaning, and interpreting culturally, it becomes possible to see power at work in text, as well as intra- and inter-textually. This language supports those who construct law; those who promote Judeo-Christian morality; and those who maintain patriarchy and middle-class values (rats are a problem of poverty). Connoting those associations tells much about our culture at a particular historical moment and about those who convey culture to us most systematically and emphatically: journalists. So I have read the newspaper articles on September 11 as discourse, or as extended, multi-layered metaphors, wherein the material form is given powerful and resonant thematic meanings and values according to the culture of the reader.

SEPTEMBER 11, 2001: REACTING AND REPORTING

The four front pages of my newspapers were strikingly similar. The *Sun,* the *Guardian,* and the *Daily Telegraph* used exactly the same photograph of the Twin Towers still standing, but both mortally wounded. The *Daily Mail* chose an image taken from across the Hudson River at about the same time—both towers are shrouded in smoke but erect. On page two, the *Mail* repeated a full page of the image from the front of the other newspapers. Only the *Daily Telegraph* had any commentary on its front page; it offered 19 pages of reports. The *Daily Mail* had 32 pages in a special edition; the *Sun* had 29 pages, also in a special edition; and the *Guardian* consisted of 25 pages. All papers were dominated by images—many full page—a rare event in the broadsheets, and indicative of the high visibility of the event. The *Guardian* used the page-foot caption "A declaration of war," and the *Daily Telegraph* used the page headline "War on America"—turning to identical explanatory discourses, despite being on opposing sides of the British political spectrum.

The *Daily Mail* super-imposed "*APOCALYPSE:* New York September 11, 2001" over the top of its image with all the associated Revelation-like connotations, while the *Sun* mixed terrorism with war in its mode of account with the foot-page title "SUICIDE HIGHJACKERS BLITZ AMERICA: SPECIAL EDITION." It also invoked crime with a brief caption to the photograph "The ultimate crime of terrorism..." Apparent similarities in form and focus are confirmed by text. In each case, the reader was reassured that this was not the United Kingdom. Only the *Daily Mail* avoided the war accounting anchor. Its use of the term "apocalypse" actually contradicted the focus on New York invited by the text, as apocalypse implies the end of the world, a theme picked up on the inside pages of many papers. It is curious that the *Mail* did not reassure readers, but rather allowed them to be threatened by the event. Some explanation for this occurred on page three, where readers are reminded of Pearl Harbor and World War II. The inference was that these are our allies and friends—we are one against the foe once more. The *Sun* alone offered multiple accounting anchors: war, terror, and crime—perhaps to attract as broad a range of opinion as possible, or perhaps to cover itself at a time when it wasn't quite clear who or what was to blame. None of the front pages attempted to attribute the act to any individual or group; even the brief commentary in the *Telegraph* resisted blame.

These similarities in papers normally diametrically opposed can be explained partly at least by the mutuality of dependence on sources, especially images from the press agencies, in the immediate aftermath of the disaster. It might also be explained by a tendency for the national press to unify in a nationalistic fervor at any moment Britain is perceived to be at risk, only reverting to their particular house affiliation when the crisis is either resolved or becomes long term and chronic, rather than acute, supporting the voicing of different opinions. This happened during the Gulf War, when public opinion began to turn against British involvement and the *Guardian* led an anti-war campaign that was initiated by a terrible front-page image of an Iraqi soldier burnt to death in a tank. Smith et al. found a similar resurgence of differences among the British press during World War II.[32] Nonetheless, on September 12, 2001, the British press subsumed its differences and "dumbed down" any trivializing within serious and unified accounting.

The massive volume of representation on the inside pages continued this seriousness. This was hard news, "macho reportage." It was characterized by the inclusion in each paper of detailed graphics demonstrating the precise trajectory of the planes, likely internal processes in the collapse of the buildings, maps, and timetables. Alongside were lists of facts about the Twin Towers. This degree of seriousness remained in place for some weeks, prompting some theorizing of a "revitalization" of journalism and abandonment of populism.[33] The immediate breadth and depth of coverage did lend a new credibility to journalism—partly because coverage, whether print or broadcast, was so vast and unilateral that it appeared to be incontrovertible: one shared vision and experience of the "apocalypse." "The image, tone and style of reporting provided only one context and outcome: 'terrorism' and 'war.' An attack of such magnitude on the United States would have global repercussions."[34]

For Berrington, the framing of news within a war paradigm quickly impelled an escalation of the blame attribution that was missing on those first front pages. It also informed the construction of an "us vs. them" accounting framework. Such was the enormity of the grief and loss inflicted, it became impossible for journalists to do other than comply with this or appear callous. Moreover, because "we" were the object of an atrocity that had no immediately preemptive provocation, "they" were vilified. So the story was told as one of good versus evil.

On that first day of coverage, accounting frames were set in place on the inside pages that defined parameters of explanation. This was war; there was therefore an identifiable enemy; we were all vulnerable so they must be stopped. By page three, the *Sun,* the *Daily Telegraph,* and the *Daily Mail* had decided Osama bin Laden and his Islamic terrorist group must be to blame. The *Sun* informed readers that "The monster, who is hiding in Afghanistan, would have been able to find a host of suicide pilots, prepared to die for the cause," and the other papers also singled out Afghanistan. Only the more liberal *Guardian* resisted naming bin Laden and Afghanistan, but only until page six. All papers used the analogy with Pearl Harbor to try and explain events, which conjured up memories, myths, and stereotypes, linked the United Kingdom and United States, and presented danger as coming from the East; the beginnings of an Occidentalism that was to typify representations of September 11. This was compounded by each of the papers referring to Arabs in Jerusalem as celebrating the attack. The *Sun* offered "Children dance as Palestinians cheer revenge on enemy."

This was the start, too, of a representational binding together of the West, or at least the old transatlantic allies, as vulnerable victims. Moreover, it was also the start of the creation of all of us as ordinary people as potential victims in a range of different ways. That vulnerability was emphasized by the publishing in all the papers of images of people jumping from the flaming World Trade Center, with one pair hand in hand. These were so terrible that they were rarely shown again in a British journalism context—yet when I mention September 11 in the United Kingdom, it is those images that most affected people and those they remember. The remaining pages made us all potential jumpers, as we were offered modes of identifying and empathizing with the victims.

The first mode was the prominence given to the ordinariness of those who were already dead or dying. These were workers, fathers, wives, sweethearts, sons, and friends—on September 12, 2001, relatives of some were already named and interviewed, and last messages of love on mobile phones were broadcast for all. President Bush was reading to school children when informed of the disaster, with the *Daily Telegraph* writing that "his tone became more somber but he continued reading."[35] The children of victims, and children as symbols of innocence and of future hope, were frequent tropes for the narrative.

The second mode was the emphasis on the fall-out beyond the immediate disaster: aircraft were grounded, public transport halted, the stock-market crashed, the subway system closed, and cell phones could not function,[36] affecting many more than those in the buildings and rescue teams. The *Daily Mail* wrote: "11am London, Canary Wharf evacuated. Workers also stream from Natwest tower, Stock Exchange and Lloyds building." So the broader public was implicated and threatened.

The third mode was the (re)building of the special relationship between Britain and United States in an invocation to all who believed in peace and democracy. Blair declared he stood "shoulder to shoulder" with the American people "in a battle between the free and democratic world and terrorism."[37] This was not portrayed as merely two leaders and governments bonded against a third force, but a collaboration of all right-thinking peoples against "the most dangerous man in the world" during which "good will prevail."[38]

So on September 12, 2001, the British press, even those papers most often in opposition or disjunction, was relatively uniform in the parameters of explanation it offered audiences: this was war, the enemy was Islamic terrorism (personified by bin Laden), and all of us in the West were united in our rectitude and vulnerability. The accounts were measured and the populism, political partisanship, and jingoism were suspended, but only to promote a Western-centric unity—binding those in power in the West into one and obfuscating the integral differences over class, race, creed, and gender. That bond also meant there was no immediate reflection on the symbolism of the attacks on U.S. military power and global trade, nor any interrogation of how investigating the impact of militarism and capitalism might provide insights into the motive for or goal of the attack.

SEPTEMBER 11, 2002: REMEMBERING AND RECONSTRUCTING

Twelve months later, the front pages of the same four national daily newspapers were very different from the previous year and one another. The *Daily*

Mail focused on bin Laden with a full-face front page accompanied by the question, "Where the Hell is He?" Of all the papers, it was the *Mail* that adhered most closely to the papers' earlier concerns—the apprehension and punishment of the presumed perpetrator of the attack. It was also the *Mail* that most overtly personalized blame on a single *criminal.* The second tabloid, the *Sun,* had a surprisingly sober image of the funeral on September 10, 2002, of one of the last firefighters to be found buried under the rubble of the towers. Neither tabloid had any other news on the front page.

Both tabloids offered special issues rather than supplements. The *Daily Mail* printed a roll call of British dead alongside the headline, "Clutching treasured mementos, they shared their grief." This was followed by four pages on "Bin Laden: Dead or Alive," reiterating the criminal and personal focus of the attribution of blame, and the build-up to war on Iraq. The tone was deeply patriotic, close to nationalistic, and racist. Photographs of Islamic radicals were placed beneath the title "The men making a mockery of Britain." It was also very pro-American. There was no criticism here of George Bush. The final page focused on the economic "fall-out," with the article "Global Economy still feeling after-shocks." This, in many ways, typified the remit of this newspaper, particularly the intense British/U.S. patriotism, underlying racial distrust (that blurs the distinction between race and religion), and middle-class concern with family and money.

The *Sun* had eight pages of recall, with only one page advocating the push to war on Iraq and none with anti-Islamic diatribe or focus on bin Laden. This was a very different *Sun* to the one that reported the Gulf War. It was measured, respectful of the dead, and empathetic with the survivors. The theme was "memorial" but also forgiveness. The editorial by David Yelland was "Why we must refuse to hate." He wrote, "no faith is inherently evil" and "the UN must be the way to resolve the Iraqi threat." He stated that he refused to frighten the *Sun*'s readers with "scare stories," and added, "we must remember" but "we must not 'hate.'" The *Sun*'s 16-page supplement, "One year on," mostly featured the bereaved and their stories, but also included a double-page spread of the *Sun*'s key front pages from the "Year that changed our lives." The *Sun* was the only paper to invoke "crime" as an explanatory discourse the year before, but it did not feature here, nor did the rampant nationalism associated with the paper's coverage of war and football. This was requiem journalism. It reminded me of the press coverage of Princess Diana's death and funeral in 1997. Its focus was grief, remembrance, family, and forgiveness. The *Sun*'s achievement was to rise above the *Daily Mail*'s ranting war-mongering, but also to rise well above its usual remit of shock, horror, probe, and populism. This appeared to be a new liberal, caring, sharing *Sun,* which was certainly surprising in retrospective comparison with the jingoism and ill-judged prejudice of it, earlier incarnation.

The *Guardian*'s front page featured an image of a cross, accidentally hewn from twisted metal in the debris of Ground Zero, that was part of a photographic exhibition, which, in fact, was part of the post-9-11 "art" so damned by Lawson in the same newspaper. The headline was "The dead and the guilty," and there was a commissioned article written by historian Simon Schama, "On the questions America should be asking on the anniversary of September 11th." This was not news as such but a serious and thought-provoking piece, partly remembrance and partly critique of the "mass reverence" surrounding the event that, for Schama, "has succeeded in making secular debate about liberty into an act of indecency, disrespectful of the dead and disloyal to the flag." One effect of this, he claimed, has been to stifle criticism of George Bush's war on Afghanistan and the threatened war on Iraq. Interestingly, this did seem to reflect an effort not to be "sickly" or "mawkish," but of course it isn't a lasting effect on journalism as Schama is a historian. There was no other news on the front page apart from brief guides to the contents. The second quality broadsheet paper, the *Daily Telegraph*, foregrounded not September 11, but Blair's recall of parliament to debate the Bush administration's drive toward war. Its main image was of the British Prime Minister in somber mode. The article commemorating September 11 was fairly brief and contained the headline "US on high alert for anniversary of September 11." It focused on the increased security within the United States on the anniversary of the attacks. There were also several other unconnected news stories on the front page. The *Telegraph* looked little different than usual and was not remembering; it was writing a daily journal of newsworthy events rather than a history or requiem.

Both broadsheets included pull-out supplements featuring images from the terrible day and how the world had changed. The *Guardian*'s 12-page enclosure was "HOW THE WORLD CHANGED," while the *Telegraph* used the phrase "THE WORLD AFTER SEPTEMBER 11" for its 12-page section. Thereafter there were no similarities between the two. The *Guardian*, rather bizarrely, offered no journalistic comment at all. It merely printed the recollections and experiences of some 50 people, some of whom had very tenuous reasons to be included; for example, a Jewish student from Manchester, and a British advertising executive, bemoaning the downturn in business. This was straight personification to try to get some kind of story out of an issue that no longer had the inherent news value of the original event. It had lost its drama, rarity, some negativity, and had become more culturally relevant to the United States rather than the United Kingdom. Only by personifying could some news value be redeemed, by reporting it as negative and dramatic for some particular British people. However, personification in news links events to individuals, often focusing on pathology or psychology as causal. It can also support a kind of domestication of events. To provide the cultural relevance, audiences are offered familial scenes and detail of affectional relationships. Both such contextualizations makes it difficult to offer broader social and historical analyses.

The *Telegraph* also personified, using interviews with heroes, survivors, rescuers, and the bereaved, but these were contextualized in carefully researched and well-written articles such as "Confusing times for eight million Muslims in the US" and "Let's roll: Americans fight back after a year of soul searching." The last four pages were devoted to the "war on terror" but were in no sense "gung-ho"; rather, they focused on integration and aid for ordinary people, such as "Smashing terrorist camps was a success, now US must aid Kabul." Both George Bush, "bird brain or ideal leader," and bin Laden, "evil smile that just won't fade," were deeply criticized.

Although the main sections of the broadsheets contained some references to September 11, they were very tangential to current events. The *Daily Telegraph* continued the story about the recall of parliament and offered a further article on Saddam Hussein, as well as a biography of bin Laden, "A cowboy fan who grew to hate America," that explained his fanaticism as inspired by Egyptian Islamists. The following page provided a list of the British victims, but with virtually no comment. The editorial was pro-British, pro-Bush, pro-war, and pro-Western democracy.

The *Guardian's* main section, completed with the front-page Schama article, offered only a further two pages and an editorial. The inside stories described the planned memorials. They also focused on the possibility of a further attack with, "World Alert on Anniversary." At the bottom of page four there was an article discussing the British artist Damien Hirst's description of the attack as "9-11 wicked but a work of art." A claim made because, according to Hirst, the event was "devised visually" and "changed perceptions." Maybe the critic, Mark Lawson, was disappointed with the art of September 11, because art can only ever imitate life, which itself so often *surprises, explains, and provokes* with no embellishment from artists. And maybe, on occasions like September 11, real life even shocks normally ebullient, partisan journalists into uniform, reverential cliché.

IMPLIED MEANING: MEANINGFUL NEWSPAPERS

News values suggested that the events of September 11, 2001, and in retrospect on September 11, 2002, might be treated in the British press as rare, negative, and the criminal actions of an evil psychopath. Journalistic profiles and practices in Britain supported, as likely, news frameworks commensurate with white, middle-class, patriotic, and masculine interests. Commercial pressures might well have prompted a simplistic account, and newspaper political partisanship should have supported significant differences between the traditional right- and left-wing publications. Yet in many ways, both in 2001 and 2002, the newspapers didn't comply.

On September 12, 2001, what was most surprising was the uniformity of the reporting, its intense visual focus, a general sense of world catastrophe, the personifying of the dead and bereaved, the obvious sharing of sources, references to Pearl Harbor, a bonding with the United States, and the search for someone or something to blame—with this tentatively highlighting Islamic terrorism, and in particular bin Laden. Seriousness, shock, respect for the dead, and distance pushed the papers into a shared language informed by news values steeped in *cultural resonance,* shared wars family grief, the *dramatic* images of contemporary media, a focus on *elitism,* the United States and George Bush, and the *personification* of blame, Islam, bin Laden, and the "other." This press emphasized common values and embraced all readers within them in a bonding of despair at death and destruction, and drive for attribution and vengeance. Differences were temporarily suspended—the West was at war, though no one was quite clear whom or what with, or even why.

These closing downs and mutualities of sensibility in some ways set down a clear conforming path for reportage, yet a year later there was some of evidence of veering back into political "stereotype" among the *Guardian,* the *Daily Mail,* and the *Daily Telegraph.* Of these, only the *Mail* retained its focus on bin Laden and its bellicose analysis. For this paper September 11 was still hard news about an evil criminal who must be caught. There were trailed racist undertones and middle class anxieties. The *Telegraph* and *Guardian* main sections offered limited and tentatively critical news accounts, and the most critical, by Schama, was not a piece of journalism. The papers were by no means as diametrically opposed as might be expected, given their usual allegiances, and focused mostly on the victims and bereaved. Only the *Sun* surprised and provoked with its pacifist and forgiving tone, which was in many aspects a-political and quasi-religious in flavor. This may be an editorial glitch rather than a sea change, or even a cynical attempt to invoke the kind of emotion that rampaged in Britain after Princess Diana's death. The funeral cortege on the front page looks very like the front pages that followed Diana's funeral, and the mood is very much about the remembrance of loved ones, loss, family, and reverence.

So was the news about September 11 as valueless a year on as Lawson felt the arts media were? Would Lawson feel these reports were "inhibited" and "sickly," showing "mawkish hindsight" and "fear of offense"? Was there a "lasting effect"? The press was certainly inhibited either by "fear of offense" or an atmosphere of censoriousness, or their own ideological parochialism, or some of these hard-bitten journalists were simply shocked into uncritical silence. The focus on the personal and familial narrowed the discursive accounts; there was an acceptance of the "war on terrorism" phraseology even though no war had been declared or identified—in fact, it was used to justify unsolicited attacks on Afghanistan; there was an incitement of "our" grief rather than a struggle for explanation for "their" actions. The effect was an inhibition and closing down of other accounts that might have looked at the implications of "our" actions in relation to imperialism, global poverty, and Occidentalism.

The news also became mawkish and sickly because, a year on, news values turned accounts of this most serious act of global slaughter (outside of declared war) into either a drama of domesticity, souvenir, and individual courage, or, in the *Mail*, the search for an individual arch-criminal. This may not be as damaging reportage as the nationalistic, racist, war-mongering that might have been expected of the tabloid and right-wing press, but they are uncomfortably close to the kind of soap-opera journalism seen by critics as characterizing the dumbing down to infotainment.

That inhibition and sickliness doesn't suggest a move toward long-lasting serious journalism impelled by September 11. If anything, the effect on journalism seems to confirm Lawson's comment about the arts as relevant to the factual media, too. But there have been effects, though perhaps not unrelated to this lack of explanation and provocation. One of those has been the almost complete lack of any criminological critique of the events of September 11, 2001, to September 11, 2002, in the United Kingdom. There has been relatively little criticism of the attacks on Afghanistan by the United States and its allies, despite a complete failure to find bin Laden or even finally establish his guilt. The assault, aimed at destroying the Taliban, who were thought to be harboring bin Laden and his followers, caused massive collateral damage to the infrastructure and civilians of Afghanistan. It also replaced the old regime with a new pro-Western regime. Some 3,700 civilians died in the first three months of the "war against terror,"[39] many more than those who died on September 11. Hundreds of surviving Taliban and al-Qaeda fighters were shipped, manacled and blindfolded, to a U.S. naval base at Guantanamo Bay, Cuba. They were declared unlawful combatants and "denied prisoner of war status," thus enabling them to be tried by U.S. military tribunals.[40] Although technically criminalized by this decision, they could not appeal to U.S. justice, as Camp X-ray is technically outside of American jurisdiction. They remain held as the "tangible manifestation of the terrorism responsible for the deaths at the World Trade Center and the Pentagon."[41] Yet they can only be held because they are not defined as "prisoners of war"—that is, the war on terrorism that justified invading Afghanistan was redefined in order to imprison without trial. There has been little fury about such contempt for the law itself and support for Bush, which has steadily grown in the United States with his inclusion of other Islamic states in his "axis of evil." In November 2002, he achieved a new record as the first Republican president to increase his majority at the mid-term elections. So closely have the terms evil, terror, and Islam been associated for the general public that the collapse of the U.S. economy and the disgrace of massive corporate corruption have all but disappeared under a deluge of patriotism, vengeance, and self-righteousness.

Also disappeared is any account of America's interest in the oil reserves of the Middle East and Bush's personal and political dependence on oil money, even though in the Autumn of 2002 the world was again on the verge of war—this time against Iraq and its leader, Saddam Hussein. Identified by Bush as part of a terrorist "axis of evil" and accused of developing nuclear and biological warfare, as well as supporting al-Qaeda, Iraq in early 2003 hovered on the brink of being preemptively attacked by the United States. Peace in the region was dependent on the UN's resistance to George Bush. Europe was divided in support for an offensive. The British government appeared to be playing a complex double bluff, both appeasing and supporting Bush while maintaining a diplomatic and political commitment to the UN.

Increasingly, September 11 has become an excuse for U.S. imperialism and a deflection from U.S. internal economic corruption and collapse. One lasting effect has been that liberals, pacifists, and anti-racists have been made pro-terrorists, because to be against American actions since September 11 is seen as an abuse of the dead. September 11 has been used politically to pursue the interests of the United States (or rather, the Bush government and the oil allies), and has been aided and abetted by journalism's failure to "surprise, explain and provoke." That failure may have been due to shared interests and sensibilities between the profession of politics and the press that stretch across the pond, complying with the political-economy model of the news; it may be because news values themselves constrained newsmakers to criteria that precluded deep, historicized, and globally contextualized accounts; or it may be due perhaps to a fear of affronting and subsequent loss of sales, so prompting adherence to a kind of safe populism, not so far from "dumbed down." Themed textual analysis revealed the evidence for this and provided the substance to expose and assess any implications. Such discursive analysis is made possible, productive, and precise when informed by the major theoretical approaches to the news.

News about September 11 has been "tweaked" to create a veil over the crises of the early millennium. Mark Lawson's comment on the arts media seems to apply well to the news media. As in the arts, there is a lasting effect evident in the British press of inhibition, mawkishness, and inoffensiveness that at best leaves intact and at worst solidifies that veil. Among journalists, *the best lack all conviction while the worst are full of passionate intensity;* meanwhile, *things fall apart; the center cannot hold; mere anarchy is loosed upon the world.*[42]

9

Creating Memories: Exploring How Narratives Help Define the Memorialization of Tragedy

Kelly R. Damphousse, Kristen S. Hefley, and Brent L. Smith

How societies respond to major historical events depends largely on the context of the event, including its outcome, the number and type of people involved, and resource availability.[1] One important aspect of the context of an event is its characterization as a "chronic" vs. "acute" incident. Acute events reflect occurrences that take place over short time frames and occur in relative isolation. Chronic events take place over longer periods of time and may occur in many different places. In the case of terrorism, the bombing in Oklahoma City in 1995 can be seen as an acute event while attacks by the IRA in the United Kingdom and homicide bombers in the Middle East might be classified as chronic events. All things being equal, acute events are likely to be treated differently by social groups than chronic events. These differences might include the extent to which the group pays attention to the event and the extent to which the event becomes part of a group's collective memory.

This distinction is especially important in the task of memorializing an event. Acute events are easy to memorialize because the "story" is easily captured. There is one place to house the memorial and usually one set of victims. Chronic events often happen in more than one location, occur over a long period of time, and have more than one type of participant. Thus, discussions about how and where to memorialize a chronic event are more complex. Acute events are also unique and thus have few distractions. As a result, acute events are more likely to garner the necessary material and emotional resources and attention that would result in a memorial. Chronic events are common and there are many distractions. Thus, memorials are less likely to be created or will be created in the light of increased controversy.

The attack in Oklahoma City, for example, resulted in a large memorial and museum that has become somewhat of a tourist attraction, part of what Schwartz calls the "heritage industry." While the process of creating the Oklahoma City National Memorial was far from simple, the task was much less complex than the memorialization of chronic events (characterized by ongoing crises), where there are many victim groups spread over time and across a wide geographical location. In chronic events, there are many "stories" to be told. The "troubles" in Northern Ireland, for example, have resulted in few formal memorials—although there has been widespread use of informal memorials in the form of murals.[2]

The building of formal memorials typically reflects the power structure of a society as various voices fight to be heard.[3] Thus, we would expect that memorials associated within a chronic context would be more likely to be controversial and complex. In this paper, we address how the process of memorializing the terrorist attacks on September 11, 2001, (September 11) was portrayed in the news media. We suggest that while the events of September 11 share many similarities with the Oklahoma City bombing, the distinction between chronic and acute events might play a role in how the events are memorialized.

While the events of September 11 were certainly startling (seemingly acute), they marked the beginning[4] of a chronic period of events. First, there were four attacks at the same time. Second, the aftermath of the 9-11 attacks was crowded by subsequent talk of a war on terrorism, the anthrax attacks, the mailbox bombings, the shoe bomber, the dirty bomber, the DC sniper attacks, and the constant talk about this being "a whole new world" where everything had changed. Thus, Americans began to see terrorism as becoming more common, more likely, and more a part of their lives. Following the Oklahoma City bombing, on the other hand, there were no further attacks and the arrest of the terrorists seemed to signal the end of the threat. Other than receiving an increased exposure by the media to militia groups, Americans did not see the Oklahoma City attack as part of an on-going social problem. Thus, the events of September 11 can be defined as a chronic event with a wider variety of "narratives," or themes, than the acute Oklahoma City bombing, resulting in greater complexity and controversy. We rely on the rich literature about the memorialization process to inform our discussion.[5]

THE PURPOSE AND PROCESS OF MEMORIALIZATION

The most important question one might ask about the memorialization process is not *how* do memorials come about but *why*. In the past several years, America has engaged in a commemoration frenzy, with many events (both small and large) deemed worthy of a memorial. The advent of roadside memorials has been cited as an example of this growing interest among Americans. The recent rush toward memorializing in modern American society might be tied to the popularity of the Vietnam Memorial and the healing felt by many in association with their visit to it. Increasingly, Americans now see the building of formal and informal memorials as "just something you do" in response to tragedy. In the moments following the Oklahoma City bombing, for example, plans were already being made for a memorial. This stands in stark contrast, for example, to the 50-year lag between the Holocaust and the museum built in Washington, D.C.[6]

In this paper, our focus is on the creation of permanent, or formal, memorials. But it is interesting also to note the use of spontaneous, or informal, memorials. One of the enduring features of the scene at the Oklahoma City bomb site, for example, was the material left behind on the fence by visitors to commemorate the tragedy. This "democratization of memorialization" has been repeated in recent years following the deaths of celebrities (e.g., John Lennon, Selena, and Princess Diana), or at the site of celebrated deaths (e.g., the D.C.-area sniper attacks of 2002). Following the events of September 11, these scenes were repeated in Pennsylvania at a makeshift fence, on a hill overlooking the Pentagon, and at fire and police stations across New York City. Although not intended as such, the photos of missing people plastered over the city soon became spontaneous memorials as well.[7]

Most often, these informal memorials are private and individual acts that commonly occur at the site of the tragedy. The material that is left behind consists of a variety of objects that seem to be more meaningful to the mourner than to the deceased. Items attached to the fence around the Oklahoma City bomb site, for example, included personalized license plates, conference name badges, and business cards. Interestingly, this fence was eventually incorporated into the formal Oklahoma City memorial, and visitors continue to attach personal items to it. This is suggestive of Bodnar's notion that the creation of public memory most often reflects a mix of *official* and *vernacular* expressions.[8]

Many historically important sites have been memorialized in America. Until recently, most were located at the site of some important battle. One of the reasons that we build memorials is so that people do not forget the tragedy or, more recently, the people that were killed. The focus of American memorials has changed over time. As opposed to symbolic edifices that rather anonymously represent event participants, American memorials have become places where each victim is reflected permanently. Linenthal has called this the "populist hagiography." The Vietnam Memorial, where the names of each

American killed in the conflict are listed, is an excellent example. Likewise, the Oklahoma City memorial represents each victim with an empty bronze and glass chair.[9]

Why are memorials important? People come to visit these memorials not just to learn about individuals and to read their stories. Instead, the goal of the visit is to become transformed into someone who has "experienced" the event. Unfortunately, while the feelings associated with the creation of memorials are generally positive, some social commentators suggest that there are some negative aspects of America's recent interest in memorialization. For example, there can be a sense of the macabre associated with these memorials; there is a fear that we might go too far with them—show too much—so that the memorial becomes more like the scene of a horrific car accident, where the passersby cannot help but look. The sale of t-shirts, bumper stickers, and coffee mugs depicting the memorials is also looked upon as the crass commercialization of grief. Finally, there is a fear that memorialization will become a cliché, where an increasing number of groups follow some formula to create memorials. Representatives from the Oklahoma City memorial traveled to New York City in the aftermath of the 9-11 attacks, for example, to "show them how to make a memorial."[10]

How are memorials developed? Scholars who study the creation of public memory frequently suggest that the process evolves through the use of *themes*. Jorgensen-Earp and Lanzilotti, for example, suggested three major themes expressed by the creators of informal shrines at disaster sites. Informal shrine makers *spontaneously* express the themes of (1) the sacredness of the death site, (2) the "specialness," or innocence, of the victims, and (3) heaven as home.[11]

In formal memorializations, the use of themes and rhetoric is even more deliberate, since the permanence of the memorial suggests there is more at stake. Actors with particular agendas use these themes to encourage others to follow their lead. Schwartz described public narratives and themes as "stories that answer ultimate questions about the origins, purposes, and fare of societies and their institutions [that] control what individuals believe about themselves collectively." Langer similarly described the efforts by victims to understand or evade the holocaust. For these scholars, the use of the term narrative is meant to describe how social groups define a situation in an effort to elicit a preferred response. It is the "story" behind the collective movement.[12]

Edward Linenthal has written extensively about memorialization in America, including the Holocaust Museum, American battlegrounds, and the Enola Gay. In his discussion of the creation of the Oklahoma City National Memorial, Linenthal described both major and minor narratives that participants used to make sense of the process. Linenthal's first major narrative is the *progressive* narrative. Here, the effects of a terrible atrocity are attenuated by focusing on all the good that accompanied the event. In Oklahoma City, some people associated with the memorial focused on how Oklahomans appeared to the rest of the country after the bombing (e.g., strong, resilient, hardy, optimistic). While the bombing was terrible, it showed what Oklahomans are "made of," and the memorial needed to reflect that. The memorial's emphasis on the "Oklahoma Standard" and the honored role of the "survivor tree"—bent but not broken—reflect this progressive narrative. Actually, the building of the memorial itself was seen as progressive in that it was an opportunity for urban renewal in an economically depressed city.[13]

The second major narrative is *redemptive*. This narrative is strongly associated with the meaning that religion can provide in times of tragedy. Here, the victim and the viewer of the memorial both find comfort in the notion that God has a plan or that things will be better "by and by." According to Linenthal, this narrative resonated especially well with those associated with the Oklahoma City memorial, because of the predominance of conservative Protestant believers in the region. Thus, the memorial would need to represent the importance of the faith of the people of Oklahoma. A prayer chapel at one end of the memorial and the "And Jesus Wept" statue at the other end of the memorial reflect the importance that the redemptive narrative played in the process.[14]

The final major narrative described by Linenthal is the *toxic* narrative. In this narrative, the focus is on the reality of the event and the pain associated with "remembering." The death and loss (immediate and eventual) associated with the event are key elements in the discussion of a memorial. Almost half of the people living in Oklahoma City knew someone killed in the bombing, while almost 1,000 were injured in the blast. Many associated with the memorial needed to have some of that hurt represented so that visitors could "appreciate" the pain. In the memorial, this is reflected in the empty chairs, the bared foundation of the Murrah Building, and the scars and blackened windows in the Journal Record Building (which houses the museum) across the street, and even a restroom that can be viewed in its damaged state. The obvious point is that visitors are meant to feel the pain.[15]

Unfortunately, the process of creating the memory is also painful—survivors are required to relive the drama, rescuers are haunted by those they did not save, and family members who desired privacy were pressured into participating. In the toxic narrative, some people express antipathy toward the process of memorialization, saying that it is too painful to remember. Some families, for example, have refused to help create the individualized mini-shrines inside the museum by donating personal items.

Linenthal suggests two minor narratives in relation to the Oklahoma City bombing. The first is the traumatic vision of the event—a medicalized view of the tragedy. With this narrative, Linenthal highlights the grief associated with loss. This grief results in the belief that the tragedy has created a whole new world where nothing is the same. At the same time, survivors, the victims' family members, and even non-affected Oklahoma citizens felt a shared trauma because of the bombing. During the recovery time, there were many critics of the large number of counselors and psychologists that descended upon the survivors and family members. There was also a fear of PTSD being over-diagnosed. The medicalized grief became the new "religion," a method of dealing with the tragedy.

The second minor narrative for Linenthal was the patriotic theme, where the seemingly senseless deaths were transformed into deaths with meaning—the victims gave their lives for their country. Political figures and the media emphasized the patriotic rhetoric while family members of victims were less inclined to do so. Many family members and Linenthal himself were actually not persuaded by this narrative. They believe that the patriotic narrative is weak because the victims did not give their lives on behalf of their country. He suggested that the Oklahoma City bombing deaths were more similar to a mass murder at a restaurant than the deaths of soldiers at Valley Forge.[16]

In what follows, we examine the narratives related to memorialization that were used in the year following the events of September 11. Our hypothesis is that many distinctions can be made between the Oklahoma City bombing (an acute event) and September 11 (part of a series of chronic events): the number of victims (hundreds vs. thousands), the victim focus (children vs. adults), the variation among the victims (people of the heartland vs. first responders, military, and business people), the geographical location of the events (one downtown location vs. the World Trade Center, Capitol, White House, Pentagon, Pennsylvania, Boston, Newark, San Francisco, Los Angeles, etc.), the scope of the story (local vs. national/international), the offenders' nationalities and motivations (American anti-government extremists vs. anti-American extremists), identification with the target buildings (an unknown office building vs. important economic, military, and cultural icons), identification with the attacks (learning second hand about the attacks in the media vs. seeing the attacks live on television), and the societal context following each tragedy (relatively isolated except for increased interest in militias vs. war on terror, war against Iraq, mailbox bombings, shoe bombers, thwarted dirty nuke bomber, Washington area snipers, anthrax attacks, etc.). Based on these differences, we would expect to find a more complex array of narratives associated with the 9-11 events than with the Oklahoma City bombing.

DATA AND METHODS

To illustrate the narratives, we examined newspaper articles (news stories, features, editorials, and letters to the editor) from the *New York Times* (for the World Trade Center memorial), Washington, D.C.-area newspapers (for the Pentagon memorial) and various sources in Pennsylvania (for the Pennsylvania memorial). We used the Lexis-Nexis newspaper database as our data source, and we collected the articles from September 12, 2001, to September 11, 2002. We searched by region using the key word "memorial" and excluded the articles that included the words "mass" and "service" to help eliminate articles that had to do with memorial services. Our interest was limited to discussions about the creation of formal and permanent memorials. We excluded any articles that focused on the creation of spontaneous memorials. Each article was read and then coded for a number of manifest variables (e.g., word count, story location, source of quotations) and latent variables (e.g., pro/con memorial).

The important latent variable for this paper was the narrative type. We defined "narrative" as a specific quote from an interview subject, or by an author, that expressed some opinion about the memorial in question. The narrative could be expressed in a single sentence or it could be reflected throughout the entire article. We read each article and coded the type of narrative (if any) that was expressed in it. Since more than one narrative was sometimes expressed in an article, the coding became quite complex and the number of narratives exceeded the number of stories collected. Some articles expressed a narrative in a single sentence within an article. This was counted as a single narrative. Other articles (especially editorials and letters to the editor) expressed a narrative throughout an entire article. If there was only one source expressing the narrative, then this was also counted as a single narrative. Some articles included interviews with several people who expressed the same narrative. In this case, we counted each quote from a source as a narrative. Thus, the single article produced several units of the same narrative. Some articles had one source who expressed several different narratives. We counted each narrative separately. Thus, some of the articles reflect several units of different narratives. Some articles had different sources who expressed several different narratives. We identified a source for each narrative in the article and counted each narrative. Thus, some of the articles reflect several units of different narratives.

Since we hypothesized a wider variety of narratives in the 9-11 events compared with the Oklahoma City bombing narratives, we needed to create the additional narrative categories. These narratives were developed by examining a sample of articles in the months immediately following September 11. In all, 16 narratives were used in news stories about the memorials. These include the 5 Linenthal narratives (progressive, redemptive, toxic, traumatic, and patriotic) and an additional 11 that do not fit precisely into any of the previous categories (commercialization, defiance, dogmatic, educational, historical, idealization, inspirational, justice, perseverance, sacred, and unity). We describe each of the additional narratives in the following section.

Using this methodology, we collected 130 articles and 382 narratives about the World Trade Center memorial—6 articles mentioned the memorial but did not express a narrative so they were excluded from the analyses. We categorized the source of the narratives as (1) a citizen of the state of New York, (2) a citizen from outside of New York state, (3) a journalist for the *New York Times,* and (4) a politician or a public figure. We collected 33 articles (90 narratives) about the Pentagon memorial and 48 articles (100 narratives) about the Pennsylvania memorial. We categorized the source of these narratives as (1) politicians or public figures, (2) journalists and editors, and (3) citizens. In the following sections, we describe the distribution of the articles about the memorials and then describe how the narratives were used to discuss each site's memorial.

NEWSPAPER ARTICLES AND 9-11 MEMORIALS

In Figure 9.1, we present the distribution of the number of memorial-based articles over the course of the year for each of the sites. The distribution follows rather predictable patterns. In the first month, there was almost no discussion of a memorial for the Pennsylvania crash site (only one story from September through November). This is probably because of the original uncertainty surrounding the cause of the crash and the location of the crash, which was fenced off in an isolated rural location. The peak in March coincides with the introduction of congressional legislation authorizing the construction of a national memorial at the site of the crash. In the last two months before the anniversary of the crash, however, the number of stories about the memorial in Pennsylvania increased dramatically. The articles were mostly in response to the impending anniversary and the creation of the Flight 93 memorial task force following President Bush's signing of the memorial bill into law. The final plan for the memorial is scheduled to be delivered to Congress by September 2005.

There were more stories early on about the Pentagon memorial, but there were never more than five per month throughout the year. The reason for this might be due to the composition of most of the victims "on the ground" and

Figure 9.1. Number of Articles per Month by Crash Site

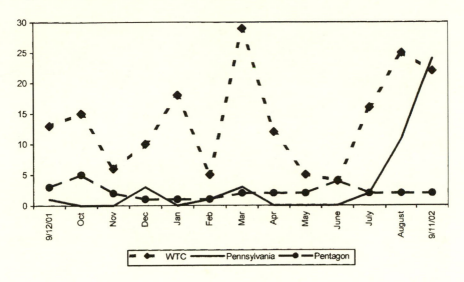

the location of the event. The majority of the Pentagon victims were military personnel and the Pentagon is not a public facility. Therefore, there was less public discussion of the memorial. In fact, about 35 percent of all the narratives associated with the Pentagon memorial were by politicians and public figures (compared to 24 percent for the World Trade Center and 30 percent for the Pennsylvania memorials). In addition, the Pentagon site was cleared and rebuilt more quickly than the other sites, and the memorial selection process was nearly completed by the anniversary of the attack. The memorial is expected to be *completed* by September 2003.

The variation in the number of articles associated with the World Trade Center memorial is much more dramatic. This is probably due to the large number of people associated with the tragedy, its location in the middle of a major U.S. city, and the hurried efforts to create a "temporary" formal memorial. In addition, the World Trade Center site was much larger and affected the psyche of the whole city. In the two months following the attacks, there were almost 30 stories about the memorial (13 in September). The number of articles then dropped, but peaked again as people began to discuss the proposed memorial commemorating the six-month anniversary of the attacks. In March, the twin lights that lit the sky over New York City generated many stories about the permanent memorial, as did the approaching one-year anniversary in July and August. Among the stories reported over the 12-month span was discussion of the bitter irony that the memorial from the

Table 9.1. World Trade Center Narrative by Person Being Quoted

	Politicians Public Figures	Journalists or Editors	Citizens from NY	Citizens outside NY	TOTAL
Commercialization	20 22%	5 7%	13 7%	1 2%	39 10%
Defiance	0 0%	1 1%	3 2%	1 2%	5 1%
Dogmatic	1 1%	1 1%	5 3%	2 5%	9 2%
Educational	3 3%	8 11%	8 4%	2 5%	21 5%
Historical	7 8%	10 14%	1 1%	3 7%	21 5%
Idealization	7 8%	1 1%	5 3%	1 2%	14 4%
Inspirational	13 14%	13 18%	31 17%	4 10%	61 16%
Justice	0 0%	0 0%	5 3%	7 17%	12 3%
Patriotic	4 4%	0 0%	6 3%	3 7%	13 3%
Perseverance	3 3%	3 4%	15 8%	5 12%	26 7%
Progressive	14 16%	18 25%	21 12%	3 7%	56 15%
Redemptive	4 4%	1 1%	6 3%	3 7%	14 4%
Sacred	2 2%	1 1%	5 3%	1 2%	9 2%
Toxic	4 4%	2 3%	12 7%	1 2%	19 5%
Traumatic	6 7%	7 10%	41 23%	4 10%	58 15%
Unity	2 2%	1 1%	2 1%	0 0%	5 1%
TOTAL	90 24%	72 19%	179 47%	41 11%	382 100%

World Trade Center bombing in 1993 had also been destroyed in the attack and would need to be replaced.[17]

NARRATIVES AND 9-11 MEMORIALS

In this section, we describe the narratives we discovered while examining the memorial-based articles for each site and then provide an example from the articles. We start with Linenthal's five narratives and then discuss our additional narratives.

We found many examples of Linenthal's *progressive* narrative—where the social group is said to have been made "better" because of the event. In the World Trade Center memorial articles, the progressive narrative was the third most popular—15 percent of the articles (see Table 9.1). Most of those narratives were made by citizens of the state of New York or the journalists (presumably from New York City). The progressive narrative was less popular in the other two sites (see Tables 9.2 and 9.3). The following quotes describe the progressive narrative:

Just as the families need the city, businesses and community groups to help us build a fitting memorial to those we lost, we need to join them as partners in renewal to restore life to the neighborhood where our loved ones died.[18]

[The 16-acre site] can never become a mere development. It should be something magnificent and inspiring that honors the dead and surpasses expectations about how Lower Manhattan can be restored and revitalized.[19]

The exceptionally fast reconstruction of the Pentagon shows that moving forward rapidly with rebuilding after a disaster can be a healing and restorative act that helps people deal with death and reaffirm life.[20]

Linenthal's *redemptive* narrative points to the importance of religion to explain the tragedy and to make it more bearable. Religion played an important role in the recovery efforts following the attacks. Many memorial services were held in churches and church attendance increased for a time following the attacks.[21] In the discussion of the memorials, however, the redemptive narrative did not seem to hold as much sway. In all three sites, less than 10 percent of the narratives had a redemptive outlook. The Pennsylvania site had the highest proportion of redemptive narratives (9 percent), perhaps because of its rural location. Nevertheless, there were redemptive narratives referring to the World Trade Center memorial. The Rev. Samuel Johnson Howard of Trinity parish, for example, said:

I'm convinced that a spiritual component is an important part of making a successful memorial statement. A wonderful church ought to be incorporated in some way. It's not only relevant to Sept. 11; it's relevant to the history of Lower Manhattan.[22]

A visitor to the spontaneous memorial on the hill above the Pentagon wrote, "God, please take care of our brothers and sisters."[23] An additional example of the redemptive narrative for the 9-11 memorials includes the following:

Table 9.2. Pentagon Memorial Narrative by Person Being Quoted

	Politicians Public Figures	Journalists or Editors	Other Citizens	TOTAL
Commercialization	0 0%	1 10%	0 0%	1 1%
Defiance	1 4%	0 0%	2 5%	3 3%
Dogmatic	0 0%	0 0%	0 0%	0 0%
Educational	3 11%	0 0%	0 0%	3 3%
Historical	1 4%	1 10%	0 0%	2 2%
Idealization	5 18%	0 0%	7 17%	12 13%
Inspirational	3 11%	1 10%	3 7%	7 8%
Justice	1 4%	0 0%	0 0%	1 1%
Patriotic	8 29%	1 10%	11 26%	20 22%
Perseverance	1 4%	1 10%	1 2%	3 3%
Progressive	5 18%	1 10%	1 2%	7 8%
Redemptive	0 0%	0 0%	6 14%	6 7%
Sacred	0 0%	0 0%	6 14%	6 7%
Toxic	1 4%	0 0%	0 0%	1 1%
Traumatic	3 11%	4 40%	11 26%	18 20%
Unity	3 11%	0 0%	2 5%	5 6%
TOTAL	35 35%	10 13%	45 53%	90 100%

Let us build the memorial on top of a tall building. Allow loved ones a place to come to mourn on a sunny day and a place for mothers to tell their children, "This is where Daddy lives with God now."[24]

There were few examples of Linenthal's *toxic* narrative (where people express antipathy toward the memorial), but these may become more evident as the memorials begin to be built. Less than 5 percent of the narratives at any

Table 9.3. Pennsylvania Memorial Narrative by Person Being Quoted

	Politicians Public Figures	Journalists or Editors	Other Citizens	TOTAL
Commercialization	1 3%	0 0%	4 6%	5 5%
Defiance	5 15%	0 0%	0 0%	5 5%
Dogmatic	0 0%	0 0%	0 0%	0 0%
Educational	1 3%	0 0%	1 1%	2 2%
Historical	3 9%	0 0%	0 0%	3 3%
Idealization	8 24%	2 40%	11 15%	21 19%
Inspirational	1 3%	0 0%	10 14%	11 10%
Justice	0 0%	1 20%	1 1%	2 2%
Patriotic	10 30%	0 0%	6 8%	16 15%
Perseverance	1 3%	0 0%	4 6%	5 5%
Progressive	0 0%	0 0%	4 6%	4 4%
Redemptive	0 0%	1 20%	9 13%	10 9%
Sacred	3 9%	0 0%	4 6%	7 6%
Toxic	0 0%	0 0%	3 4%	3 3%
Traumatic	0 0%	1 20%	12 17%	13 12%
Unity	0 0%	0 0%	3 4%	3 3%
TOTAL	33 30%	5 5%	72 65%	110 100%

of the sites expressed toxic tones. Our findings include excellent examples, however, of the anger people experience over the creation of a memorial. A widow from Princeton, New Jersey, who lost her husband in the World Trade Center attack said:

What do you do when on the one hand you have the economic necessity of moving Lower Manhattan forward and on the other a group of victim families that say, "You may not build on my loved one's head?" It will never be resolved.[25]

Raymond Gastil, the co-chairman of the task force for the memorial process at "New York New Visions," reported a similar experience regarding the World Trade Center memorial when he said:

What we have to get past is people saying they are going to form a human chain to stop building on the site.[26]

Concerning Linenthal's *traumatic* narrative, it was common in the days following September 11 to hear people say that "everything had changed." In fact, these comments were also prevalent in many of the discussions about the 9-11 memorials. More than 15 percent of each site's narratives suggested a traumatic narrative. This is probably expressed best by the following quotes:

The city and the country have undergone a trauma that cries out for an external, tangible architectural expression that will succeed in embodying the injury, the grief, the remembrance and the surmounting of tragedy that this horrible event will require of us.[27]

At the recovery site, firefighters and construction workers said what they were seeing was too horrific to describe without causing the families more hurt.[28]

The use of Linenthal's *patriotic* narrative in the 9-11 memorial discussion falls in line very closely with his sentiments. Among the discussions of the Pennsylvania memorial (where the victims were thought to have acted heroically to save the White House or the Capitol) and Pentagon memorial (where the victims were targeted because they were military personnel), the patriotic narrative was prevalent (15 percent and 22 percent respectively). When talking about the plans for a memorial for the Pennsylvania crash, for example, President Bush said:

To me, that was one of the most defining events of Sept. 11 . . . It shows me what a great nation we have. It reminds me of the character of the American people. And that's why we're so unique—not because of our government, but because of our people.[29]

Among the World Trade Center memorial narratives (where the victims are more similar to the Oklahoma City bombing victims), only about 3 percent of the stories had a patriotic emphasis. The World Trade Center memorial discussion seemed to struggle to make the connection between the emphasis on commerce and patriotism. The problem was to make the World Trade Center as symbolically important from a patriotic standpoint as the Pentagon, Capitol, and White House. The solution was to equate the buildings as representing "all that is America":

For the generations born after their completion, the towers of the World Trade Center were as representative of fundamental American values as the Capitol and the White House.[30]

When former Mayor Giuliani discussed the World Trade Center memorial, he likewise suggested that the towers represented America:

This place has to become a place in which when anybody comes here immediately they're going to feel the great power and strength and emotion of what it means to be an American.[31]

Of course, the famous picture of the firefighters hoisting the American flag at Ground Zero added to the resonance of the patriotic narrative, especially because of its resemblance to the Iwo Jima memorial.

In summary, we found evidence that the narratives suggested by Linenthal's description of the Oklahoma City bombing were also used by those engaged in the 9-11 memorialization process. There were many other narratives, however, that we were not able to classify according to his taxonomy. Thus, we created 11 alternative narratives that were also used in the discussion of the 9-11 memorials. Some of these could be classified as subcategories of Linenthal's five narratives. In the rest of this section, we briefly describe these alternative narratives and provide an example of each one.

Our first alternative narrative is *commercialization,* which reflects a concern that people have begun to use the tragedy as a means to make money. This is closely related to Linenthal's toxic narrative. Since the World Trade Center both represented capitalism and existed in the heart of the world's major financial district, it was inevitable that people would express concern about the commercialism of the future memorialization. Would the memorial fully *replace* the economic structure that existed before, or would it *coexist* with some other commerce-centered structure? After looking at the first six proposals for redevelopment of the World Trade Center site, an architect and co-founder of "Rebuild Downtown Our Town," said:

These plans are all driven by hard economics. There's no heart in them and no recognition of what we all had been led to believe would occur, that we would wind up with something wonderful on this site.[32]

Along with the concern about the memorial, some news articles described a revulsion associated with the commercialization of the disaster site.

These days, visitors to the giant, gaping hole are no longer covered in a grimy coat of dust, and only a faint hint remains of the burning stench that once pervaded Lower Manhattan. Vendors selling rhinestone American flag pins are joined by vendors hawking "designer" sunglasses. And for every cluster of tourists with disposable cameras or silver video cameras, there is one New Yorker clutching a plastic shopping bag bearing the red-lettered logo of Century 21, the discount department store across the street from the World Trade Center.[33]

Not surprisingly, most of the commercialization narratives found expression in the discussion surrounding the World Trade Center memorial. Still, there was some limited use of the narrative in the other sites. For example:

Shelley Walker says her gift shop, A Time to Remember, fills a need. People feel closer to the site if they can leave with a "Hearts of Steel Bracelet" or a "Let's Roll" T-shirt, she says. "I'm not trying to make money on this," Walker says, moments after noting that people paid $3.50 for buttons she bought for 65 cents.[34]

Another alternative narrative that was similar to Linenthal's toxic theme is the *defiance* narrative. In this narrative, we hear the expression that became trite in the months following the 9-11 attacks: "Doing [this or that] would be letting the terrorists win." People who wanted a specific type of memorial would use this narrative to goad others into agreeing. Some, for example, argued that simply re-building the World Trade Center towers (or building bigger ones) would be the best memorial:

The terrorists succeeded in wiping an American landmark off the map; building nothing in its place will simply affirm their crime. Putting up an uninspired development, like four 50-story buildings, doesn't cut it either. Building the tallest buildings in the world on the portion of the site not occupied by the memorial will let the terrorists know that we can't be pushed around and that we will rebuild what is destroyed, better than ever.[35]

The twin towers of the World Trade Center should be rebuilt taller and stronger than before and each brick should bear the name of someone whose life was taken by terrorism. In this way, the towers could still stand as a memorial to the victims but would also be reborn as a symbol of America's strength. We need to send the message that we won't fold under acts of terrorism.[36]

A Navy captain commenting on plans for the Pentagon memorial suggested that the memorial would make a statement to the terrorists:

They who did this will hear our battle cry of freedom.[37]

Also, the Pennsylvania representative who initiated the bill authorizing the Pennsylvania memorial commented on the importance of creating the memorial:

The terrorists miscalculated, thinking Americans were soft. They found out that the people on board were not going to give up that easily.[38]

Some people used the discussion about the memorial to make another point or push another agenda. We refer to this as the *dogmatic* narrative, and it only existed in the World Trade Center memorial narratives. One person suggested that the memorial could be combined with another dire need in New York City:

As a New York resident and an avid sports fan in my mid-20s, the tragedy downtown has sparked an idea that must be considered...I have an alternative plan. Build the stadium that New Yorkers have been fighting about for the past decade.[39]

Another citizen attached his comments about the memorial to his dissatisfaction with President Bush:

Since President Bush has repeatedly told us how much he dislikes Washington, why doesn't he come live in New York? We know he has no great love for this place, but by moving to our city, he might learn something about the country he is trying to govern. He might learn, in spite of his reservations, that we are the true heartland.[40]

Some of the narratives in the discussion of the 9-11 memorials suggested that *education* should be a key part of the memorials. This is similar to Linenthal's progressive narrative in that one could say that the end result of the terrorist attacks could have a benefit. New York City Mayor Michael Bloomberg specifically suggested that the best memorial might be a "phenomenal school."[41] Another source took direct aim at the Oklahoma City memorial, suggesting that it erred on the side of ambivalence to avoid controversy:

I wonder if New York will do any better than Oklahoma City in memorializing our new tragedy...How will a New York memorial...confront the men who instigated our suffering? Will it portray the jihad cultists simply as barbarians arrayed against our liberal values...or will we allow for some complexity in the portrait, some examination in how the world could have bred people so violently disaffected.[42]

The curator of the Somerset County Historical and Genealogical Society said about the Pennsylvania memorial that

People don't want just a granite monument; they also want a place to learn about what happened and to learn about how to prevent it.[43]

Related to the educational narrative, we discovered an *historical* narrative about the 9-11 memorials. In the historical narrative, efforts are made to link the events of September 11 to other important historical events in order to provide context. In addition, the historical narrative points to the fact that the memorials will record history for future generations. We believe this to be important, because today's memorials will define current culture to those in the future.

We should use the time to visit the memorials we already have, to learn about victims, heroes and events that came before us. This will teach us how Sept. 11 fits into the landscape of the New York—and the American—experience. And it will comfort us to learn that those who gave their lives in the trade center rubble had some worthy company.[44]

One feature great cities have in common is the capacity to recreate themselves after an assault. Under traumatic circumstances, New York has joined an ancient and illustrious roster. The dialogue about cities is synonymous with history. This discussion is now global. Young as we are, history is calling on New York to lead it.[45]

Many who spoke about the 9-11 memorials worried that not all victims were being treated equally, even though all should be treated as heroes. Part of this *idealization* narrative could also be called a subcategory of Linenthal's toxic narrative, since it refers to the problem of some victims being honored less than others. In this narrative, the sources described their victims of interest as special but ignored. For example, much of the focus of the World Trade Center tragedy was on the firefighters and police officers that were killed while heroically trying to save people's lives, while most that died in the building remain anonymous. In the Pennsylvania plane crash, only a few of the 40 passengers are thought to have participated in the heroic efforts to bring down the plane, while the other passengers are ignored. As an example:

Some family members say that while there were many heroic acts that day, society's fixation on the hero tale denigrates the majority of people who were simply doing their jobs and who now risk being dismissed from the nation's memory as second-class victims.[46]

What distinguishes the idealization narrative from the toxic narrative, however, is that the key point is that *all* of the victims were special or heroic. A visitor to the temporary memorial near the Pentagon said:

We have come here today to honor those brave souls who gave up their lives so we may live in a free country.[47]

The memorialization of those on Flight 93 was especially likely to be described in the idealized narrative. For example, the delegate to Congress from American Samoa referred to the Flight 93 victims as follows:

Many members of Congress may not be alive today if it had not been for the heroic acts of those passengers willing to sacrifice their lives.[48]

We defined many of the 9-11 narratives as *inspirational,* similar to Linenthal's progressive narrative in that the goal is to create beauty out of ugliness. The difference is that the goal is to make the memorial itself be uplifting (not necessarily to show how society "got better"). More than 15 percent of the narratives for the World Trade Center memorial were coded as inspirational. Milton Glaser, for example, the creator and copyrighter of the slogan "I ♥ NY," said that the memorial should reflect New York City's key strength—its imagination.[49] Another source, arguing for a light-based memorial in New York City, suggested that the memorial would soothe the city:

Imagine twilight falling each evening, and ghostly, towering columns of light gently, gradually appearing where the towers once stood. Not only will they fill the achingly empty spaces of the downtown skyline, but I can easily imagine a collective hush coming over the city as the silent specters appear—a daily pause in the city's mad rush, a chance to reflect and recommit to the ways we vowed that we would change after that horrible day.[50]

Some clearly stated that the memorial needed to have the twin goals of reflection and inspiration:

While new offices on the site should be of moderate height, I suggest that they be topped with majestic, skyward-reaching spires—open and light within—that would offer sanctuary for reflection and inspiration to visitors. They should rise just a bit higher than the previous towers.[51]

Finally, some argued from an aesthetic point of view, that for the memorial to be inspirational, it needed to be beautiful. A woman who lost her parents on Flight 93 stated that:

We all believe that this area in Shanksville, PA is the final resting place for our loved ones. We would really like it to be a place of beauty.[52]

A few of the narratives associated with the memorial were identified with the idea of *justice,* where the focus was on striking out against the offenders. Some examples of the justice narrative seem more rhetorical or tongue-in-cheek. For example, a spontaneous memorial had the following words written in the dust a few days after the World Trade Center towers collapsed: "Our tears will be their blood."[53] Another source suggested that the memorial take on a more practical role than most suggestions:

Amid the preserved rubble, construct a court building. In that court, situate the United Nations war crimes tribunal. Bring the suspected terrorists there for justice.[54]

Many of the narratives suggested a *perseverance* narrative—similar to Linenthal's progressive narrative except that the goal is not in getting "better" but in remaining the same. At times, the reference was to the perseverance of the people:

You can imagine that the [remains of the World Trade Center] above [aren't] just the debris from a successful attack—it's the building hanging on, still refusing to fall, just like New Yorkers.[55]

Don't keep [the Tribute in Light] lighted permanently, and don't turn them off this month and bring them back later. Just give us their steadiness now, for a few more months, while it feels most precious.[56]

Other times, the narrative referred to objects that were meant to commemorate the events of September 11. The man who designed the "Freedom Flag," for example, suggested that it was "born of a reaction to statements, in the days that followed the Sept. 11 attacks, that things needed to go back to normal and people needed to return to their lives."[57]

Like many informal memorials, we found that narratives of the formal memorials for the 9-11 events suggested that there was something *sacred* or holy about the site of the tragic events. This is not a redemptive narrative because it is not talking about the transformation to a "better place," and it is not traumatic because it is not always associated with sorrow. Sources that used the sacred narrative sometimes referred to the sites as being a cemetery, "a smoking funeral pyre containing the remains of thousands, and that nothing should be built on it."[58] Similarly, the secretary to the Somerset County commissioners in Pennsylvania referred to the crash site as:

Unique...it's hallowed ground...It literally is a cemetery and always will be.[59]

Similarly, the brother of a man killed while working in the Pentagon said that he wanted the memorial to represent

hallowed ground...a place where the families and everybody can go and feel the sense of loss, but still come away with a sense of hope.[60]

The final alternative narrative suggests a focus on *unity.* This narrative is a blend of Linenthal's progressive and patriotic narratives. The focus was on how the memorials would point to the brilliance of the country and its people, while also providing for a sense of togetherness. The unity narrative is suggestive of Durkheim's notion of collective sentiment, where participation in rituals brings members of a society closer to each other. Since the attackers in the 9-11 events were foreigners, and so many people felt victimized because they viewed the attacks, it makes sense that discussions of the memorial would include how the events unified the nation. While there was much talk about how the attacks of September 11 had united the country, there was relatively sparse use of the unity narrative in the discussion of the memorials.[61] Some sources noted the distinctions between Oklahoma City and New York City (with its focus on "revenue and commerce over humanistic concerns") to suggest that the memorial could bring the whole country together:

One can hope that this tragic event, which has led to a sense of community spirit unprecedented in recent New York history, will indeed result in a sensitive and inclusive project on the site of the former World Trade Center.[62]

DISCUSSION

The goal of this project was to compare the process of memorialization of America's two major terrorism events: the Oklahoma City bombing and the events of September 11. We used the narratives suggested by Linenthal as a baseline, hypothesizing that the narratives associated with the 9-11 attacks would be more varied and complex. We recognize, of course, that Linenthal adopted his narratives through the use of personal interviews while we are focusing on newspaper articles. Still, it is interesting how similar our findings are, even given this different methodology. Our data suggest that the five narratives used in the in the process of memorializing the Oklahoma City bombing were used for the 9-11 memorials and can be supplemented by an additional eleven narratives (mostly because of the complexity of the stories that need to be told).

It is important to recognize, however, that the 9-11 events are not a monolith. Each site has a different story to tell (and different story tellers) and thus requires different narratives. While each site has victims on an airplane, two sites have competition between victims on the planes and victims on the ground for memorialization "rights." The Pentagon had mostly government (military) victims on the ground and few people saw it happen. Thus, there was less competition for how the memories were to be created. Some victims in the Pennsylvania crash were highlighted because their acts are thought to be known. Special attention is more likely to be focused on these plane victims than on the plane victims at the other sites. The World Trade Center is also unique because of its geographic location, the large loss of life, and the variety of victims (e.g., people on the planes, first responders, and a national community of witnesses). Thus, we also expected to find variation among the 9-11 sites.

For the World Trade Center memorial, the top three narratives used were inspirational, traumatic, and progressive. Two of these are Linenthal's narratives, suggesting that the memorialization reaction to the World Trade Center attacks is similar to the reaction to the Oklahoma City attack. Considering the World Trade Center memorial narrative sources, we found that the politicians and public figures were more interested in the commercialization narrative, while the journalists/editors focused on the progressive narrative. Citizens living in New York were more likely to express a traumatic narrative, while citizens from outside New York emphasized the justice narrative.

The top three Pentagon memorial narratives were the patriotic, traumatic, and idealization narratives. Again, two of these narratives reflect Linenthal's minor narratives. The fact that the Pentagon was a military target likely made the patriotic narrative more suitable than it was for the Oklahoma City bombing. Politicians and citizens both emphasize the patriotic narrative while journalists emphasize the traumatic narrative.

The top three memorial narratives for the Pennsylvania crash were the patriotic, idealization, and the sacred. The suspected acts of the passengers on Flight 93, of course, lead perfectly into the first two narratives, while the isolated and rural location might have created a greater opportunity to discuss the "sacredness" of the site. The journalists and public figures emphasized the patriotic and idealization narratives, while citizens emphasized the sacred narrative.

What makes the memorialization of the Oklahoma City bombing and the 9-11 attacks so different from the study of other memorials (e.g., Lincoln, World War II, and Korean War memorials) is that these memorials were being created concurrent with the recovery efforts. Most other memorials resulted in commemorative symbolism that defined the past—engaging in revisionist history, if you will.[63] Recent work on the revised memory of Lincoln and the Korean War memorial is also illustrative.[64] Instead of revising history, those people who were responsible for the 9-11 and Oklahoma City memorials, on the other hand, were *creating* history in the wake of the events. Because those who were creating the terrorism memorials did not have the benefit of the passage of time to dull the voices of any opposition, the use of narratives was likely to be more pervasive.

The interesting challenge for the student of memorializing is to capture how the narratives are being used. Clearly, in cases where acute events occur, the need for a variety of narratives is not as strong as when there are chronic events that "need" to be memorialized. Those who intend to create a memorial for a chronic event need to use a greater variety of narratives to compete with wider variety of voices staking a claim to memory.

Popular Narratives

10

Step Aside, Superman...This Is a Job for [Captain] America! Comic Books and Superheroes Post September 11

Jarret Lovell

The iconic age is upon us.

—Marshall McLuhan

A contemplative, if not forlorn, Superman flies high above the planet earth while struggling to make sense of his superhero status. Like Kryptonite, the events of September 11 render him powerless, and this realization frightens him. Against the dark backdrop of space, he ruminates upon his newly discovered limitation.[1]

I can defy the laws of gravity. I can ignore the principles of physics. I can breathe in the vacuum of space. I can alter the building blocks of chemistry. I can fly in the face of probability...But unfortunately, the one thing I can *not* do is break free from the fictional pages where I live and breathe...Become *real* during times of crisis and right the wrongs of an unjust world.[2]

Indeed, as Superman flies off into the sky, the specter of the unreal surrounds him like a fog from which he cannot escape. When this post 9-11 vignette draws to a conclusion, the seemingly larger-than-life, realistically drawn action figure disintegrates into a mere sketch, one drafted with rudimentary artistic talents and constrained by the panel borders that typify the comic medium.

Superman did not die in the tragedy of September 11, but the events of that day did much to undermine his status as the world's true superhero and the most able defender of truth, justice, and the American way. Still, even if international terrorism did nothing to weaken the man of steel, even if Super-man could rise to the occasion and defeat these evil-doers, even if he could ensure that no civilians would be harmed as a result of collateral damage, it is likely that Superman would not be called upon by the U.S. military to fight the American cause of justice. Who is this Superman, anyway? This outsider from a distant place? This man living among us in disguise? This being who masks his true identity and conceals his ulterior motive? This "other" who blends into society too nicely? This person who claims America as his home? Citizen or not, whomever he is, he is no longer trustworthy, for he is not a purebred patriot. In an era dominated by visual imagery, where the patriotic icon reigns supreme, Superman as our nation's hero simply will not do. What is needed is a new hero: an icon cultivated from within, one of our own; a leader in whom Americans can place their complete trust, someone whose commitment to the homeland will surely be unwavering; someone whose very costume screams patriotism. What is needed is a hero whose loyalty is to America only; someone willing to win the war on terrorism whatever the cost and regardless of scruples.

For over 60 years, Superman has served America well, representing the embodiment of the comic-book medium's necessary heroic icon. He is strong, yet vulnerable; he is made of steel, but has a soft spot for romance; he is an exceptional man, though he is a workingman and at one with the people. Appearing incognito as a mortal, he is uncomfortable around women, and his false persona fails to win the affection of his primary love interest—Lois Lane. But being true to himself, he very ably wins the admiration of not only Lois Lane but also countless others. And though possessed with super-human powers, he channels those powers not for personal gain or profit, but for the collective benefit and the common good.

Yet Superman is wholly unfit to lead the American battle against global terrorism. In this age of pervasive and unabashed suspicion, Superman too closely resembles the enemy. Like the very terrorists with whom he should be opposed, Superman came to America from a distant land (a distant planet, actually), following the destruction of his home, and he now lives quietly and privately within the United States under the assumed identity of Clark Kent. It is interesting to note that in the first issue of *Action Comics*,[3] the reason provided for Superman's emergence on earth is rather brief and vague, adding an air of mystery to his persona. ("As a distant planet was destroyed by old age, a scientist placed his infant son within a hastily devised spaceship, launching toward earth".) Working as a reporter for the *Daily Star* newspaper, located in the fictional city of Metropolis, this "foreigner"-turned-superhero has direct access to one of the most powerful of wartime weapons: the mass media. As a result, his ability to sway public opinion against a full-scale military assault renders him untrustworthy. In fact, the idea that Superman might use the mass media as a counter-weapon for ideological purposes is not far-fetched. In *Action Comics* 12, Superman hijacks Metropolis radio station WVUX.[4] Threatening to "make a bee-line for his gizzard" if the control engineer shuts him off the air, Superman is intent on notifying the public of potentially fatal traffic hazards after the city's mayor suggests that nothing can be done to rectify the problem. Finally, and most significantly for the comic medium, Superman is unfit to conquer international terrorism under the banner of the United States simply because he lacks the iconography that communicates the superiority of American culture and the glory of American strength.

He does not don the stars of the American flag on his cape, nor does he shield himself behind the red, white, and blue. He does not have the letter "A" emblazoned upon his brow as a reminder of national heritage, and he did not even lead the American cause against our foes during World War II. As will be shown, Superman has been a rather fierce critic of American capitalism; and both visually and historically (and therefore, iconographically), Superman is simply less emblematic of the "American way" than he is of "truth and justice."

And it is for this reason that Superman must step aside for a more patriotic hero, a hero who fights not for global justice, but for American justice; a hero whose costume is comprised of both the Stars and Stripes and the "red, white, and blue"; a hero whose costume, therefore, is unmistakably and unwaveringly iconic of the American dream; a hero who never thinks twice about using racial slurs when making reference to our nation's enemies ("Here come some China Boys. And they're not waving laundry tickets!");[5] a hero who killed off the "Red Skull" in what can only be called a successful regime change;[6] and now, a hero who will—through the hegemonic use of iconography and through the medium of comics—garner enough national support to launch an unmitigated assault upon Al-Tariq and the ever-expanding axis of evil.[7] And that someone is [Captain] America.

But, as the fate of great superheroes is always left in a state of perpetual uncertainty as the demands of each passing challenge increase in complexity, so too is the fate of [Captain] America left standing over a political and moral abyss as he once and for all confronts the true face of terrorism.

UNDERSTANDING ICONOGRAPHY

Perhaps more than any other form of media, comic books are dependent upon iconography to communicate ideology to a mass audience. An icon is any image used to represent a person, place, thing, or idea. They can be symbols, archetypes, or even personas used to communicate concepts and philosophies. Historically, icons have been central to religious practice. Appearing in the mosaics and stained glass windows of orthodox churches, they were designed to serve as a visual reinforcement of ecclesiastical teachings and scripture. Today, in an increasingly fast-paced and media-filled culture dominated by visual imagery, icons are universally abundant in advertising and film as they quickly and succinctly communicate themes through myriad visual metaphors.[8] Thus, lemons and sunshine dominate the iconography of advertised cleaning products, while films like *Rocky I–III* (Carl Weathers as "Apollo Creed," Mr. T. as "Clubber Lang") and *Star Wars* (Darth Vader, the "Dark Side") use color as iconic of race relations and—in particular—"blackness" as iconic of dangerous and aggressive adversaries.

Icons arguably work best when they can convey ideas and themes to the broadest possible audience by transcending the barriers of language or narrative context that are often required to provide meaning. Thus, as visual icons, the ♥ almost universally communicates themes of love and passion, while the ♥ has become a recognized metaphor for unrequited love, disappointment, and melancholy. Moreover, sketches, drawings, and illustrations are often more iconic than photographic representations. This is because the lack of detail or specificity renders the image more widely identifiable and less specific to a real time, place, or person. It naturally follows, then, that ideology in comic books is often more pronounced than in any other form of media. McCloud summarizes the inverse nature of this formula as a process of "amplification through simplification," where the simplicity of even the most detailed comic art still requires the audience to mentally connect the dots.[9] And this is precisely what McLuhan meant when he noted that comics— caught "in an iconic grasp"—are low in definition and therefore necessarily highly participatory, as they require the audience to form connections with both the image and, by extension, its ideology.[10]

Through the use of iconography, then, comic books are rich in ideology, and this ideology is most often visually anthropomorphized as a superhero whose costumes and colors, posture and physique, and situations and context combine to communicate the major ethos of an era. In his study of heroes within American popular culture, Orin Klapp identifies various hero character archetypes that communicate "The kinds of things people approve."[11] Two of these heroic personas maintain a prominent role in the language of comic books, and although imbued with different and sometimes conflicting goals, they both are met with widespread public support. Moreover, as they are both cast as heroes, they are seldom pitted against one another. The first of these heroic archetypes is the *winner*, a figure that communicates the importance of getting what you want, beating everybody, and being a champ. Conversely, the *group servant* is a special breed of hero who endorses helping people, personal sacrifice, and social solidarity. When appearing in comic books, both character types convey themes and ideas through a combination of visual iconography and narrative context. It follows, then, that one can readily come to appreciate the dominant ideology of a given historical moment by examining its representation in the most easily grasped popular form: the comic-book superhero.

SUPERMAN AS *GROUP SERVANT*

As a character archetype, the *group servant* comes closest to the traditional impression of what a hero should be. S/he has a "strong arm and a heart of gold" and is the personification of social solidarity. One of the defining features of the *group servant* is the practice of self-sacrifice, as the collective is always of greater importance than the individual. As such, the *group servant* often performs as a social worker when the political system fails to promote social or economic justice. It naturally follows that the *group servant* is imbued with a strong sense of moral high-mindedness. S/he is always pushing for broad-based reform and is always working for the public, but it is important to note that the *group servant* always struggles for justice in purely "nonmilitant ways."[12]

If the *group servant* does indeed bear the closest resemblance to what a hero "should be," then Superman is most assuredly a *group servant*. Although he is often thought of as working exclusively for the American way, and while some scholars argue that American hegemony is quite safe in the hands of Superman,[13] throughout his career, Superman has been rather critical of the American political structure, a structure that he recognizes as one contributing to the successes of some at the expense of others. Superman emerged as a heroic icon in the aftermath of the Great Depression at a time when the American ideals of individualism and the free market were never more in question. What was promised as a dream attainable by all proved to be an utter nightmare for many, and the public turned to Superman to fix the seemingly intractable problems of a class-based system.

In *Action Comics* 2, Superman uncovers congressional malfeasance by foiling an attempt by the munitions lobby to push the United States into a foreign war. In a subsequent issue, this critic of American capitalism destroys a car factory after discovering the use of low-grade metals to increase corporate profits. In April 1939, long before the days of Enron, Superman swindles stockbrokers out of millions after they sold millions in worthless stock to the masses. Superman also understood what forces lay at the root of crime and delinquency. In *Action Comics* 8, he tells an inner-city boy, "It's not entirely your fault that you're delinquent—it's these slums—your poor living conditions—if there was only some way I could remedy it!"[14] Superman does remedy the situation. He uses his superpowers to destroy the slums and force the city to build anew, while fighting the National Guard and local police who try to stop him. More recently, Superman's criticism has been directed toward the American military when he discovered it had ties to international terrorists ("How many innocent people were killed with American money and weapons?"). When military leaders expect him to show his loyalty to the United States and be loyal to a single nation, Superman is both blunt and direct. Reaffirming his status as *group servant*, Superman speaks the following: "I value *all* life, regardless of political borders."[15]

Superman, then, is above political posturing. Living life as an American citizen, he certainly has contributed to the national cause. Yet when forced to choose between justice and the American way, time and again he opts for that which is in the interest of the common good. Like the American military—which has amassed an arsenal of near epic proportions—Superman represents a figure of awesome power and strength. Unlike the American military, however, Superman does not kill, "or at least not more than was [ever] absolutely necessary."[16] Superman is neither subservient to any political doctrine, nor is he imprisoned by any nationalist ideology. As a result, the history of U.S.-Kryptonic relations is one where the United States has often had to succumb to the will of Krypton's earthly leader, who uses his powers to replace self-interest with self-cleansing.

But if ever there was a new world order, surely it can be found in the post-9-11 climate. Shocked to the core, the U.S. government now answers to no one, not to its own Constitution, the provisions of the Geneva Convention, the international community, or to those working on behalf of human rights—and certainly not to the kind of superhero likely to question U.S. ties to the Taliban prior to that fateful September day. It is noteworthy that there was once a time when even the president of the United States conceded his powerlessness in the presence of Superman; as a 1960s issue of the comic book—released posthumously—finds President Kennedy in need of Superman's assistance in launching his presidential physical fitness program.[17]

Today, it is America that is all-powerful while Superman is weak. Rolling up his sleeves and ready to fight, Uncle Sam leaves a solemn, mournful, and less eagerly combative Superman behind him. For what follows is not for the sympathetic or humanitarian at heart, nor is it a task for the hero iconic of universal principles. Instead, what follows is a job for none other than [Captain] America.

CAPTAIN AMERICA AS *WINNER*

In the spring of 1941, with the ruthless warmongers of Europe focusing their eyes upon a peace-loving country, President Roosevelt suggests to his cabinet that a character out of the comic books might be best suited to lead America to victory against its foreign enemies. "Perhaps the *HUMAN TORCH* in the army would solve our problem." Roosevelt was so serious that he authorized FBI director J. Arthur Grover to conduct secret experiments upon young American males deemed unfit for military service. The hope was that a special serum would create an American soldier with superhuman strength. With members of the cabinet by his side, Grover leads the president to a secret laboratory where one Professor Reinstein injects a secret formula into a young and lanky American named Steve Rogers. What follows is a most remarkable transformation, a transformation both of the American soldier and of the patriotic spirit. As the young man quickly becomes a patriot extraordinaire, one of the scientists declares:

Behold, the first of a corps of super-agents whose mental and physical ability will make them a terror to spies and saboteurs...We shall call you CAPTAIN AMERICA, son! Because, like you...Americans shall gain the strength and the will to safeguard our shores.[18]

And thus marked the birth of one of America's most potent wartime weapons and one of comic book's most popular *winner* archetypes.

"Oligarchic," "authoritarian," and "Machiavellian" are all words used to describe the iconic *winner* social type. By definition, the *winner* must beat everybody, get what is wanted, and come out on top. With a grin and a smile, s/he is invidious, competitive, and ultimately cannot be stopped. Yet these qualities, even when viewed negatively by the public, do not prevent *winners* from achieving mass popularity. This is particularly the case in the United States, where Americans are by no means squeamish about accepting some pretty rough customers as heroes. According to Klapp, what allows this morally ambiguous social type to rise to the top is the fact that the *winner* typically emerges during uncertain times when moral definitions are unclear. Without a universally recognized umpire, it may be impossible for the public to be entirely certain about the limits of right or wrong.[19]

Despite the popularity of the *winner,* superheroes are typically *group servants,* and they are thus imbued with a strong and immutable code of morality. As such, the dawn of World War II, the first war following the rise of comics, posed a significant problem for the writers of American comic books. Were the United States to unleash its superheroes upon its international foes,

American audiences would naturally expect the war to end in a matter of days, if not hours. Yet such a quick resolution to the war was—in reality—unlikely to occur. At the same time, these *group servant* superheroes operate according to universal principles, not nationalistic ideals. Were the typical comic book hero to be called to duty, s/he would only contain the enemy, not eradicate him/her.[20]

All of this likely explains why Clark Kent failed his military fitness exam upon enlisting to fight with the Allies during World War II. Technically, Clark Kent failed his eye exam when he accidentally used his X-ray eyes to read the eye chart in an adjoining room. But there was nothing to fear over his failure to make the cut. As Kent himself explained to readers, the "United States Army, Navy, and Marines are capable of smashing their foes without the aid of Superman."[21] Now, some 60 years later, Superman is still unfit for war, and he is once again portrayed by comic book writers as internationally frivolous. As explained in a post-9-11 comic book dedicated entirely to the terrorist attack, what is needed today is action, not compassion. "We need people who are going to *DEFEND* [American] life, not discuss the *MEANING* of it."[22]

Fortunately, comic book readers continue to find a patriot in the form of Captain America. Emerging in the pages of American comic books in March 1941, Captain America was the creation of Jack Kirby and Joe Simon, whose objective in creating this superhero as *winner* was consciously political. A reaction to a growing isolationist movement against war, Simon and Kirby used their fictional character to wage a metaphorical war against Nazi oppression. "The opponents to the war were all quite well organized. We wanted to have our say too."[23] And between 1941 and 1949, Captain America did have his say.

In an iconographically brilliant presentation of red, white, and blue, [Captain] America encouraged young boys and girls to join his "Sentinels of Liberty." He tirelessly fought against "*FANG:* Arch Fiend of the Orient." He triumphantly declared Germans to be "rats" in his moment of victory. He battled "the fiendish ghoul of ancient Egypt." All the while, he reminded readers that the threat to America's security was on both foreign and domestic soil. This threat could be found "deep in the shadowy heart of San Francisco's Chinatown." It occupied the stage of an American theater where "an ominous whistling fills the small auditorium." Like the anthrax threat of the new millennium, it manifested in the form of a fast-killing poison. And threats to American security even resided within the halls of high schools and academia:

To the utter amazement of the class, Captain American leaps at Professor Hall! By day a respectable schoolteacher, by night a marauding killer! A startling change comes over the meek little professor as he listens to Captain America: 'I'll tell you, Mister Jekyll and Hyde!'[24]

As a heroic *winner* created in a time of war, Captain America's sole purpose was to both literally and iconographically represent the United States and only the United States, while garnering support for America's military efforts abroad and often-questionable domestic policies at home. War knows no compassion, and the military is therefore no place for those—like Superman—who question authority for the sake of humanity. Rules change during times of war (or so we're told), and so, too, must there be changes to comic book superheroes. Captain America, then, became the symbol of patriotism for a country needing a patriotic symbol. Designed in deliberate fashion, he was the ultimate national icon. He was created to fight the war, not question it. He didn't need to carry the flag because he *was* the flag. So iconic was he that it would be positively un-American not to salute Captain America when he walks by.[25] After all, the Captain was America personified.

But while each of his 1940s comics concluded with a caution that, like the war on terrorism, the war might be one without an end ("But is the Red Skull really dead, or will he return once more...?"), World War II did come to an end, and with it came the end of Captain America's career as an agent of the State. By 1949, the need for a patriotic icon had passed. With no imminent threat on the international horizon, the Captain no longer had a purpose, and he quickly disappeared from America's newsstands. During the 1960s, Marvel Comics revived the character of Captain America, but the superhero no longer served the State in any realistic capacity. Instead, he became part of the fictional "Avengers," an elite team of superheroes that included such fantastic characters as the Wasp and the Sub-Mariner. And while the Captain would time and again return to serve the FBI in an official capacity, he no longer resembled the wartime hero of the past. When a formidable foe injects him with a mysterious potion that turns him into a werewolf, the Captain both literally and figuratively struggles to gain a sense of his own identity. By the mid 1990s, [Captain] America had outlived his iconic calling, and his patriotism was simply nowhere to be found.[26]

AN OLD HERO FOR NEW TIMES?

In a comic panel dominated by colors of black and ash-gray, a tattooed arm bearing the inscription "Steve Rogers" tosses aside debris in a desperate attempt to locate any survivors. Behind him, a stalwart medic approaches, his face concealed beneath a layer of protective clothing. Unaware of the identity of this Good Samaritan, he puts his hand on Captain America's shoulder in a comforting manner and asks of him the question so many of us asked when recounting the events of September 11: "Where were you? When..." With eyes cast downward and his head turned away, our heroic *winner* is emotionally crippled by the devastation in front of him. Collapsing to his knees, he has no choice but to acknowledge his dereliction of duty and accept the consequences of his absence. Remorsefully, and with the meekest of voices, the patriot finally responds, admitting to himself what he considers the most awful of truths: "I wasn't here."[27]

For [Captain] America and his military superiors, the implications of this national tragedy were all too apparent. For years, the "evil empire" threatened to destroy the American ideal, yet America's patriotic spirit was nowhere to be found. The conflict in Vietnam found its way onto domestic soil as young citizens burned their draft cards and refused to fight, an action that tore apart the very essence of American pride. Yet throughout this turbulent era, America's patriot remained in retirement from the FBI. Now, with the events of September 11 flickering in an endless video loop on Americans' television screens, the time is ripe for a full-force patriotic reemergence. Like unacknowledged FBI memorandums, the warning signs were there: the country was losing its patriotic zeal; as icons, flags were becoming a thing of the past. But never again. This time around, there shall be no complacency. This time around, [Captain] America will prove his patriotism once and for all. This time around, [Captain] America will unleash his strength upon the international community with an awesome display of jingoistic pride. And this time around, [Captain] America will ensure a victory, for this time, he has vowed not to play by the rules. After all, [Captain] America is a *winner,* and winning is everything.

Don't let the enemy choose the battlefield. Or the time of engagement. Don't let the enemy anticipate the strength or the direction of your attack. Don't let the enemy see you coming. Strike without warning... [V]iolate *half* the tenets of *classical warfare* before you've even *seen* the *battlefield.*[28]

Thus, in the pages that follow, Captain America fights tirelessly in a patriotic attempt to triumph over his foreboding nemesis, Faysal Al-Tariq. With the sky behind him a brilliant red, he parachutes into a desert on the outskirts of Kandahar. Shielded by the Stars and Stripes, he makes his intentions clear: "The sky should be burning—or bleeding." Eyes cast upward toward heaven, and with bombs bursting in air, our hero hopes and prays that "God's watching this." All the while, and without any trace of irony, the Cap' struggles to understand the mentality of the true believer that believes in a God that takes sides during times of war. Imagining what he would say if confronted by Al-Tariq, the Captain speaks: "Is this your offering to your God? Your worship? Your prayer?"[29]

Yet despite the initial zest with which he fights, something is different about the Captain this time around, something quite profound. Has the Captain begun to question his patriotism, or is the task at hand simply unpatriotic? It has been years since he's seen the front lines and experienced the ravages of war (it was during World War II, to be exact). Whether it was at all possible for that war to have been averted, by the time [Captain] America got involved, there was little question that something simply had to be done. For years, armies had amassed and ethnic cleansing had begun, while the Captain stood silently by conducting business as usual until he was drawn into the conflict with little choice but to act. Throughout his efforts, the "good" war revealed many horrors, and now the Captain is being asked to once again lead the nation into battle to conquer among the most dangerous of all foes: international terrorists.

Where Issue 1 of this six-part series finds the Captain leading the troops into battle, by Issue 3 his patriotism wanes as he begins to recognize the true face of international terror. Face to face with Al-Tariq's disciples for the first time, he begins to contemplate the truth upon hearing one of the "terrorists" speak, a truth wholly excluded from American media. "I am a messenger here to show you the truth of war. *You* are the terrorists. When innocent *Americans* die, it's an atrocity. But when we die, *We* are collateral damage." Reflecting upon this, the Cap' begins to waver: "Are we only hated because we're free, free and prosperous and good? Or does the light we see cast shadows that we don't...?" Beginning to recognize the terror inherent in the practice of holding "a *NATION* accountable for the actions of a *MAN*," by Issue 4 the Captain relinquishes all of his military duties and strips himself of his *winner* status, removing from his body the mask of the red, white, and blue.[30]

No longer identifying with [Captain] America, Steve Rogers finally broaches to his superiors the rationale behind current U.S. military practices, such as the dumping of cluster bombs on a small town, or how cutting-edge American military technology found its way into the hands of the very terrorists with whom he was at war. The response the Captain receives, however, proves less than satisfactory. Like the rationale for the Patriot Act and for "military combatants," for news blackouts and for Guantanamo Bay, for vague terrorist warnings and for mass deportations, for secret military tribunals and for expanded racial profiling; like the justification given for so many injustices, the government adheres to its current shibboleth as the top brass simply inform the fallen hero "That's privileged information. A matter of national security."

Vowing to uncover on his own the motive behind the U.S. military strategy, the Captain leaves the military compound. Yet as he sets out on his quest for truth, a team of uniformed assailants quickly confronts him. The American flag clenched in his fist, the patriot with a conscience is fired upon. As he falls to his apparent death, his hold upon Old Glory loosens until he is finally disconnected from the red, white, and blue. [Captain] America and the flag are no longer iconographically one.[31]

CONCLUSION

> My name is Steve Rogers. I'm a citizen of the United States of America, but I'm not America.[32]

Spoken only moments before his impending doom and with news cameras pointed directly toward him, Captain America for the first time addresses an international media audience. His heart filled with shame, he publicly removes the mask from his face and vows to no longer take part in an unjust war where no rules apply. In so doing, he relinquishes his status as the ultimate comic book *winner* and as the iconic patriot. Just as Superman before him had to remain Clark Kent during times of war, because his patriotism was suspect, even the ultimate patriot is seemingly not patriotic enough during this time of unrestrained military aggression. After all, his military superiors were quite explicit: this is a new kind of war, and it requires a new kind of patriotism.

Like the very war that brought him out of retirement, at the time of this publication, it remains unknown how the saga of [Captain] America will play out. As the course of history remains to be written, Issues 5 and 6 have yet to appear at the time of this publication, but with their publication will likely come the answers to so many questions: Is Al-Tariq really the most dangerous of all international terrorists? Is Steve Rogers a traitor to his nation, or is this new and endless war simply unpatriotic? With iconic flags adorning all public places, what will happen to the most powerful of all national icons? Will demands for [Captain] America to remain unreflective in his actions bring about his ultimate demise, or are there countless others willing to take on the role of the iconic *winner* under the banner of patriotism? Will the arrogance of the nation's political and military leaders really cause [Captain] America to perish? And if so, what will this portend? Or, will Clark Kent break his silence and flex some muscle of his own? Will he finally emerge as the patriotic icon of our age by rising to the occasion and—in true *group servant* fashion—demand that the "American way" once and for all take the back seat to "truth and justice"? Find out as the saga of [Captain] America continues.

11

Of Heroes and Superheroes

Amy Kiste Nyberg

Superheroes and September 11, 2001—it seems a natural fit, somehow, to have creators who work in a medium whose dominant genre is devoted to explorations of what it means to be a hero reflecting on the events of that fateful day and the days that followed.[1] After all, the superhero is an American creation, born on the eve of World War II. Literally thousands of costumed heroes have filled the pages of American comic books in the decades since the debut of the first superhero: Superman. Today, the superhero remains the dominant genre in American comic books, as heroes are invented and reinvented for each new generation of readers. The five special-edition comic book collections produced by various publishers in the wake of September 11 were selected for analysis because they were created specifically in response to the terrorist attacks.

As comics scholar Christopher Murray notes, "In (the superhero) genre, comics are often used to explore certain ideas about heroism and morality, and these ideas communicate much about the values and culture of the society that produces and consumes these adventure stories. In this context, the superhero can act as a metaphor for American identity."[2] Two stand out in that respect. For DC Comics, it's Superman who best epitomizes America, with his fight for "truth, justice and the American way." In the Marvel Comics Universe, the champion is Captain America, whose red, white, and blue costume marks him as the quintessential American superhero. His origin story is set in World War II, when Steve Rogers is injected with a serum that will turn him into a "supersoldier." In the patriotic culture of post-9-11

America, Marvel reports that Captain America has enjoyed a resurgence of popularity.[3]

It's not surprising that these characters, these metaphors for America, serve as vehicles for comics creators who wished to tell stories of September 11. In the various tribute comics offered by comics publishers in the wake of the terrorist attack, images of superheroes are paired with other icons of America—Superman flies with a bald eagle perched on his forearm, an American flag as the backdrop; Batman drops between buildings, each balcony sporting an American flag; the Hulk clutches a standard flying an American flag in one immense fist, and above his head the words "strongest one there is"; Superman, Batman, and Wonder Woman pose atop a globe, stitching the flags of the world together, and in her hands, Wonder Woman holds the familiar Stars and Stripes; Superman and Uncle Sam, in a pinup piece supporting the American Red Cross, stand at the foot of the wrecked World Trade Center, and Uncle Sam is rolling up his sleeves—inscribed on a memorial marker in the foreground is this promise, "First things first, then we come for you."[4]

What is surprising, however, is that superhero narratives and images are largely absent from the tribute comics. Of the five compilations published, two feature almost no superheroes. In the other three, only about a quarter of the pieces—including both pinup art and stories—evoke the superhero in some way. Instead, the tribute comics are dominated by narratives of the reaction to the events of September 11. Some are told from the viewpoint of people directly affected—people at Ground Zero, or people who lost loved ones. Others are written from the viewpoint of the vast majority of Americans, who could do nothing but watch television and call their family and friends. Many are written in first person, and several are autobiographical, intensely personal accounts of that moment when the creator(s) first learned of the events of September 11.

Part of the explanation for the absence of the superhero lies in the publishers and creators themselves. The volume published in 2002 by Alternative Comics, *9-11 Emergency Relief,* features artists whose work, by and large, falls outside the superhero genre. The same can be said for many whose pieces were included in the first volume of *9-11,* subtitled *Artists Respond,* a joint venture of Chaos! Comics, Dark Horse, and Image, and published by DC Comics. The other three collections, however, were the work of mainstream comics publishers whose output is primarily superhero comics. The second volume of *9-11,* with the lengthy subtitle *The World's Finest Comic Book Writers and Artists Tell Stories to Remember,* was published by DC Comics. Marvel Comics published *Heroes* late in 2001, followed by *A Moment of Silence* in early 2002. These books featured work by prominent creators in the superhero genre, not limited by copyright considerations. Where, then, are the superheroes?

The answer to that question is that the superhero narrative structure and genre conventions did not readily lend themselves to telling stories of September 11. Therefore, many creators bypassed superhero characters and narratives altogether, finding a different vehicle for the stories they wished to tell. This non-superhero material is excluded from my study—not because it lacks importance, but because it is not unique to the comics medium. Accounts of people's actions on and reactions to September 11 were the staple of all media coverage. What set contributions to the tribute comics apart from stories told through other media was their use of the superhero narrative as a lens through which to view and respond to the events of that day. Therefore, this essay will focus on those creators who chose superheroes as a framework for telling the stories of September 11 through a textual analysis of the superhero narratives and imagery that do appear in the tribute comics.

The conventions of the superhero have been expanded and modified in the years since the archetypal Superman established the genre beginning in 1938, but there are still certain well-established expectations that accompany such stories. Even those who don't read comics can list them: a colorful costume, a secret identity, a moral imperative to fight for justice on the side of "good," and super-human powers that set superheroes above humanity and allow them to triumph over evil in circumstances where mere mortals would fail. Except for the examples cited above, where creators invoked themes of patriotism, linking superheroes with other icons of America, the superhero images and stories in the tribute comics deviated significantly from genre conventions that structure such narratives. Four related themes, each representing a break from the traditional superhero narrative, emerge from a close reading of the superhero material. First, superheroes are shown in positions of weakness or helplessness; second, superheroes are contrasted with the "real" heroes of September 11, sometimes as partners, but usually either distanced from events or subordinate; third, children are shown rejecting their superhero fantasies in favor of heroes such as firefighters and police officers; and finally, the superhero narratives themselves are deconstructed in ways that bring the reader face-to-face with the inadequacy of the narrative to deal with a world where September 11 is a reality.

SUPERHEROES OVERWHELMED

Superheroes, by their very nature, are invincible. They possess abilities beyond those of mere humans. However, in reconciling the world of the superhero with the events of September 11, creators produced images that broke with the established convention of an all-powerful hero. Images of Captain America, in particular, illustrate the helplessness of the superhero. In one pinup, he is crouching, his knees almost touching the ground. His shoulders are hunched, and he is flinching from some unseen threat from above. His costume is torn, and chunks are missing from his shield. Even its edges are notched and cracked. His expression, one of apprehension, is: What next? At first glance, another pinup of Captain America, this time looming larger than life above the Manhattan skyline, would seem to belie the suggestion of weaknesses. But his red-gloved hand covers his face, and his head is bowed. His figure is ghostly, no more substantial than the clouds that hang over the skyline or the smoke that rises from the site of the World Trade Center. He cannot help; he can only grieve. A third image of Captain America shows him kneeling on top of a pile of rubble, head bowed, tears dripping to the ground, his shield on the ground beside him. The dominant figure is a fireman, who grasps Cap's left hand, trying to raise the superhero back to his feet, pointing with some urgency to where they must go. A police officer rests a hand on Cap's back. A woman, with tears streaming down her face, stands in front of him, reaching out to touch his bent head, while a girl places her hand over his clenched right fist. The real heroes know what must be done, and even women and children are stronger than Captain America.[5]

Captain America isn't the only superhero to be overwhelmed. Marvel Comics editor-in-chief Joe Quesada's introduction to *Heroes* is accompanied by an illustration of the Hulk, shown kneeling, his forearms resting on his thighs, weighed down by events. Despite his size, he is made to appear small, his hulking shape folded in on itself. His head is bowed, and his expression is one of sorrow, of grief. His large hands are touching an upside-down fire helmet. He is surrounded by rubble; the horizon is indistinct.[6]

All of these illustrations show the superhero character in positions of weakness. Kneeling and crouching signify smallness and inadequacy. These postures run counter to the traditional superhero pose—feet spread apart, hands on the hips, shoulders thrown back, head held high. These images can be read on two levels. As suggested, these illustrations acknowledge that for all their powers and abilities, superheroes were helpless in the face of events on September 11. On a more abstract level, these characters are representations of America. The world's remaining superpower has been shown to be vulnerable, ill-prepared, momentarily defeated by unseen forces. Superheroes, and by extension America, are not invincible after all.

UNREAL AND REAL HEROES

The relationship between the mythical heroes found in comic books and the "everyday" heroes of September 11 is the subject, directly or indirectly, of most of the superhero narratives and images found in the tribute comics. The elevation of the "real" hero over the fictional one is the predominant theme in much of the material. This is made explicit on the back covers of the two Marvel Comics tribute books. This passage is from the back cover of *A Moment of Silence:* "For years, comic books have given the world a chance to see brightly clad super heroes in action—saving the innocent, preventing disasters and making the world a better, safer place. Mythical heroes with one mandate—to honor the heroic ideal. On September 11th, the world changed. We found that the real-world heroes went beyond the ideals of our imagination . . . the heroic acts that will define this generation as well as the heroic ideal for the new millennium." Almost identical words can be found on the back cover of *Heroes:* "Comic book universes are populated by colorful characters that possess fantastic powers. But on September 11th, 2001, an untold number of real men and women amazed the world with their phenomenal acts of bravery . . . They can't stick to walls. They can't summon thunder. They can't fly. They're just HEROES."

Contrasting superheroes with heroes is done in several ways. In some instances, the superheroes and the "real" heroes join forces. For example, echoing a common scene in the days and weeks after September 11, one piece shows a wall holding posters of those missing, the background for an impromptu memorial featuring flowers, a fireman's shovel propped up, holding a coat and helmet—and Captain America's shield. Smoke rises from behind this memorial, and the entire pinup is done in sepia tones. In a portrait of heroes, the familiar faces of the Marvel Universe—including Captain America, Spider-Man, and members of the X-Men—are interspersed with a firefighter, a police officer, and rescue workers. Perched on the shoulder of the Hulk is a boy in a baseball cap, sporting a FDNY T-shirt.[7]

A more subtle representation of this theme is an image of a firefighter, waving others on. His helmet is decorated with the face of Wolverine, a popular hero from the X-Men series. In a similar piece, a man with a physique like that of a superhero is helping to lift a piece of concrete off a trapped victim. On his arm, tattooed in red, is the Superman emblem. In another illustration, the heavily muscled arm of Thor clasps the very ordinary arm of a firefighter—both are raised high. Even Krypto gets into the act with the "real" canine heroes. In "A Hard Day's Night," Krypto brings a giant dish of water to the dogs that are sniffing through the rubble looking for survivors—or bodies.[8] This is a departure from the traditional superhero narrative, where the primary function of mortals in the storyline is to be either rescued or protected. Sometimes, such as in the case of Lois Lane and Jimmy Olson in Superman, they can assist the superhero, but they are never his (or her) equals.

Sometimes the contrast is made, not in the images, but in the text accompanying them. A man and a woman struggle from the wreckage in an image fractured by long vertical panels, a reminder of the towers. The text that accompanies the image: "Moving through a cloud thick with smoke, glass, concrete, and murder, a city and its people wrap their arms around each other—and rise! Super heroes exist."[9]

In some instances, the superheroes stand aside, looking down upon the "real" heroes. While this could be read as an attitude of superiority, it's actually a distancing mechanism. The superheroes in these stories note that they are not really needed; America has its own heroes to call upon. For example, in *Heroes,* Silver Surfer looks down on the earth, noting the "sacrifice of a noble few" and observing that "history will recall them with a single name...heroes." The image of earth, with the sun rising behind it, is one of serenity and hope. His position, outside earth, also serves to separate him from the "reality" of September 11. In a similar image, the figure of Storm, an X-Men character, hovers above figures of police officers, firefighters, and rescue workers. At the top is a quote from Ralph Waldo Emerson: "Heroism feels and never reasons and is therefore always right."[10]

In one pinup, Captain America, Thor, and Ironman are a ghostly presence, holding candles in a vigil scene repeated countless times in America in the days following the attacks. Below them are firefighters helping a wounded man. Kurt Busiek's text begins, "There Came a Day, A Day Unlike Any Other...when Earth's mightiest heroes found themselves united against a common threat." Busiek explains, "Those words were originally written about the Avengers, a band of fictional heroes batting fictional foes. But they apply as well to the harrowing events of September 11, 2001, and to the men and women who responded to those events." His tribute ends with, "We will never forget your heroism."[11] These superheroes are there in spirit, if not in flesh. And they honor those who have taken up their fight, for real.

BEYOND SUPERHERO FANTASIES

Comic book characters have long been associated with children—one illustration shows a teddy bear clad in a Superman T-shirt.[12] A study by Steven

White and Joseph O'Brien found that for young children, a superhero character is often the first that comes to mind when they are asked to name their heroes, and their definition of a hero is often someone who possesses super powers.[13] It is telling, therefore, when these superheroes are cast aside, rejected in favor of those proclaimed heroes on September 11. Implicit in this is the recognition that such superhero fantasies are "childish," and when children are confronted with the horrors of September 11, they must grow up a little, putting aside their hero worship of fictional characters in favor of true stories of heroes.

In one *Heroes* piece, two children look out their bedroom window at smoke billowing from the World Trade Center. On the wall are posters of Captain America and Spider-Man, but the children are dressed as a police officer and a firefighter. The little girl, her back to us, wears a leather jacket. She has pinned the word "Police" to the back of the coat, written in a childish hand, with the "E" backward. The boy wears a firefighter's hat and boots that are too big for him. At their feet are a toy fire truck, police car, and ambulance. Clutched in their hands are dolls. Discarded on the bed, and beneath it, are superhero action figures.[14]

Discarding the superhero for the "real" hero also is the subject of a three-panel untitled story in *9-11, Stories to Remember*. In the first panel, a little boy wearing a Superman T-shirt ducks into a telephone booth. In the second panel, all that's visible inside the telephone booth is a hand and the top of the boy's head as he wiggles out of his shirt. In the final panel, the boy is standing in front of the telephone booth in a typical superhero pose: legs spread, hands on his hips. He has changed into a T-shirt bearing the letters "FDNY."[15]

In "The Call," the characters are young adults, not children, but the theme is the same. The first panel of the five-panel story shows Superman, Wonder Woman, and Batman responding to a call for help. In the second panel, drawn in a completely different style, a young woman demands, "Are you just going to sit there reading?" The third panel reveals a young man sitting on a bench, holding a *JLA* comic book, the source of the image in the first panel. The young woman tugs on her companion, telling him blood donors are needed: "We can finally help!" In the final panel, the two run, arms pumping, resembling superheroes. The young man is wearing a Superman shirt, and the young woman is dressed in a Wonder Woman shirt. The young man says, "Yeah, a job for a REAL superman. . . ."[16]

There are two messages here. The first is that children—and by extension, all of us—should put aside hero worship of fictional characters for that of real heroes. Fantasy worlds and the heroes who populate them are a poor substitute for the "real thing." It's interesting that this assertion echoes early criticism of comic books that spurred the rise of educational comics. Publishers of these comics hoped stories of true-to-life characters in a comics format would lure young readers away from the lurid adventures of the superhero, which were dismissed as having no literary merit or intellectual value.[17] The second message, of course, is that while we can never become Superman, we can all aspire to be "real" heroes.

So many of the stories in the tribute comics, not just the superhero stories, are about children. Children can signify so many things in our culture: innocence, vulnerability, and finally, hope for the future. In many ways, it is images of children that signify America, not images of superheroes. Two pieces featuring children and superheroes demonstrate this clearly. An illustration of Superman with children shows the superhero on the floor. With him are three children; together they are building two towers out of blocks. Superman adds a block to one stack, and a child next to him adds a block to the other. Superman's hand rests on the boy's back, and the superhero is smiling. The children are helping to rebuild the Twin Towers and, along with them, the hopes and dreams for the future. The restoration of hope, of the promise for the future, is the theme in a story of a young boy who must come to terms with the loss of his father. In the story "This, Too, Shall Pass," the empath Raven appears to 10-year-old Andy Adigun. In a story reminiscent of Dickens, Raven and Andy visit the future, and he comes to understand what Raven means when she tells him, "You feel everything good in your life is over, but it is just beginning."[18]

DECONSTRUCTING THE SUPERHERO UNIVERSE

Probably the strongest evidence of the difficulties faced by artists and writers in using the superhero narrative to tell the story of September 11 comes in two stories where the creators begin with what seems to be a traditional superhero story, only to reveal to readers the fictional—and therefore powerless—nature of these stories. Structurally, these creators present a story within a story. What is significant about this structure is the way it is used to deconstruct the very nature of both the superhero myth and, literally, the comic book universe they inhabit. Not only are these superheroes revealed as nothing more than figments of imagination, powerless in the face of reality, but even their stories cannot serve as an escape from the horror that is the world after September 11.

In *9-11 Stories to Remember,* the first page of the story "Unreal" features six panels, with Superman in deep space, putting the space shuttle back on a safe course. As he works, he thinks about his abilities. "I can defy the laws of gravity," reads the opening panel. On the next page, the panel frames a comic book page. As each subsequent panel pulls back, revealing more and more of the image, we see a little boy reading a Superman comic, tears on his cheeks. He's being carried by a firefighter, who returns the boy to his mother amid the flames and rubble that look like a scene from hell itself. Superman's musings continue: "...the one thing I cannot do...is break free from the fictional pages where I live and breathe...become real during times of crisis...and right the wrongs of an unjust world." In the final panel, as the firefighter walks back into the inferno, an American flag grasped in his left hand, we see Superman, still on the comic book page, saluting: "A world, fortunately, protected by heroes of its own."[19]

This self-referential treatment of Superman is a common storytelling device for creators who wish to comment on the nature of superheroes and the universe they inhabit. In this case, the story blends aspects of fiction and reality in such a way that while we initially accept a universe in which Superman exists and is aware of the "real events" of September 11, ultimately we are forced to reject that universe as a fictional construct that is powerless in the face of those same "real events." Superman's inability to "become real" somehow diminishes him; he's not a hero for our world at all. The final panel suggests that, in times of true crisis, fiction, and the power of imagination, provide poor role models, and we must look elsewhere for our heroes.

The second of these stories opens with Superman in his classic pose—legs apart, one hand on his hip—surveying the destruction of the World Trade Center. Beside him is fellow Justice League of America member Martian Manhunter. Narration in a dialogue box in this first panel is provided by reporter Alexander Jackson, who explains that the team rescued everyone from the Twin Towers seconds before the terrorists attacked, and now they're preparing to rebuild the towers. In narrow vertical panels symbolic of the towers themselves, the team erects steel beams taller than the original buildings. Green Lantern calls forth a giant green vacuum cleaner to clear the wreckage, and the Flash works at his characteristic super speed to finish the towers, using a cosmic "reintegrater" to recycle debris into building materials.[20]

This is the opening sequence of "If Only..." The first page of the four-page story is rendered in the realistic style comic-book readers expect to see in professionally produced comic books. There is nothing, yet, to suggest this is any different from countless superhero narratives.

But in a panel on the second page, behind an image of Green Lantern wielding his magic ring, there is a crudely drawn picture of the sun, rendered as a child might draw it—a yellow circle with black lines radiating from it. It seems out of place in this professionally crafted superhero story. The sun appears again, in the first panel of the story's third page, behind the shoulder of the Flash. Two panels later, the Flash himself is drawn in this amateur style as he promises the team will head to Washington next to "fix the Pentagon." In the next panel, as narrator Alexander Jackson comments, "Great work, Flash. Will the Teen Titans assist you there?" Two word balloons intrude from outside the panel border: "Alex? Alex!"

The final panel on this page is drawn in the same childlike style, as Superman tells the reporter, "Everyone has a job to do in times like this Alex." Wonder Woman chimes in: "You can NEVER have too many HEROES." But the final two word balloons, coming again from outside the panel border, draw the reader out of the superhero story altogether: "Alex, would you PLEASE come and set the table?" "But—Mom! I'm not done!" The panel on the top of the next page repeats the image, this time clearly a drawing on a large sheet of paper, rendered even more crudely. A child's hand is in the lower right-hand corner of the panel. The next panel pulls back to reveal this superhero story as the work of a young boy, dressed in a Superman shirt, who pleads for more time, telling his mother that "nobody likes a story without an ending!" Alex wants to finish the story before his father comes home. "He hadda walk out of New York," he tells his mother. From the expression on his mother's face, readers know she doesn't believe Alex's father is coming home. In the final panel, though, she encourages him to finish his story, thus keeping hope alive. As his mother takes Alex into her arms, their figures are no longer contained in the comic book story at all. Rather, they are superimposed on the page, separating them physically from the story and returning them to reality, where there are no superheroes.

This story is analogous to DC Comics' classic "imaginary stories," where creators took characters out of the continuity of their comic book universe to speculate on key events (e.g., what if Superman had been raised by criminals?) It is the only story, of all the superhero narratives and images in the tribute comics, that directly addresses how a world in which superheroes exist would have responded to the events of September 11. But the narrative literally falls apart; it cannot be sustained. In the superhero world, September 11 never would have happened. At the last minute, the planes would have been stopped, the death and destruction would have been averted, and the perpetrators surrendered to the appropriate authorities. The fictional triumph cannot be reconciled with the reality of September 11 and therefore is abandoned, unfinished, because we know the "real" story.

CONCLUSION

The discussion up to this point has focused on *how* images and stories of superheroes presented in the tribute comics deviated from the conventional norms of such narratives, but it is equally important to consider *why*. One might argue that the horror of September 11 is just too much reality for the superhero genre to handle. While the superhero narrative falls in the category of fantastic literature, if you are able to suspend your disbelief and accept a universe populated by superheroes, their world very closely resembles our own. Readers recognize cities such as Metropolis as an American city (although which one is sometimes the subject of lively debate). Even the events of "our" world are often mirrored in the superhero universe. In fact, World War II, coming as it did soon after the birth of the modern comic book in the late 1930s, was quickly incorporated into superhero comics, as the Nazis and the Japanese replaced super villains. The war spawned a group of superheroes as super-patriots; foremost among them Captain America. Notes scholar Matthew Pustz: "Superman fought the enemy at home and abroad...Other heroes, from Captain Marvel to Spy Smasher, fought the enemy whenever and wherever they could as U.S. enemies provided easy models for villains." He suggests that depicting the war in comic books allowed younger readers to "feel involved in the war effort."[21]

The answer lies not so much in what the superhero story is about, but in the way in which superhero characters in general embody heroism and in the structure of the superhero narratives. While the creators worked against genre conventions to a certain extent in order to incorporate superheroes in some way into September 11 narratives, those conventions also serve, through the representations of superhero characters, to define the very nature of heroism. In a universe where a hero is defined as someone who possesses superpowers and uses those powers on the side of "good" to ultimately triumph over evil, there is no recognition of heroism as an act of sacrifice. Superheroes are never called upon to die (or, even if they are, they are usually resurrected). September 11, however, defined heroes as those everyday (read "real") people who, in many cases, made the ultimate sacrifice. Structurally, too, the superhero narrative proved to be problematic. Read on their most basic level, superhero narratives are power fantasies, and power used in the service of good always triumphs over power used for evil purposes. The superhero narrative allows us to identify, understand, and eventually conquer evil. The outcome of the struggle is never in question. The satisfaction of the traditional superhero narrative, the pleasure in reading the text, comes in how the victory is achieved. Structural analysis of fairy tales and myths has revealed that while the characters and situations change, the structure of the narrative remains the same. The events of September 11, however, don't fit neatly into this structure. In "What If...," narrator Alex protests: "Nobody likes a story without an ending." The terrorist attacks are a story without an end; or, at least, a story whose end has yet to be revealed and whose outcome—the triumph of good over evil—is still very much in question.

Narrative Reconstruction at Ground Zero

Randy Frances Kandel

Personal stories and narratives, with their ability to distance and witness simultaneously, have become the folk art form of the World Trade Center disaster and its aftermath. They emerged immediately and informally through art, poetry, biography, and testimony adorning walls and makeshift shrines, spreading by cell phone, e-mail, television, and then by bound volumes of print.

The diverse narratives of the immediate events, the planes hitting the buildings, the buildings burning, the people crossing bridges covered with ash, resonate with an effort to document the surreal, and to emotionally assimilate the unthinkable. Assembled, like the AIDS quilt, the infinity of individuals and idiosyncrasies in chorus stand as a popular cultural production that defies the literal fragmentation of human bodies and steel towers, parallels the real unity of New Yorkers in crisis, and mimics the questionable and querulous national unity of the moment.

The sharing of one another's narratives, in creating a cultural script for a newly figured world to stand on, and the necessity to believe what had been unbelievable and what the subconscious tried to keep unbelievable—has been as important as the creation of the narratives themselves.[1] Speaking of "fiction," but broadly, to include essays and poems, Ulrich Baer says it "sears the event into the collective imagination by embedding the initial shock in narratives, poems, theater, and tales."[2]

On the first anniversary of September 11, the five-story-high Barnes and Noble book store at Lincoln Center in New York sports a display of more than 20 books of real life stories, written in the first and third person, about sur-

vivors of the World Trade Center, women police and firefighters, ordinary people and public safety officers, young journalists, writers living in downtown
Manhattan and nearby New Jersey, and others, even as the authors both celebrated the "heroes" and deplored the media cannibalism.[3] Some are second-
generation narratives, such as journalists writing their experiences of collecting
the narratives of victims, families, and other interviewees.[4] "Literature," says
Baer, again speaking broadly, "is called upon here as the unconscious history-
writing of the world: as a form of expression that uncannily registers subtle
shifts in experience and changes in reality before they can be consciously
grasped or have fully taken place."[5] With time the narratives diverge by occupational perspectives, as September 11 and professional narratives roll into
each other.[6]

This article is about the narrative reproduction and re-envisioning of professional identity in the wake of September 11 by three different groups
involved with issues of law and society: legal anthropologists, mystery writers,
and administrative law judges, as they draw upon key questions and themes,
moral understandings, and tasks of craft. I am a member of each of them, so
the lenses and filters through which these groups view the intersection of law
and society are also parts of my evolving self and should be acknowledged.

THE END OF NARRATIVE, THE MYTH OF THE UNREAL MOMENT, AND THE STORYING OF THE EVENT

Sometime after 8:00 A.M., on the morning of September 11, 2001, I was in
the office of the matrimonial clerk at Brooklyn Supreme Court, waiting to
pick up an order to stay proceedings in a family court case. The matrimonial
part of Brooklyn Supreme Court is squashed into a "temporary annex" in the
Municipal Building. The clerk's office is cubbyhole-like, but has large windows and good views from the seventh floor. An unusually smiley and cheerful clerk with dirty-blonde hair checked the computer, and said that no stay
had been entered. He said that he would go look at the in-box in the other
room to see if the stay had been put there after hours the day before, and suggested that I knock on the judge's door, meanwhile, to see if she had it. "Just
quietly like," he pantomimed, the judge in question being well known to be
feisty tempered.

I walked down the hall, knocked to no avail, and returned to the clerk's
office. Within the time that took, the mood of the clerk, and of the world,
had changed. His face was hysteric; he was banging with both fists on the
counter, crying and screaming, "How could anyone do this? It's terrorists! It's

terrorists! They've hit the second tower!" I looked at him with incomprehension and asked, "Did you find the stay?" Like any attorney psychically prepping for an uncertain court hearing, my mind was in tunnel vision, tuning out all distractions. "Two planes have hit the World Trade Center. It's going up in smoke. Look!" he said. That was the end of ordinary narrative.

Several minutes later I was in a taxi on the Brooklyn-Queens Expressway, trying to get home to the Bronx. We saw the first tower melt down. Traffic slowed to a standstill. The driver was looking in the rearview mirror. "Turn around," he said. I saw the second tower, smoking, buckling, and melting down. "Look at it," he said. "It looks like television, doesn't it? It looks like Disneyland." Maybe for fifteen minutes, maybe for half an hour, maybe for half a week, or a lifetime, we watched the towers melt. "Like a video game. Like television," he said.

When we finally reached the bridges to the Bronx, they were closed. The driver, a Pakistani, was translating the news and gossip of the attack from the two-way radio to his base. "I have to go home to my family," he said. "Where can I drop you?"

I asked him to drop me at the largest Marriott at La Guardia airport. I entered a lobby with thousands of people, coming from or going to all over, who had been taken off planes, or not allowed to board for their respective destinations. The lobby was filled with urns of coffee and tea, rolls, and croissants. The conference rooms were opened wide. Several large televisions were set up side by side. And each of the televisions played, again and again and again, the attack on the towers, and the towers melting. For hour after hour after hour, replaying the unreal moment again and again and again until it was possible to leave. The unreal moment was burned into the lives of everyone.

Although my experience was not a particularly dramatic one for that day, I have begun with my story of the end of the ordinary narrative and the mythologizing of the unreal event, because in the wake of September 11, storying became a metaphor for experience. That day's stories of "where I was when" became the successors to the "where I was when John Kennedy was shot" and "where I was when the Challenger went down."[7]

After the "where were you" stories came the survivor stories, the miraculous exception stories, the hero stories, and the biographies of the missing, with their pictures posted on walls and windows everywhere, made into shrines with candles and offerings.

Immediately following 9-11 we went through various stages of story telling. First there were the stories of those who survived (usually told with a "miraculous" disbelief). They were generally followed by stories of those who barely escaped (including people who missed the entire event by random occurrence—i.e., oversleeping, a doctor's appointment, late to work, bringing a child to kindergarten). As time moved on, we began to hear stories of those who didn't survive. We ultimately arrived at the point where most of our stories were dominated by heroics—first the rescue workers that were killed, followed by people in the towers, and now, increasingly, about the surviving families and children. We are now also hearing stories about Posttraumatic Stress Disorder, and the longer-term effects on people. However, these are not as dramatic or pervasive as the early stories because our need to use the metaphor as a defense is greatly deceased.

Thus, we create stories that are metaphors for our experiences. Stories report about our experiences, they protect us against the attack of raw fear.... By telling stories we transfer these powerful, potentially devastating psychological terrors to one of our most basic and primal metaphors (the story).[8]

But after the storying of the event came the authoring of self, as professional identities both stabilized and came to be questioned. Much of the conversation and statements discussed here took place in, or refer to, the three months following September 11. Informal conversations took place in the similar circumstances of work contexts among colleagues, where the normal work agenda was temporarily partially suspended because of, or in memoriam of, the event: the October monthly meeting of Sisters in Crime, where, instead of the usual formal meeting about forensics or writing craft, we congregated at our favorite post-meeting restaurant and talked about how we felt as mystery writers; in November, during the American Anthropological Association's annual meetings, when the legal and political anthropologists had a round table discussion instead of a business meeting; and during down time at the New York City Taxi and Limousine Commission administrative court.[9]

The Mystery Writers

The working mystery writers quoted and discussed in this section are members of a professional organization of women mystery writers, the New York/Tri-State chapter of Sisters in Crime. These writers, who, like the legal anthropologists discussed below, deal with and write about law and justice in local context, felt a self-conscious need to collaboratively discuss the significance of September 11 and its aftermath to their professional identities and craft.

The discussion began when the October field trip to the New York Police Academy was canceled (because the police were on 24-hour emergency duty and the academy was being used as a command headquarters), and in its stead we met for dinner at Gus's, a Greek restaurant in Greenwich Village. One member of the group, Dr. Jeri Fink, who is both a mystery writer and a family therapist, approached the question obliquely by saying (in the midst of everyone's tale of "where I was when") that she "found it fascinating that (since the attack) stories had become a metaphor for experience." The challenge to engage with the powerful symbolic reality was not immediately taken up. It was still the time of the myth of the end of narrative, of the self-distanced repetition of the unreal moment. The time when many of the writers could not write.

In the fall issue of the *Bloodletter,* the Sisters in Crime newsletter, editors Irene Marcus and Marge Mendel recognized and echoed the repetition of shocked stories:

The impatient words die before they reach our lips, we step back; we make eye contact (brief to be sure; the pain is too close to the surface, and no one wants to touch another's tender places); we listen to each other, share stories we strangers.[10]

They wrote of the inability to fictionalize in the face of an almost unbelievable truth:

How do we find words with which to respond to the unspeakable tragedy of September 11, 2001? How do we writers of fiction muster the strength to spin our imaginary worlds when the real-life stories all around us are so powerful?... To conjure fictional death in the midst of so much actual death seems an impossible inappropriate act... As writers, we create worlds, throw them into chaos, and bring them back to order. In the face of the unfathomable, we continue to live.[11]

But gradually the narratives resurfaced. Members were invited to write about their experience of September 11 and its aftermath in the winter newsletter. Some of the mystery writers explained that they used their writing to distance and control reality, a perspective perhaps analogous to an anthropologist stepping into a participant-observer mind-set.

Writing for me has always been a means of escape.... I would turn to writing... and create a more comforting orderly world that made sense. September 11th was no different. While the sirens screamed on 34th Street and Second Avenue, I was holed up in my apartment in front of my computer, encased in a fictional world in which violence took place, but the perpetrator was caught and justice was done.[12]

For the most part they expressed no interest in writing about the attack itself.

I'd like to think no one will write a "rock 'em, sock 'em" thriller about all this—that would truly be disrespectful to those who died. For now, I think this is a job for journalists and essayists. It is still too raw to transmute into fiction.[13]

But most recognized that their characters would feel the effects, and thus the experience would be integrated in, and integral to, their writing.

I have no desire to write about terrorism or to recreate these events, but the attacks will inform the minds, hearts, and spirits of my characters from this point forward, just as they will continue to do for me and for everyone I know.[14]

My books are light... so it's more a matter of remembering to include the new realities of our everyday life. Nobody's going to rush through an airport onto a plane at the last minute any more. And they won't be filing their nails as they take off.... and nobody who is armed is likely to breeze past the metal detectors so one more plot device is scratched.[15]

Some understood that this integration might even be imperceptible to the authors themselves.

I think all our writing will undergo subtle changes as September 11th becomes an integral part of us. But I doubt if we will even be aware of them. It will be up to the next generation of readers and critics to discover, interpret, and understand them.[16]

We are too close to this tragedy to have historical perspective on it to tell the "whole" story in some easily digestible way with a nice pat ending that ties up all the loose ends. Especially for those of us who write about New York City, our job for now is to chronicle the lives of the ordinary people who have to go on living amid the rubble, and to describe the effects of this destruction on a few real people, even if we have to invent the real by assembling the fragments of a thousand different shattered lives, just as Harriet Beecher Stowe did.[17]

Rather than focusing on the event itself, the mystery writers saw the event through its fallout on individuals and emotions they would create.

In the case of 9-11, the events are so much bigger than anything you can write that the question becomes "What can you write that approaches the emotions (some of which we've never felt before) without trivializing the events?" In my case I came over time, to think of it like this: the events themselves are like a horrifyingly bright light, a light too bright to look directly into. But that light will fall on other objects, and those objects will cast shadows. The objects, and the surfaces they shadow, were already there, but this new light changes the way we see them.... I've just started a book...about the shadows.[18]

The events drew out a moral meaning to the mystery writer's craft.

At the beginning of September, I was finishing a wonderful book, David Denby's *Great Books,* the account of a middle-aged journalist's return to the "great books" courses he took in college.... One of the lessons I took from it is that the politicians and their issues, the generals and their wars, all pass away and are forgotten. Words live.... For me, that is the only answer we need to the question of whether what we do matters. It doesn't matter less now. It matters more. Okay, most of us aren't Dante, or even close. Nevertheless mysteries can be a way to address the biggest moral questions, if we choose to write that. And if we write books that are essentially diversions, why would we think there is no need for them now?[19]

Something I think I've always known, but perhaps lost sight of...Mystery writing isn't just entertainment, an appeal to our jaded attitudes toward life and death, but a kind of sympathetic magic that invokes our ability to confront danger and draw on our inner strengths in order to bring evil to justice.[20]

Yet there was also a business-as-usual concern about the significance of the next book. Despite their own disclaimers, the World Trade Center disaster had made life a little harder in the world of fictional justice, where evil is controlled.

I know that eventually I will have to incorporate some of the recent events into my character lives. Who would have believed those two bland words—recent events!— could acquire such rich and fearsome resonance? With a May deadline I have a little more time to decide how.[21]

Ultimately the question is between you and your editor. If my editor tells me she wants my character Dr. Sutcliffe to be in or near the World Trade Center on September 11th, I'll find some reason for Dr. Sutcliffe to go there. There are so many published reports of people escaping it wouldn't be hard to make up a fictional escape.... Then the book could go wherever it's going not specifically about September 11th, but in the aftermath of it, Dr. Sutcliffe can go about her business while she deals with the effects of PTSD.[22]

The Legal Anthropologists

At the American Anthropological Association's annual meetings in Washington, D.C., in November 2001, the legal and political anthropologists suspended the ordinary order of business in favor of an open discussion on what September 11 and subsequent events meant for us. The concerns through which the legal anthropologists steered and storied their professional identities were both similar to and different from those of the mystery writers.

Sharing the belief that we could comprehend, to some lesser or greater degree, through the other's mind and eyes, there was a general nodding of heads and hearts that we could understand why the World Trade Center was attacked and that now Americans were experiencing a reality and possibility that has long been commonplace around the world.

I have been where those people live.[23]

With that comes a concern about maintaining, explaining, and storying a nuanced understanding of the cultural others in the face of their public vilification and public fear.

When did it become the only good Muslim is a peace-loving Muslim?[24]

Implicitly but surely, using the knowledge of the other's reality becomes a moral purpose, not always appreciated by colleagues or students. The sensed ethical imperative is to keep focusing on the multiple systems of cultural meaning; the individual agency of human beings; the local, national, and global inequities of power, economy, and wealth. Keep trying to understand and explain how these things happen; caution against authoritarian and univocal responses; and, perhaps above all, research, witness, and write what happens.

One anthropologist, working at a university in the Midwest, found her mission in informing her students, most of whom gathered around the patriotic banner, of the facts and situations of the countries from where the pilots had come. Instances revealed the differences between New York, where the attacks were first and foremost a local disaster, and other localities, where they were primarily viewed as a national threat. For example, in a collaborative conversation, several legal anthropologists based in small New England schools, with liberal-to-left traditions, described the unusually harsh treatment (lack of faculty and college president's support, unusually steep sentences) for students who had participated in flag-burning demonstrations shortly after September 11. In contrast to the hardening of positions, in New York, reciprocity, shared experience, and concerned communication were dominant. The communal responses called up the sensitivity of culture to local context and global ties.

There was talk of other times—World War II, the cold war, the Vietnam War—when anthropologists had made difficult choices: to speak about the lives of the people they worked with or to keep silent, or to stand with or against the U.S. government position. There was discussion about having a panel at the next annual meetings about living in the security state. Longstanding anthropological concerns with multiple systems of meaning and values also shaded into somewhat less-vocalized concerns regarding academic freedom.

I was not-exactly being silenced (but my colleagues did not exactly want to hear or understand what I had to say).[25]

Anthropologists' strivings to be at once insider and outsider is roughly analogous to mystery writers' efforts to distance and control a strange reality by creating fiction. In novel, difficult, or strange situations, calling simultaneously for hard, quick choices and complex reflection, anthropologists, I think, draw upon their participant-observer training both as a personal defense mechanism and a practical tool for balancing moral relativism and moral choice. Anthropologists, looking around them, struggled in a characteristically anthropological way.

It heightened my sense that human life is complicated—sometimes it is so hard to accomplish things. We had a community meeting here—because one of our neighbors had been killed and there was some talk about trying to have a community vigil, or a community ceremony acknowledging the pain that people had been through. But since it is a neighborhood with a significant Pakistani presence, there was an idea that people from the Pakistani community should be definitely included.... The idea was to search out people in that community that share a common view but it is not easy to negotiate the complex terrain of another community especially where there may be people in that community that have a mix of attitudes you wouldn't find particularly laudable.... It struck me how difficult it was to have an easy, simple, multicultural moment.[26]

As in the above statement, these observational stances were strongly mingled with a sensibility, both politicized and professionally primed, to project changes in social and political institutions and to be concerned about the despotic possibilities about governments and hegemonic institutions.

I had just come from observing the trial of those accused of bombing the U.S. Embassy in Nairobi, trying to make sense of what had happened. I was in the embassy at that time. My husband was killed in that bombing. Watching the trial, I wondered about the fairness of it, the way that the language foreclosed certain possibilities. Now looking at what has happened since, especially the decision to use military trials, with relative summary procedures, and hearsay evidence, I realize how much openness there was in that trial.[27]

One of the people in the police department really undermined the effort to do something as a community. He was the local community relations officer and he said that while there were "a lot of good people in the community there were also bad people there too." He was referring to people who had been supportive of terrorist activities that the FBI was paying attention to. It made it kind of complicated.... [Yet] when a lot of people have lost their lives you don't search so much for the idealistic answer.... You feel more sympathetic to the complexities of people living under the stresses of war—when you recognize to some degree that you are willing to allow police and government somewhat more leeway in handling the problems of threat, in ways that you wouldn't if you weren't under threat.[28]

As is evident from the anthropologists quoted above, the work, the lives, and the writing of anthropologists are intimately intertwined. David Rosen is writing a book on child soldiers. Susan Hirsch is writing a book on the trial of the embassy bombers. At the "Law and Society Meetings" in May 2002, Susan Hirsch spoke about her research on the trial, stating her own refusal to give victim witness testimony because she would not be allowed to speak against the death penalty, and elaborating on the distortions in victims' testimonies when inserted into prosecutorial strategy. To me, her words were foreshadows.

In addition to the anthropological perspective as a way of storying the concerns of September 11 and its aftermath, there were individual stories made, or being made, public that resonated in the anthropological chorus. The reader who recognizes the names may hear in the explanations and concerns addressed above the continuing voices of those who have written and will write on religious legal systems; law and language; the resistance of virtuous citizens to hegemonic legal systems; the landscape of children at war; and, like the mystery writers perhaps, self-interested hope that their books may be published sooner, distributed more widely, or rendered more significant as the events of September 11 and its aftermath are, explicitly or imperceptibly, incorporated into their larger understandings and the continuing questions of their professional selves. The stories, both of continuity and change, are told through the stories of the culture of anthropology.

The grand questions of anthropology—the characteristic participant-observer, insider-outsider stance in which anthropologists are trained, and the use of its perspective in decoding figurative worlds and the landscape of ideologies—are a cultural inventory used both to distance, manage, and explain reality, and to make large issues palpable through describing ordinary human beings as they instantiate, complicate, and explain larger questions, much in the manner and to the purpose that mystery writers create fiction.

The Administrative Judges

The balance of myth, life, and work was very different for the administrative judges of the New York Taxi and Limousine Commission. The New York Taxi and Limousine Commission (commonly referred to as the TLC) is a municipal agency that regulates the New York City taxis (called "medallion" or yellow cabs) and other for-hire vehicles licensed by New York City.[29] The court in Long Island City, Queens, is largely pro se, although there are a number of attorneys and specially licensed industry representatives who practice regularly there. To me, it is usually an endlessly fascinating venue of legal argumentation between police officers and TLC inspectors on the one hand, and the multi-cultural thousands who drive for hire in the city. It is a true people's court at the intersection of the public culture of the New York streets and the perspectives of Africans, Indians, Latin Americans, Middle Easterners, Europeans, Asians, and others, including native-born New Yorkers, making their strong cases on behalf of their vehicular occupations and entrepreneurship.

September 11 abruptly, if temporarily, put an end to this narrative. At first there were no hearings, then virtually none. The police were on emergency duty. The TLC inspectors replaced the police for ordinary traffic duty in the streets. When respondents appeared, instead of contesting the summons and arguing about their cases, they came in to plead guilty, smiled, and said, "Thank you for letting me go so quickly." The drivers and owners of vehicles and bases (dispatch centers), like many other people in New York, avoided the streets and public buildings, including the TLC court. The judges adjourned and adjourned. Many of the respondents, who are Muslims and/or from Pakistan, North Africa, or the Arab countries (or believed they might be mistaken for such), were reticent to appear anywhere. One day it seemed I adjourned more than two-dozen hearings where the respondents had names like Mohammed or Islam.

As the ordinary narrative ended, the myth of the unreal moment became perpetual. The main offices of the TLC were located within three blocks of the World Trade Center. Many judges and other personnel were there at the time, and some saw much of the meltdown from the windows before evacuating. The story of "where I was when" was circulated and shared again and again.

Another judge and I were in different rooms at the TLC offices on Rector Street, within three blocks of the World Trade Center. Each of us was looking out the window and watching the building buckle. At the same time, but independently, each of us thought, the building is going to fall down on us, it's time to get out of here. Both of us left the building at the same time, and got away before it crashed.[30]

I saw the towers hit, I saw the smoke from the train. (The No. 7 elevated subway that runs near the TLC court). I didn't know what it was.[31]

As the hearings thinned out, the court became crowded with personnel. Those who worked at Rector Street were temporarily transferred to Long Island City. There were more identity card checks, daily meetings where the

Commissioner informed everyone whether there was any news from the Mayor, and a safety evacuation when an unidentified car appeared in the garage next door (that turned out to have been rented by a nearby factory owner whose own luxury car was in the repair shop). Many public spaces and places in New York seemed to be vacillating between extra regulation of the ordinary and fear of chaos and destruction.

As there was less work to do than usual, there was time to talk about how the United States should respond, to express concern for those drivers who were scared and facing backlash, and to ask who had trouble sleeping at night. Most of the talk was of the most ordinary kind. Judges writing out adjournments en masse complained that their fingers ached. There was little work, yet most people came to work. And some said it was sort of like a family.

It was good to be working there at that time because we were with people. Because most of us are sole practitioners (when not being judges), it was good to be with people and share stories. What happened? Where were you when? The various little stories we heard and shared with other people.[32]

But, as the above quotation shows, the collaborative dialogue recycled the myth of the unreal moment. It was the workplace, not the work, that was comforting. It was the people, as people in the same space, that was significant. The dialogue never progressed toward a shared renewal. The issues were there of course, and the judges were wise enough to see them: the strange, strained emotions; the physical and financial fears of the drivers; the tightening of security and control; and the continuation, if not intensification, of routine as a counterpoint to chaos, even though few police or TLC inspectors or respondents were there. The TLC passed out American flags for the licensed vehicles. Attached to car antennas, for some drivers, they doubled as amulets and patriotic badges.

But when I asked the judges whether they felt any connection between what they were doing at the TLC and the other events, they answered with one word: "No." A shared workplace did not make a collaborative calling, nor did the calling become an anvil for the cognitive and emotional integration of the events. Eight months later, one judge spoke of her emotions at the time as entirely solitary.

There was a general atmosphere of depression and I was personally depressed because I had the most horrible romantic breakup in my life because it happened pretty much concurrently (with September 11)...A general atmosphere of malaise, misery and depression—a bleak empty landscape.

Now things are back to normal. The inspectors, police officers (some mellowed and chastened from the tough work of the emergency) and the respondents, no longer much afraid of the streets or the TLC court, again vigorously debate the propriety of street hails and wrong turns. The ordinary narratives are back.

COMPARING

The mystery writers and legal anthropologists have surprisingly much in common. Both write stories as metaphors of experience. Both groups self-consciously felt a need for some collaborative revising. Both groups simultaneously involved and distanced their personal selves in the books that will be made of the aftermath of the experience. Both found a moral purpose in their work, one analytical, the other creative, as a means of communicating experience to others, which somehow gave them the impetus of "now more than ever." Both groups understand, and write about, the larger experience as instantiated and embodied in individual human lives.

Fiction, like anthropology, stories a metaphor for experience. Both anthropologists and mystery writers renewed their professional selves and craft by finding a challenge and a kind of moral purpose in the core themes and questions that dominate their disciplines, both distancing and integrating their personal selves into the books they continued to write as reflections and extensions of human experience. It was not the event, but the afterwards that was significant.

There were differences, of course. The mystery writers emphasized emotions of their own and their characters, and found their solace in a world of good and evil they could control. Anthropologists worried about the institutional, governmental, and political powers they could not control, and the over-simplification of explanation. The mystery writers (almost all of the members have other occupations as well) work separately and independently, and in that sense they have no workplaces. The legal anthropologists spoke also as academics, of the need to teach and support students, the engagement with or isolation from colleagues, and the specter of chilled speech.

In contrast, the TLC judges, who, in ordinary times preside over and determine cases at the intersection of governmental power, New York public culture, and global migration, did not look through their professional lenses to story their own personal or professional bridge across the 9-11 aftermath. When the ordinary stories disappeared, and the work became routinized, the court became only a workplace, where co-workers could share their personal stories of who was where when.

When the inspectors', officers', and respondents' stories reappeared and the court was busy again, the judges stopped chatting about their personal selves, donned self-perceived impartiality, and listened to the ordinary stories of others. To an extent, these stories integrated others' 9-11 and post-9-11 experiences. One police officer, who had previously added charges of non-compliance to many summonses, after working months of emergency duty, testified he had no "blues" (his records of summonses) before September. Drivers explained they picked up illegal street hails because they had no business, owing from the absence of tourists in New York. To the extent we wrote opinions deciding innocence and guilt, the judges were also storying the experience of September 11 in the light of law and justice, but without a conscious, a visible investment of personal narrative.

Of course, that judges story experience is no news to legal anthropologists or mystery writers, or even judges, although their professional myths may not always let them say so. But the "where were you when" narratives that were the stock-in-trade of conversation at the TLC for many months remained as first-order narratives of the "unreal moment." The stories, by organizing, plotting, and distancing the trauma, and incorporating it into our personal narrative selves, did the work of psychological healing.[33] And the rounds of repetitive narration engendered a collective memory, an intimate but public cultural reality that might be laid safely in the past.

By contrast, the mystery writers and legal anthropologists, for whom the personal and professional are more tightly intertwined, were inclined to engage in still more complicated ways in what Bakhtin would call dialogism,[34] interrogating the master narratives of their disciplines with those of the new cultural reality and vice versa, as well as authoring both their cultural selves and their written works in the spaces of uncertainty.[35] As such, they continued to embed their narrated selves in their books, creating fourth-order narratives.

CONCLUSION

Now, in the calm before the storm, the closing paragraph of a book I use for my crime and culture class, with a substitution of "9-11" for the word "trial," seems appropriate:

And in the mornings, I write, telling the story, trying to tell the story; and it isn't until the end, the very end, as I look at the writing, as I leave the desk, that I see (and I see it sharply, suddenly) that the writing has been, all along (without my knowing), the doing of the thing I wanted so badly from the start, that the writing has done the thing I wanted so badly from the start—it has made (September 11) into words, a thing to read, to interpret, to circle back through. A text. Like art. Meaning something different to each person. Keeping the large questions open. But (September 11) was not that.[36]

Agony and Art: The Songs of September 11

Mark S. Hamm

The terrorist attacks of September 11 were responsible for more cultural productions than any other single event since World War II. They inspired
countless books, poems, plays, paintings, sculptures, dances, documentary
films, television specials, and memorializations, both real and virtual. Yet
none of these creations would approximate the role that music assumed as
America struggled to recover in the wake of September 11. Whether it was
the sound of a lone saxophonist playing John Coltrane's "In a Sentimental
Mood" in New York City's Union Square hours after the World Trade Center
fell, or the sound of Congress singing "God Bless America" on the steps of the
Capitol building the day after the attacks, or the sight of a weeping crowd lis-
tening to the Harlem's Children's Choir singing "Wind Beneath My Wings"
at a memorial service for fallen firefighters, music accompanied many unfor-
gettable moments that are now seared into our collective memory. In the
days, weeks, and months that followed, music not only became an effective
way for many Americans to express rage against extremist elements of the
Muslim world, but it also enabled Americans to cope with their fragile existence in world that has never been more dangerous.

The sheer magnitude of this music is one measure of its consequence. After
sending out an open call in September 2002, the *Village Voice* received some
800 submissions for a benefit compilation of new love songs for New York
City; the vast majority of them were about September 11 and its aftereffects.
The Web site MP3.com lists another 520 songs with "9-11" in their titles,
plus 83 more called "September 11," or something similar.[1] Add to this
another 80 songs contained in four tribute albums, and another two dozen

topical songs featured on various CDs, and that totals roughly 1,500 songs about the attacks. While I have made no attempt to review all of these songs, a purposive sampling of 50 of them does reveal some meaningful patterns in the ways musicians responded to the attacks and their aftermath. Those patterns are discussed in the following pages, along with a brief historical note for context. The songs are organized along three broad lines: American standards and pop hits selected by artists and record companies to commemorate the tragedy (examples include such war horses as "America the Beautiful" and Frank Sinatra's "New York, New York"); songs written after September 11; and an eerily foreboding set of songs released on the day of the attacks. I shall begin there.

TALKING WORLD WAR III BLUES

The release of Bob Dylan's *Love and Theft* on September 11, 2001, was entirely coincidental. But that misses an important point: how many people heard the album during the week of September 11 and immediately thereafter. For *Love and Theft* is riddled with images of hopelessness, war, and apocalypse: splintered ships, the end of summer, storms and floods, bloodthirsty soldiers, poison whiskey, and other things that are, in Dylan's words, "too terrible to be true." Had any other artist released a record with these images on September 11, it would have gone unnoticed. Yet because it was Dylan—arguably the most influential songwriter of the past fifty years—the themes take on historical significance. This is where he began, way back in the early sixties, as the original troubadour of an American apocalypse with such classic protest sirens as "Masters of War," "Hard Rain's Gonna Fall," "With God On Our Side," "Blowin' in the Wind," and "Talkin' World War III Blues." With the terrorist attacks of September 11, the so-called "voice of a generation" returned as a Doomsday prophet. At least that is how I heard *Love and Theft*, and how others heard it as well.

One was music critic Mikal Gilmore. "I've talked with several people in the time since [9-11]," he wrote, "who have turned to *Love and Theft* because they find something in it that matches the spirit of dread and uncertainty of our present condition."[2] Another was Sean Wilentz, who recognized the ageless beauty of the record: "Dylan shuffles space and time like a deck of playing cards. One moment, it's 1935, high atop some Manhattan hotel, then its 1966 in Paris or 2000 in West Lafayette, Indiana...then it's 1927, and we're in Mississippi, and the water's deep as it comes...Then it's September 11, 2001, eerily the date this album was released, and we're inside a dive on lower Broadway, and, horribly beyond description, things are blasted and breaking up out there, nothin's standing there."[3] Then there is critic Greg Tate, who says that "Before [September 11], *Love and Theft* was an abstract expressionist painting. Dylan could never have intended to carry a topical frame. Funny what a little moonlight can do: Now poets are bringing us the news."[4]

That news begins with a line from the album's second song, the drifter's lament "Mississippi." When Dylan sings about the fire and pain dropping down from the sky, who could not contemplate the terrible sight of the Twin Towers in flames, men and women leaping to their deaths from the upper reaches? Dylan returns as Jesus in the breezy romantic ballad "Bye and Bye," rendering an even more portentous line where sin is eliminated by a baptism of fire and civil war. In "Cry Awhile," and other songs on the album, he presents strangely eerie images of bodies, bones, flesh, and caskets.

The apocalyptic ramble continues in the juke-joint round of "Lonesome Day Blues." When I listened to this song on September 11, it immediately brought to mind the image of the evil plot of Osama bin Laden and the first hero of the 9-11 saga, Northern Alliance leader Ahmad Shah Massoud, killed by bin Laden operatives in Afghanistan on 9 September, just in time for reports about his death to make the September 11 *New York Times.* The song emphasizes a hero not deterred from being exposed to the evil and death that crosses his path.

Soon after the attacks, learned discussions would turn on Samuel Huntington's clash of civilizations thesis—the idea that much of the Arab world is irredeemably out of touch with modernity and will inevitably seek to annihilate it, thus creating a cataclysmic counterattack from the west. The immediacy and dread of this thesis is on full display in the upcountry rockabilly of "High Water (For Charley Patton)," a song describing the elimination of different perspectives and points of view, arguably the best song on the album if not the most nightmarish. Once again the poet brings the news: In the wake of September 11, many Americans would realize that, no, they couldn't open their minds to every conceivable point of view (radical Islam), as U.S. President George W. Bush resorted to Wild West newspeak, aspiring to get bin Laden "dead or alive."

It is here that *Love and Theft* breaks with a longstanding tradition of American protest music. Against the backdrop of Vietnam and the civil rights movement, for instance, Dylan and other protest singers of the era favored the dispossessed over the privileged, harshly criticizing the fanaticism and zealotry of the U.S. military industrial complex. Dylan saved his special brand of venom for the masters of war, hoping that they would die and then celebrating their death. Now he sees the cowards coming from afar, bounding out of a barren land with their enigmatic weapons of death and destruction.

Dylan appreciated the fear behind this threat months before September 11 when he wrote "High Water (For Charley Patton)"; the same kind of fear would soon consume the national psyche as we anxiously waited for the next shoe to drop after the attacks. In fact, the paranoia filtering through *Love and Theft* sounds like a minstrel's version of what has become the bizarre, color-coded Homeland Security warnings.

On "Lonesome Day Blues," "Floater (Too Much to Ask)," "Summer Days," and "Sugar Baby," Dylan focuses on creating, believing in, and moving based on fears that are not real. And if you listen closely at the places where Dylan weds the personal with the apocalyptic, you can hear him bravely confronting this fear. For Dylan's America is a place where people still tenaciously cling to the promise of honest work, love, and divinity. As greater details about the terrorist attacks became available to the public, more than one critic would examine these prescient, bombastic lyrics and ask: What did Dylan know and when did he know it? But there is a far more serious issue here, and that concerns the relevancy of art to the explosive times in which we live, a point that Dylan himself made in his 2001 *Rolling Stone* interview. When asked to comment on the events of September 11, the poet responded:

I mean, art imposes order on life, but how much more art will there be? We don't really know. There's a secret sanctity of nature. How much more of that will there be? At the moment, the rational mind's way of thinking wouldn't really explain what's happened. You need something else, with a capital E, to explain it.[5]

THE FOUNDATION

Although September 11 was a singular event in American history, the presence of catastrophe in the United States is nothing new. From its inception, the nation has experienced natural disasters, plagues, and man-made tragedies. And while pop music's response to September 11 would also be unprecedented, it too would be part of a rich musical tradition of dealing with calamity. In this tradition, disaster, terrorism, and war have been addressed in a straightforward manner: songs about these topics have been unapologetically honest and are often of a rare artistic caliber. Examples abound, cutting across all musical genres, but four songs are especially meaningful.

Mississippi, 1927

One of the most destructive natural disasters to ever occur in the United States was the floods that hit along the Mississippi River during the spring of 1927. After nearly a year of above-average rainfalls across the entire Mississippi River basin, the Mississippi and many of its tributaries were already at flood-stage by late-March 1927. Then, during the first three weeks of April, nine inches of rain fell in southern Missouri and in most of Arkansas. The heavy rain combined with melted snow coming down from the north, crashing levees in more than a hundred places along the river. By 23 April, the Mississippi had flooded more than 26,000 square miles of land in seven states; in some locations, the river was 80 miles wide. This was before national flood relief, and the extent of desolation reached biblical proportions. The waters forced more than 600,000 people from their homes, thousands of farm animals starved or drowned, and some 250 people were killed.[6]

Many of the homeless were impoverished blacks of the Mississippi Delta region—the birthplace of the blues. This led to a natural predilection among blues musicians to deal with the flood's devastation. Thirty-six-year-old Charley Patton was a pioneer of the Delta blues tradition and the first artist to address the disaster in song. Patton sang in a heavy, bold voice, typically about personal experiences, such as being a witness to a murder, or a railroad strike. He played several instruments and his repertoire included spirituals, ballads, and breakdowns. Following the great flood of 1927, he wrote his most famous song, "High Water Everywhere."[7] This became the model for other blues songs written about the flood, and, inevitably, the object of Bob Dylan's love and theft. Patton was affected directly by the flood, allowing him to express the story inside the song's lyrics, thus revealing their true menace. In a single verse, the flood spreads, upending lives, homes, and businesses, and in Greil Marcus's inimitable words, "that your freedoms under the Constitution are nothing compared with what God wants from you this night."[8]

Florida, 1935

Influential as they were, blues songs of disaster raised few questions about the relationship between art and politics. That would not hold true, though, for songs about terrorism. America's experience with terrorism began in the aftermath of the Civil War, when the Ku Klux Klan imposed a reign of violence against southern blacks that included an untold number of murders, shootings, whippings, rapes, tar-and-featherings, acid brandings, and other forms of mutilation. Yet the favored method of terror was the lynching; historians estimate that between 1867 and 1935 some two thousand African American males were hanged to death, many in public view.[9] A photograph of one lynching would profoundly influence American protest music.

That photograph, of one Rubin Stacy, hanging dead from a tree in Fort Lauderdale, Florida, on July 19, 1935, was the catalyst for "Strange Fruit," a political poem written by a New York City school teacher named Abel Meeropol (aka Lewis Allen) in 1937, and set to music two years later by Sonny White and the legendary jazz singer Billie Holiday.[10] The words to the anti-lynching song are powerful, but it is what Billie Holiday did with those lyrics that made "Strange Fruit" perhaps the most disturbing recording ever made. It is clear that for Billie Holiday, this song, too, had a deep, personal meaning. "When Billie sings it," wrote a critic, "you feel as if you're at the foot of the tree."

The history of "Strange Fruit" reveals that American art dealing with the agony of terrorism is often vulnerable to broader social and political influences. "Strange Fruit" was simply too radical for its time. After the song's release, nightclub owners prohibited Holiday from singing it; the song was banned on many radio stations, and *Time* magazine denounced it as "a prime piece of musical propaganda" for the National Association for the Advancement of Colored People (NAACP). Clearly, for these audiences, and for Billie Holiday herself, "Strange Fruit" was not only a song about lynching, it was a protest against all racism and bigotry. But the sheer power of the song eventually forced many Americans to face their stark and shared history. And in time, "Strange Fruit" was seen as a noble expression of hope that was ultimately reconstructed as the first cry of the civil rights movement, inspiring such huge talents as Sam Cooke, Curtis Mayfield, Marvin Gaye, Stevie Wonder, and Bob Marley. (The cry for social justice was also passionately embraced, of course, by folk singers of the era, including Dylan, Pete Seeger, Odetta, Phil Ochs, and Joan Baez.) Ironically, sixty-one years after condemning the song, *Time* declared "Strange Fruit" the best song of the twentieth century.

Pearl Harbor, 1941

The Japanese attack on Pearl Harbor was the defining event of a generation. Its impact was immeasurable, sparking significant changes at every level of society, including the world of pop music. One significant change involved the ways in which bedrock American values found their way into popular songs. Prominent among these values were the indomitable American spirit and a statement of American beliefs and inspirations. This served as the basis for a series of patriotic songs, most of which were written in the early period of World War II and reflect the nationalistic fervor arising out of the attack on Pearl Harbor.

One of the earliest was Denver Darling's country-music event ballad "Cowards Over Pearl Harbor," recorded two weeks after the attack.[11] "Cowards" was important because its mood (extremely somber and slow so as to evoke sympathy and sorrow for the victims) and its themes (that God is on

the side of America, and that Japan is evil) would set the tone for more popular patriotic songs celebrating the war effort. And they followed, by the
dozens, ranging from the jingoistic to the sentimental, and occasionally
humorous. These included songs that encouraged men to enlist in the armed
services, such as "America Calling" by Fred Waring and his Pennsylvanians;
songs to raise the spirit of the American worker, such as "On the Old Assembly Line" by Glen Miller and his orchestra; songs that praised the American
family, such as "There's a Blue Star Shining Bright" by Red Foley and "Don't
Worry Mom," by Sonny Dunham and his orchestra; and numerous songs,
like Cole Porter's "Something for the Boys," the Andrews Sisters' "Boogie
Woogie Bugle Boy," Frank Loesser's "Praise the Lord and Pass the Ammuni-
tion," and country singer Carson Robison's incendiary "We're Gonna Have
to Slap the Dirty Little Jap"—all intended to boost the morale of the fighting
Yank. Although most of these would be forgotten by war's end, one song
from the patriotic genre would emerge as an enduring relic of Americana.

"God Bless America" was written by Irving Berlin in 1918, yet he shelved
it for another twenty years. In the fall of 1938, as war threatened Europe,
Berlin decided to write a peace song, which led him to rework the music and
some of the lyrics for "God Bless America." Singer Kate Smith introduced the
revised song in a radio broadcast on Armistice Day 1939, and it became an
immediate sensation. Yet with America's entry into the war, "God Bless
America" achieved even greater popularity; and by 1943, the song threatened
to replace the national anthem because of its patriotic theme. The defining
feature of the song was the chauvinistic declaration that God, in wartime,
would bless America and stand beside her.

A second change brought about by the war was the inclusion of a heartfelt
sentimentality into pop music. By and large, these songs dealt with longing
for the time that soldiers could return home to their lovers. Such songs dominated the music charts between 1942 and 1945, and they included the towering hit "White Christmas," written by Irving Berlin and performed by Bing
Crosby, as well as the Andrews Sisters' "Don't Sit Under the Apple Tree (With
Anyone Else but Me)," Doris Day and Les Brown's "Sentimental Journey,"
and Frank Sinatra and the Tommy Dorsey Orchestra's "Let's Get Away from
It All." In these songs, all skepticism about domesticity was suspended in
favor of a highly idealized image of "home" as a place where yearning and
grief no longer existed. Rendered with utmost sincerity, singers of these sentimental old chestnuts provided comfort and hope to soldiers overseas, and
reminded those back home of the importance of love, family, and country.
The songs are rife with images of friends and neighbors, fireplaces and moonlight, home-cooked food, a sweetheart's kiss, and a good night's sleep. This

romanticized image would dominate American culture for years to come. Foremost among these odes was an auburn standard that commanded the charts during the darkest hours of America's involvement in the war. This was "I'll Be Seeing You," written by Irving Kahal/Sammy Fain, and performed by Bing Crosby. "I'll Be Seeing You" is the story of a man's tender desire for reunion with his lover in a small café by the chestnut trees and wishing well. There, life will bloom again, in a lovely summer day.

POP MUSIC AND THE MEMORIALIZATION OF SEPTEMBER 11

Immediately after the 9-11 terrorist attacks, most songwriters took the position that the acts were of such magnitude that they could not be responded to in song so soon. Accordingly, there would be no "Cowards Over Pearl Harbor" for this generation. That does not mean, however, that it was impossible to find a fresh angle in existing songs that could be used to bring some perspective to the attacks. And that was the purpose, albeit a secondary one, of *America: A Tribute to Heroes,* a star-studded telethon (and subsequent double CD) held in New York City on September 21, 2001. The primary purpose of the concert was to honor the thousands who died on September 11, to strengthen the national resolve to transcend the catastrophe, and to raise money for victims' families.

The concert featured more than two dozen pop music performers who conducted their songs with subdued sincerity. With the ruins of the Twin Towers still smoldering, each performer chose one song that either reflected on loss, called for love, or celebrated the human spirit. In so doing, some of the performers dug deep into the oeuvres of disaster, terrorism, and war songs. Yet in other songs, you can hear a search for something new, something that was always just below the surface in previous pop music attempts to grapple with unfathomable darkness, but never quite made it to the fore. This is the notion of spirituality, not direct pleading with a universal God, but a more humble artistic attempt to articulate the sacred qualities of soul needed to comprehend the mysteries of human holocaust.

Nowhere is this more evident than on Bruce Springsteen's somber opening performance of "My City of Ruins," a song introduced as "a prayer for our fallen brothers and sisters." Plaintively rendered with acoustic guitar and har-monica, and supported by backing singers from his E Street Band, "My City of Ruins" is a gospel-tinged folk song written late in 2000 about Springsteen's hometown of Ashbury Park, New Jersey. The song is about urban deteriora-tion, spiritual desolation, and rebirth. Springsteen approaches the destruction with the same kind of despair testified to by the Delta bluesmen after the great flood and the only way he knows how, it seems: with the working-class mettle that has defined his career since the glory days of *Born to Run*. He will begin with his own hands, and prays for strength, for faith, and for love. His bravery grows with each iteration until Springsteen is irredeemably consumed by his spiritual strength. With it, he will persevere and, somehow, so will we.

As inspiring as it is, "My City in Ruins" stops short of finger pointing. That task is taken up by others who cleverly perform the trick of establishing historical context for the attacks by focusing on the root causes of terrorism. In fact, some of these lyrics read like selections from a college textbook on the subject. The first trickster is Stevie Wonder, who introduces his soulful "Love's in Need of Love Today" by saying, "When you kill in the name of God or Allah, you are cursing God." Wonder turns his pop hit into a protest against the grievances that inspired the 9-11 attacks, interpreted with the spiritually uplifting grace that has come to define his work. Taking the role of a news broadcaster, he sings of a dire warning and tells us what Dan Rather and the other talking heads of the day only wish they could: Stop the Hate. This is not only a song about the personal dangers of fanaticism, but I read it as a plea to governments to take responsibility for ending those dangers as well. The same can be said for U2's "Walk On."

Originally written in honor of Burmese activist Aung San Suu Kyi, "Walk On" became the most played song on U.S. radio in the wake of September 11, its universal sentiments capturing the spirit of the moment.[12] Here we have Bono, arguably the world's most famous rock star, seducing us with a prayer for salvation. What is good for the wretched of the earth is good for the fortunate, including those who control most of the world's wealth. And with the ragged glory of Edge's electric guitar driving him on, Bono ends the anthem with a litany of sins to be left behind in our hour of darkness.

The lessons on terrorism continue in Neil Young's interpretation of John Lennon's "Imagine." Commenting on the state of pop music in the post-9-11 era, critic Alexis Petridis writes that "Rebellion, the lifeblood of rock music for over 40 years, is suddenly off the agenda."[13] I could not disagree more. In what is perhaps the most courageous performance on the album, Young turns the idealism of Lennon's anthem into a personal and political challenge. For to imagine, just ten days after the calamity of September 11, that killing, dying, and separateness can be eliminated was to denounce both the Islamic fanaticism behind the attacks and the calls for revenge then sweeping America, a different but equally dangerous kind of fanaticism. Especially at the highest level of the American political order, the government was preparing for war. Because of those disjunctions, Neil Young's shaky interpretation of "Imagine" is transformed into a first-class protest song.[14]

Younger artists also rise to the occasion. Limp Bizkit and the Goo Goo Dolls' John Rzeznick turn in a haunting acoustic cover of Pink Floyd's "Wish You Were Here," appended with a new verse that asks what may be the twenty-first century's most compelling question of a willingness to change. From here the album sandwiches Wyclef Jean's cover of Bob Marley's "Redemption Song" with a chillingly somber acoustic take of "Livin' on a Prayer" by Bon Jovi, before offering up the subtly ironic benediction of Willie Nelson's "America the Beautiful." If there was a more parsimonious commentary on the causes of terrorism in the tender days following September 11 than the one delivered by this American musical icon—I have missed it.

Other artists were less controversial and eager to please the body politic. Canadian Celine Dion sang "God Bless America." Also drawing from the pop scripture of war songs, Tom Petty and the Heartbreakers transformed their defiant "I Won't Back Down" into a statement of patriotic resolve. Playing the song softer than usual, with the rhythm section chugging along like a freight train and guitarist Mike Campbell floating ethereal licks above him, Petty makes such declarations as the need to stand one's ground and fight for what one believes is right. Finally, the album features a number of unobtrusive contemporary pop expressions of romantic sentimentality. These songs range from the Dixie Chicks' country ballad "I Believe in Love," to populist rocker Dave Matthews's "Everyday," to love songs for the community most affected by the terrorist attacks, including Billy Joel's tear-jerking "New York State of Mind."

There would be other pop music tributes to September 11, but none would come close to capturing the social significance and emotional gravity of *America: A Tribute to Heroes*. None would be as daring, none as intelligent. While some of the songs—especially U2's "Walk On" and Neil Young's "Imagine"—were not necessarily anti-patriotic, they did ask the universal question, Why do people want to keep killing each other? And it was asked at precisely the same moment that much of the world community was asking the same thing. With each new memorialization, however, came a repetition of the more traditional themes found on the original tribute album, and with repetition came a deadening of the images and ideas of September 11. By the time Billy Joel sang "New York State of Mind" for the second tribute, *The Concert for New York City*, for example, September 11 was recast as "September 11." And "September 11" effectively drove away the burning significance of September 11. Despite some stunningly urgent performances by such senior statesmen of rock as The Who, Paul McCartney, David Bowie, Mick Jagger, Keith Richards, and Eric Clapton, the second tribute represented a dissociation of September 11's political and strategic aspects from its social and emotional aspects. One only has to compare the gritty reality of Springsteen's "My City of Ruins" with the bubblegum banality of Backstreet Boys' "Quit Playing Games With My Heart" (on the second tribute) to appreciate the ways in which popular culture can concentrate the American spirit and disperse the American will to *rise up*.

It was time for something new.

THE EARLY 9-11 POP SONGS

Stuart Hall and other cultural studies scholars argue that any attempt at understanding the significance of a cultural product must take into account its relationship to a broader societal discourse.[15] As we have seen, this was certainly true for earlier American pop songs about terrorism and war. Similar considerations would apply to the first wave of songs written about September 11. The most influential force in the music business would become the music business itself. As such, artists who aimed to reach a broad audience were forced to work within some well-defined parameters that would initially define pop's response to September 11.

Immediately following the attacks, radio stations and music video outlets tempered their play lists, opting to not play songs with themes of violence and terrorism. While MTV and VH1 pulled a number of videos from programming, Clear Channel Communications, owners of the largest share of the nation's radio stations, distributed a list of more than 150 songs considered questionable in light of September 11. That list included such famous standards as Louis Armstrong's "What A Wonderful World," Cat Stevens's "Peace Train," Elton John's "Rocket Man," and John Lennon's "Imagine" (which further underscores Neil Young's courage to sing the song before millions of Americans in the first tribute concert). For the artists who *did* attempt to address the tragedy, the message was clear: they would have to be circumspect.

This put a strain on the heart of pop music's response to September 11, initially creating two unsatisfying polar opposites: songs that were either overly abstract or overly realistic. In the first instance, the songs shout a lot but say little; in the second, they say a lot but shout little. Paul McCartney's "Freedom" is a prime example of the first case. Debuting at the *Concert for New York City,* "Freedom" is a feisty, mid-tempo pop song of unadorned patriotism in the "God Bless America" tradition. McCartney—who once held the belief that all we needed was love—now insists that he's ready to fight for freedom. The song leaves me flat. Freedom from what? Lousy airline security? Future intelligence failures? While the song is of the "changed world" vintage, its message is so muted that it fails to say anything about the preeminent issue of that world: the conflict between a superpower and an almost invisible enemy.

An example of the second case is Dawn Landes's "A Well Dressed Man" from *Vigil: N.Y. Songs Since 9-11* (produced by Suzanne Vega and the Greenwich Village songwriter's exchange). Where "Freedom" leaves me frustrated with McCartney's twisting and shouting about an unspecified danger, "A Well Dressed Man" leaves me withering in horror over its specificity. Accompanied by a simple drum and bass, affecting a dirge-like quality to the music, the teenaged Landes addresses one of the most horrifying aspects of the attacks: the "jumpers," as they were called by the firefighters and reporters on the scene, those men and women who dove to their deaths from the upper floors of the World Trade Center. This is a topic for which there can be no universality. Such concerns should never have to cross the mind of anyone, let alone a young girl. When they do, agony overwhelms art.

After the initial horror of September 11 subsided, other songwriters would find a middle ground between these extremes, seeking comforting modes and arrangements typically associated with their various musical traditions. The most aggressive group out of the box was country music performers. In mid-2002, country singer Toby Keith stirred up a storm of controversy when he delivered *Unleashed*, an album celebrating the bombing of Afghanistan. Dedicated to "The Lord," the record included "Courtesy of the Red, White and Blue (The Angry American)," a career-defining hit intended to express the emotions of ordinary Americans in response to September 11. As much as liberals hated Keith's unrepentant anger and jingoism, conservatives loved it, as did soldiers on several U.S. military bases where Keith performed the song, because he celebrates everything American, from the Statue of Liberty, the bald eagle, Mother Freedom, and the Red, White, and Blue.[16]

"Courtesy" fits squarely within the country music tradition of responding strongly and topically to war and other challenges to the nation, ala Carson Robison's "We're Gonna Have to Slap the Dirty Little Jap." So, in that sense, there is nothing new about Keith's song, nor is there anything original about other flag-waving country songs written about September 11, such as Aaron Tippin's "Where the Stars and Stripes and the Eagle Fly," Charlie Daniels's pro-war ballad "This Ain't No Rag, It's a Flag," or Ray Stevens's track mocking the al-Qaeda leader, "Osama Yo-Mama." These songs are intended to get our attention by speaking directly from the gut rather than appealing to any thought-provoking dialectic. An exception is Alan Jackson's "Where Were You (When the World Stopped Turning)."

One could argue that there are two defining features of a good 9-11 song. First, a good song will generally enhance our understanding of the event better than a flawed one; a good song is more eloquently written and more coherently conceived. And second, a good song will help people move toward catharsis. (This is the shortcoming of songs like "A Well Dressed Man," in my opinion. Instead of offering catharsis, they simply re-summon powerful emotions.) Not only does Jackson's "Where Were You" conform to these particulars, but it is, quite simply, one hell of a country song. While Jackson follows country's populist tradition of truthfully expressing the emotions of every man and woman, he defies that tradition by assuming a pacifist world view. Played in traditional country flat-picking style, the song's tender rumination owes more to the disaster genre than anything else. It is indeed a rare kind of flag-waving song that joins the political complacency of Hank Williams with televised images of world conflict and the Gospels to arrive at social commentary on September 11. In the song, Jackson refers to himself as a simple man—not political, but a believer in God, justice, and love.

Another challenge facing songwriters, in addition to those posed by the music industry, is that post-sixties American culture is an insufficient starting point for understanding the deeper truths exposed by the events of September 11. Many attempted to bridge this gap by relying on pop's foundation for expressing the vagaries of disaster, terrorism, and war. This happened in gospel music, folk music, rock, and rap. And again, there would be some good songs and some not so good.

Time is too precious to waste on the second category (only to mention that veteran folkie Tom Paxton's "The Bravest," a tribute to the fallen firefighters and police officers, and United States Attorney General John Ashcroft's gospel ode, "Let Eagles Soar," are exemplars). So, I'll focus instead on several songs that offered original takes on the complex social and political factors underlying the attacks. The first is Neil Young's "Let's Roll."

Although some critics panned the song as unduly patriotic and "bellicose" for a "former hippie" like Young, I'm not sure that there's a good alternative given its ominous content.[17] (To say nothing of the subjective assertion that former hippies can't be patriotic or bellicose when situations demand it.) "Let's Roll" is an homage to Scott Beamer and the other heroic passengers who took on the terrorist hijackers aboard American flight 93, the so-called "fourth plane" of the 9-11 attacks, foiling their presumed plan to strike a Washington, D.C., target. The jet was brought down in a Pennsylvania field, killing all on board. Here, the enemy is actual, brutal, and deadly. Young takes us inside the plane with the hijackers guarding the doors. This terrifying image is accompanied by Young's "timeless brand of fossil fuel: love that burns, faith that endures, and guitar solos that keep searching for a heart of gold," as a critic put it.[18] The pivotal point occurs midway through the song when Young transforms the war on "evil" into a concrete image of the predator stalking its prey, and the brave response that followed: responding to evil by facing it down, going after it, and conquering it. It was time to roll.

"Let's Roll," then, is a song about terrorism in the "Strange Fruit" tradition, offering an artistic testimony on both the deadly tactics used by terrorists and their final consequences for victims. It is a song of human torment, trimmed with hippie soul rhythms. Equally unique, though virtually unknown, is Ina May Wool's "Boxcutters and Knives" from the *Vigil* CD. Accompanied by a spooky electric guitar riff, in just a few well-chosen words Wool gives us a creative, thought-provoking lesson on the ingenuity of the hijackers (taking flight instruction) and the simplicity of their tactics (using box cutters and knives) versus the technology of the Western world. It is what they used, of course, to contrive the agony of September 11.

These issues are further explored by renegade country artist Steve Earle in "John Walker's Blues," from his album *Jerusalem*. There is perhaps no contemporary artist who writes about outsiders as well as Steve Earle. Like Howard Becker, Earle understands that criminals usually do not accept the rules by which they are judged and "may not regard those who judge him as either competent or legitimately entitled to do so."[19] As critic Robert Christgau states more bluntly: "Earle identifies with any unlucky asshole who makes the wrong choice at the wrong time."[20] This trait is important for present purposes, because terrorists are not created in a vacuum. Rather, they are forged by a complex mix of social pressures, social pulls, and psychological pressures. Earle investigates these forces from the point of view of the so-called American Taliban, John Walker Lindh, a contemporary outsider if there ever was one. The song is a broadside about the 21-year-old's interest in music videos, boy bands, and religious fanaticism. Alienated from mainstream American culture, Earle's confused young man found peace by reading the words of the prophet Mohammed. Where Neil Young and Ina May Wool set original ideas about the hijackers and victims to rock and folk music, Earle's country blues tackles a broader issue that lies at the heart of the current conflict between Islam and the West: the inability to accept one another's religions. Earle investigates that chasm in the song's powerful, climactic verse, featuring Earle's recitation of an Arabic prayer and a snippet of mullahs reading from the Quran.

Several artists addressed the U.S. war on terrorism, yet this was by no means a common subject taken up by the American pop-music community.

In fact, most 9-11 songs are distinguished by their absence of commentary on the war. And that in itself is rather unique. In times of conflict, musicians can usually be counted on to offer some opposition to the rhetoric of war. The turbulent 1960s, of course, created a watershed of anti-war songs. "Pop culture is almost instinctively pacifist," observed Neil McCormick, "rallying around the flag of universal love and, certainly at its edgier, lyrical extremes, deeply suspicious of political leaders."[21]

In the United States, the most flammable anti-war songs came from alternative folk/rock singers and non-gangster rappers. These included such underground hip-hop artists as Mr. Lif, whose "Home of the Brave" rebukes the U.S. government's rhetoric that demonized all people of Afghanistan or indie emcee Sage Francis's "Makeshift Patriots"—a rap that skewers George W. Bush's speech during the Ground Zero cleanup.

Also entering the fray was folk singer Stephan Smith. As the United States prepared to expand the war beyond Afghanistan, Smith released the "The Bell," an antiwar ballad featuring a child unwilling to fight in the war. On the record, Smith is accompanied by 83-year-old Pete Seeger, America's patron saint of lost causes. A more direct assault on the political class was expressed by the alternative-rock trio Sleater-Kinney in their post-9-11 protest song, "Far Away," from the CD *One Beat*. Against a backdrop of angry, angst-ridden grunge rock, singer Carrie Brownstein recalls the irony of September 11, a day when the president was hidden away and working men responded and died because of it. Yet the most combustible, ahistorical, Bush-bashing song of the post-9-11 era is no doubt Ani DiFranco's "Self Evident," from her *So Much Shouting, So Much Laughter* CD. In a long statement on September 11, DiFranco weds the personal with the political to explore the chauvinism that she sees as the root cause of the attacks. This is Toby Keith in reverse. After berating the Bush administration's calls for freedom and liberty, DiFranco verbally executes the entire news media establishment; then gives a shout out to the freedom fighters of El Salvador, to prisoners on death row, and to nurses and doctors who offer abortions. She ends by mourning the 9-11 victims—they are people, not pawns used by Bush (i.e., the Asshole).[22]

But, in the main, all of this was a failed attempt to ignite dissent against the war. And for good reason. The paucity of post-9-11 protest music in the United States actually says more about the peculiar nature of the "war on terrorism" than it does about artistic opposition to military conflict. Because the war was primarily fought with precision-guided missiles and laser targeting devices, soldiers never had to face the actual result of their killing. And neither did musicians. Both soldiers and (most) singers were part of a generation that grew up on video games—like "Command" and "Conquer"—that made such "killing" easy. Like these video games, the war on terrorism was dehumanized and distilled onto digitalized battlegrounds. Not only were soldiers and singers, then, far different than their counterparts a generation ago, but the absence of a military draft and the influence of the Internet—a fundamentally conservative phenomenon—further led to a homogenization of American attitudes toward the war which favored the status quo. During the Vietnam War, music was used for an anti-establishment purpose, making it "hip" for American youth to rise up against authority; during the war on terrorism, youth flocked to a venue devoid of protest but full of patriotic aggression. To be sure, 2002's top-selling recording artist, controversial rapper Eminem, not only released an extremely popular video lampooning Osama bin Laden ("Raping in a Cave"), but during the war the U.S. government broadcast his songs in the Middle East as part of its propaganda campaign to enhance America's image to young radio listeners in the Arab world.[23] The young critic Matt Rubin said it best: "The uniquely revolutionary weapon of music has been co-opted by the same powers that control all the other weapons."[24]

There were, however, several 9-11 pop songs that successfully challenged this stale conformity, and most of them originated overseas. In England, agit-prop veteran Paul Weller recorded "A Bullet for Everyone," which moralized that killing Afghan women and children isn't right.[25] British pop star George Michael reincarnated himself as a protest singer with an assault on U.S. foreign policy in "Shoot the Dog."[26] And in Germany, various rap artists weighed in with a compilation CD, *Pandemonium Against Terrorism,* some of which was also critical of the U.S. assault on Afghanistan.

Yet the most interesting, and arguably the most important, protest songs emanated from Arab lands. One Arabic folk singer is reported to have sold more than 20 million CDs featuring songs that express adamant hatred of U.S. foreign policy in the Middle East and Afghanistan.[27] One of the most daring Arabic pop songs was "No More" by the Pakistani band Junoon. Written from the perspective of a person who had actually seen people killed in the war, "No More" is nonetheless a statement of equanimity. It was this sympathy with victims on both sides of the conflict—those killed in Afghanistan *and* New York City—that provoked a thunderous response when Junoon debuted the song in Karachi during the U.S. bombing campaign. "No More" set off a full-scale riot, as angry young Pakistanis threw rocks and bottles at the band, burned American flags, and stormed local businesses. Not only did Junoon strike a raw nerve among Arab extremists, but their anti-war anthem also struck pop gold with its lyrics. The song ends with the singer wondering why love remains despite great horrors—that question would now be addressed by America's working-class poet laureate.

THE RISING

By the first anniversary of September 11, cultural productions about the terrorist attacks had surpassed the point of critical mass. Book publishers, for example, had released more than a hundred titles related to September 11, ranging from commemorative editions and tomes on heroism and patriotism, to investigative reports and historical readers. With the market saturated, interest in "September 11" began to fade fast.[28] Meanwhile, pop culture was demonstrating a resiliency to tragedy (September 11, the war on terrorism, the anthrax attacks, *and* suicide bombings in Israel all received saturation media coverage), and so pop music reverted to its old tricks, as sex, violence, and irony returned to center stage. It was at this (rather ironic) point, to once again quote Neil McCormick, that "perhaps the first post-9-11 masterpiece in any medium" was released: Bruce Springsteen's *The Rising*.[29]

The Rising picks up right where Springsteen left off with his stirring rendition of "My City of Ruins" at the *America: A Tribute to Heroes* concert: by speaking for ordinary men and women. The firefighters, police officers, rescue units, and victims of September 11 were of a class and character that Springsteen's music revolves around. They were the inspiration for *The Rising*. The songs resound with the emotional chaos of September 11, embracing each perspective with compassion and bewilderment before arriving at the central message of the work: that life, with the passage of time, will eventually be okay, our hearts will be healed, and the memories of those who paid the price will never be forgotten.

Much has been written about *The Rising*, and much of it has been written very well. Therefore, instead of rototilling this fertile ground, I'll end this essay by trying to do something original: explain how *The Rising* builds on pop's foundation of confronting catastrophe to achieve something truly unique. And in this sense, the most important thing about *The Rising* is that, like Charley Patton's encounter with the great flood or Billie Holiday's experiences with racism, Bruce Springsteen was directly affected by September 11: his New Jersey property offered a direct view of the burning towers. Days later, he began reading the *New York Times*' touching series of obituaries for the victims of September 11. Springsteen told a *Time* reporter that he learned from reading those obits that some of his previous hits—especially "Thunder Road" and "Born in the U.S.A."—were played at countless post-9-11 memorial services for many blue-collar victims. Working like a good ethnographer,

Springsteen then called the widows of several of the victims who had appeared in the obituaries. It was through those interviews that he fleshed out the intimacies of September 11.[30] Those intimacies appear on *The Rising*, and they allow some of the songs to rise to greatness, especially those that penetrate the unique horror of having a loved one burned to death by terrorists.

And that marks the album's true distinction. Love songs interpreted against the backdrop of war differ from those that are interpreted during peacetime. And love songs interpreted against the backdrop of terrorism are unlike those interpreted during war or peacetime. Indeed, they are unlike anything else. The sentimental love songs of the forties, like "I'll Be Seeing You," were about hope—hope that families would survive a war. *The Rising* captures the quiet suffering that occurs when a family is torn apart in an instant, when men and women see everything they believe to be true turned upside down in a flash. It is quite possible that death associated with terrorism, which is totally unexpected, is more excruciating for survivors than death suffered in war, where it is always a possibility. This agonizing loss is everywhere on *The Rising*.

Springsteen adorns his love songs with images of loss in the way that a painter would sparingly use colors to warm the lights and shadows of a portrait. The images are both physical (a ticking clock on the wall, an empty bed, a pearl-handled gun on the night table) and emotional (deceit, dread, empathy, and redemption), making his songs earthy yet spiritual. At his best, Springsteen combines the images, as he does in the heroic opener "Lonesome Day," and in them he searches for revenge against an enemy that is close by. In other love songs, Springsteen plumbs deeper into the depths of despair. In a simple, pleasant melody, "You're Missing" conveys details known only to a bereaved lover: a shirt in the closet, a television playing in the den, too many phone calls, and hopelessness and tears.

This sentimentality is also used to frame the darkest subject of *The Rising*. "Paradise" is a new take on the classic story of lost love, only in this case one of the lovers is an Islamic terrorist. "Paradise" is more introspective and complex than any other 9-11 song about terrorists (such as "Let's Roll" or "John Walker's Blues"). Set to a delicate guitar run, "Paradise" begins with the final thoughts of a young suicide bomber (sung in the first person) as he walks through a crowded marketplace with his lover. Then the song shifts perspectives and suddenly we're inside the mind of a woman who lost her husband in the Pentagon attack—inspired by a conversation that Springsteen had with a Washington widow. The song ends with the realization that the afterlife—paradise—is no comfort to the living.

Springsteen moves effortlessly from lost love to heroism and transcendence without losing sight of the details. "Into the Fire" is an uplifting gospel tribute to the emergency workers who climbed up the burning Twin Towers never to emerge. "It was this vision of ascension, of them going up as everyone else was coming down, that struck me," Springsteen told reporter Ted Koppel. But it is another song about the fallen firefighters, "The Rising," that chokes me up every time I listen to it. This song represents everything Springsteen fans have come to love about his music: layers of slash and burn guitar licks, swirling keyboards, screaming harmonies, thundering percussion, and lyrics that pack a wallop. Springsteen's soul is burning here, his incredible blues-soaked voice erupting like a snake charmer channeling Phil Spector. "The Rising" is a mini-epic about a firefighter's last day on earth, rendered in one mordant yet graceful stroke that links fate and will and the ordinary. Hell hound on his trail, he's rising into the flames, rising on wheels of fire like a blessed saint. Now we're in the physical space of the crumbling towers; no need to talk about the hero's courage because that's understood. No need for anything, because the faces around him have all disappeared. All that matters now is the power of a hard life lived well. For now is the moment of death and resurrection.

With these songs, Springsteen linked September 11 to a broader societal discourse reflected in the two near-opposite feelings of most Americans in the days and weeks after the attacks: on the one hand, a deep grief for the lives lost; on the other, a belief that we will "rise up."[31] That belief is based not on optimism or even hope, but on faith: faith that people can set aside their differences, join together, and struggle through hard times. Because this is a common, populist struggle and not an iconoclastic one *The Rising* is a subtle testament to patriotism; thus the record would avoid the crippling social and political influences visited upon a countless number of more controversial songs about terrorism. By offering up this utopian dream, then, Springsteen's heartfelt stories of love lost accomplish nothing less than the broadening of pop music's tradition of dealing with human catastrophe. Stated more simply, *The Rising* is what Bob Dylan would call "something else, with a capital *E*."[32]

Notes

CHAPTER 1: INTRODUCTION

1. David Halberstam, *Firehouse* (New York: Hyperion Books, 2002), 5–6.

2. Austin Sarat, *When the State Kills: Capital Punishment and the American Condition* (Princeton: Princeton University Press, 2001), 213, 245.

3. John Fiske, *Media Matters: Everyday Culture and Political Change* (Minneapolis: University of Minnesota Press, 1994), 4.

4. Stuart Hall, "Encoding/Decoding," in *Culture, Media, Language,* ed. Stuart Hall et al. (London: Hutchinson, 1980).

CHAPTER 2: HOLY WAR IN THE MEDIA

1. "Speech meant to tell real meaning of 'Jihad'" CNN.com (June 6, 2002), retrieved from the World Wide Web December 2002 http://cnn.usnews.

2. See Edward W. Said, *Orientalism: Western Conceptions of the Orient* (London: Penguin, 1995).

3. For recent discussion of the concept, see John L. Esposito, *Unholy War: Terror in the Name of Islam* (Oxford: Oxford University Press, 2002); Hilmi M. Zawati, *Is Jihad a Just War? War, Peace and Human Rights Under Islamic and Public International Law* (Lewiston, Queenston and Lampeter: Edward Merlin Press, 2001).

4. See Edward W. Said, *Covering Islam: How the Media and the Experts Determine How We See the Rest of the World* (London: Vintage, 1997).

5. Samuel P. Huntington, "Clash of Civilizations?" *Foreign Affairs* 72, no. 3 (1993): 22–49.

6. This is further complicated because the United States and the West in general had been sponsors of groups in Afghanistan waging "Jihad" against the Soviet Union in the 1980s. See Christian Parenti, "America's Jihad: A History of Origins," in *Beyond September 11: An Anthology of Dissent,* ed. Phil Scraton (London: Pluto Press, 2002), 10–19.

7. For a sensitive investigation of the complexities of Muslim identity in a multicultural contest, see Yvonne Yazbeck Haddad, ed., *Muslims in the West: From Sojourners to Citizens* (New York: Oxford University Press, 2002).

8. Zeyad Yasin, "My American Jihad," retrieved from the World Wide Web October 2002 http://www.beliefnet.com/story/107/story_10725.html.

9. Ibid.

10. See Abdullahi Ahmed An-Na'I, "Upholding International Legality Against Islamic and American Jihad," in *Worlds in Collision: Terror and the Future of World Order,* ed. Ken Booth and Tim Dunne (Basingstoke: Palgrave, 2002), 162–71.

11. Dave Marash, *War of Words: Harvard Senior Wants to Reclaim the Word "Jihad,"* (June 5 2002), retrieved from the World Wide Web December 2002 http://abcnews.com.

12. Ibid.

13. Ibid.

14. "Speech meant to tell real meaning of 'Jihad'" CNN.com (June 6, 2002), retrieved from the World Wide Web December 2002 http://cnn.com/2002/US/06/06/american.jihad.cnna/.

15. Kate Zernike, "Harvard Student Drops 'Jihad' from Speech Title," *New York Times,* 1 June 2002.

16. Nader R. Hasan, "Jihad and Veritas," *New York Times,* 5 June 2002.

17. Ibid.

18. Ibid.

19. Ibid.

20. Ibid.

21. Ibid.

22. The idea that Islamic law and values have been perverted and need to be reclaimed by a return to a pure original from of Islam is held in common by Islamists like Osama bin Laden and Islamic reformers. See Qudsia Mirza, "Islamic Feminism, Possibilities and Limitations," *Law after Ground Zero,* ed. John Strawson (Sydney, London, Portland: Glasshouse Press, 2002), 108–22.

23. Daniel Pipes, "Harvard Loves Jihad," *New York Post,* 11 June 2002. This article was also published in the English-language *Jerusalem Post,* 12 June 2002, retrieved from the World Wide Web December 2002 http://www.danielpipes.org/article/419.

24. Ibid.

25. Ibid.

26. Ibid.

27. Daniel Pipes, "Jihad and the Professors, Commentary" (November 2002), retrieved from the World Wide Web December 2002 http://www.danielpipes.org/article/498.

28. Ibid.

29. For a chilling account of Western militarism see Sven Lindquist, *A History of Bombing* (London: Granta Books, 2001).

30. John Strawson, "Islamic Law and the English Press," in *Law after Ground Zero,* ed. John Strawson, 205–14.

31. Farid Esack, *Qur'an, Liberation and Pluralism* (Oxford: Oneworld, 1997).

32. John Strawson, "A Western Question to the Middle East: Is There a Human Rights Discourse in Islam?" *Arab Studies Quarterly,* 19, no. 1 (1997): 31–58.

33. Aziz Al-Azmeh, *Islams and Modernities* (London: Verso 1993).

34. R. Stephen Humphreys, *Islamic History: A Framework for Inquiry* (Cairo: American University in Cairo Press, 1992).

35. Joseph Schacht, *An Introduction to Islamic Law* (Oxford: Clarendon, 1964), 23–68.

36. Majid Kadduri, *The Islamic Law of Nations: Shaybani's Siyar* (Baltimore: Johns Hopkins Press, 1966).

37. The Abbasid period ends in 750 C.E. and the Ummayad in 1258. The founders of the main sunni schools of law were: Abu Hanifa (700–67 C.E.); Malik ibn Anas (710–95 C.E.); Mohammad al Shaifi'I (767–820 C.E.); and Ahmad ibn Hanbal (780–855 C.E.).

38. Khaled Abou El Fadl, *Speaking in God's Name: Islamic Law, Authority and Women* (Oxford: Oneworld, 2002), 12.

39. Khaddiri, *The Islamic Law of Nations,* 10–14.

40. Ibid., 15–16.

41. W. Michael Resiman, "Allocating Competences to Use Coercion in the Post-Cold War World: Practices, Condition, and Prospects," in *The Use of Force in the New International Order,* ed. Lori Fisler Damrosch and David Sheffer (Boulder, CO: Westview Press, 1991).

42. This is essentially the development of the law of war. It should be noted that Islamic jurisprudence is far in advance of the West in this area, which only began to develop a systematic approach to the issue in the second half of the nineteenth century (e.g., the first Geneva Convention, 1864).

43. Zawati, "Is Jihad a Just War?"

44. Martti Koskenniemi, *From Apology to Utopia: The Structure of International Legal Argument* (Helsinki: Finnish Lawyers Publication Company, 1989).

45. Quoted by Ibn Khaldun, Bidayat al-Mujtiahid—*The Distinguished Jurist's Primer,* trans. Imran Ahsan Khan Nyazee (Reading: Garnet, 1994), 455 Quran 9:122.

46. Majid Khadduri, *The Islamic Law of Nations: Shaybani's Siyar* (Baltimore: John Hopkins Press, 1966), 76 (This is from Khadduri's translation of the original text).

47. Ibid.

48. See Peter Fitzpatrick, *Modernism and the Grounds of Law* (Cambridge: Cambridge University Press, 2001).

49. The Hanaifi School is one of the four surviving schools of the sunni branch of Islam and has widespread influence in much of the former countries of Ottoman empire and the Indian subcontinent. The Hedaya dates from the twelfth century. See Charles Hamilton, *The Hedaya,* 4 vols. (London: T. Bensley, 1791).

50. John Strawson, "Islamic Law and English Texts" in *Laws of the Postcolonial,* ed. Eve Darian-Smith and Peter Fitzpatrick (Ann Arbor: University of Michigan Press, 1999), 109–126.

51. Lawrence Rosen, *The Justice of Islam* (New York: Oxford University Press, 2000).

52. For example, in Europe, the *London Guardian,* 1 June 2002; the German *Der Speigel,* 7 June 2002; in the Islamic world, the Turkish *Hurriyet,* 31 May 2002; in Pakistan, the *Dawn,* 8 June 2002, and *Pakistan Today,* 14 June 2002; and in Bangladesh, *News from Bangladesh* (on-line news forum), 14 June 2002.

53. Ibid.

54. Ibid.

55. Ibid.

CHAPTER 3: BETWEEN ENEMIES AND TRAITORS

1. S. Sengupta, "September 11 Attack Narrows the Racial Divide," *New York Times,* 10 October 2001, p. B1.

2. J. Rhodes, "Fanning the Flames of Racial Discord: The National Press and the Black Panther Party," *Harvard International Journal of Press/Politics* 4, no. 4, 95–119.

3. R. N. Jacobs, "Race, Media and Civil Society," *International Sociology* 14, no. 3 (1999): 355–73.

4. These include the *Atlanta Inquirer,* the *Baltimore Afro-American,* the *Chicago Defender,* the *Chicago Independent Bulletin,* the *Indianapolis Recorder,* the *Hyde Park Citizen,* the *Los Angeles Sentinel,* the *Miami Times,* the *New York Beacon,* the *New York Amsterdam News,* the *New York Voice/Harlem,* the *Mississippi Link,* the *Philadelphia Tribune,* the *Pittsburgh Courier,* the *Portland Skanner,* the *Sun Reporter,* the *Tennessee Tribune,* the *Tri-State Defender,* and the *Washington Informer.* Selected pieces from the *ADC Times* published by the American-Arab Anti-Discrimination Committees are also included.

5. R. Walters, "Blacks and American Super-Patriotism," *Indianapolis Recorder,* 28 September 2001, p. A11.

6. K.D. Richards, "Middle Eastern People Being Booted off Planes," *Columbus Dispatch,* 28 September 2002, p. 1A.

7. Ibid. Since September 11, the Council on American-Islamic Relations, based in Washington, D.C., has received more than 1,700 reports of workplace bias, airport profiling, discrimination in schools, physical assault, and other incidents, compared with 322 in all of 2000. By March 2002, the U.S. Department of Transportation had received 98 discrimination complaints from airline passengers, including 26 who said they were kicked off flights as a result of racially motivated passenger panics. See

M.B. Sheridan, "Backlash Changes Form, Not Function: Sept. 11 Aftereffects Include Less-Visible Discrimination Cases," *Washington Post,* 4 March 2002, p. B1.

8. T. Bartimus, "Are We Headed for More Paranoia and Profiling of Innocent Parties?" *Seattle Times,* 29 September 2002, p. M2.; Richards, "Middle Eastern People Being Booted off Planes,"

9. Richards, "Middle Eastern People Being Booted off Planes."

10. C.E. Mayer, "Passenger Fears, Bias Laws May Clash: Terrorism Raises Legal Concerns," *Washington Post,* 29 September 2001, p. A12.

11. Ibid.

12. Journalists reporting these incidents have noted that Arab American victims of such racism have, in most cases, received no apology and little compensation from the offending parties. Instead, Arab victims are typically asked to tolerate, endure, and be understanding of such assaults. Thus, when a Gaithersburg construction worker of Middle Eastern origin informed his boss of insults and threats he had endured from coworkers, the supervisor replied, "Well, don't you think these people have a right to be angry?" As if such a response were not bewildering enough, the construction worker, a U.S. citizen employed by the company for more than a decade, was also told that filing a complaint would be "detrimental to [his] career" (M.B. Sheridan, "Backlash Changes Form, Not Function").

13. Bartimus, "Are We Headed for More Paranoia."

14. Ibid.

15. M. Parenti, *Land of Idols: Political Mythology in America* (New York: St. Martin's, 1994), 26.

16. T. Lewin, "Sikh Owner of Gas Station is Fatally Shot in Rampage," *New York Times,* 17 September 2001, p. B16. After killing Sodhi, Roque then fired shots through a window at a Lebanese American clerk working at a second gas station and into the home of an Afghani family. Roque did not injure any of the others. Nationwide, the FBI was investigating forty possible hate crimes, including killings, assaults, and arsons that occurred within two weeks after September 11, 2001 (See J. Trevi-o and G. Alimurung, "The Hate Files," *LA Weekly,* 21 September 2001, p. 21.)

17. M.W. Potts, "Sikh, Pakistani Businessmen Killed in Wake of Attacks," *India-West,* 21 September 2001, p. A24.

18. "PUSH Forum Focuses on Threats to Americans' Civil Liberties," *Hyde Park Citizen,* 20 December 2001, p. 2.

19. "Blacks React to Terrorism," *Sun Reporter,* 13 September 2001, p. 1.

20. Ibid.

21. Ibid.

22. M. Omi and H. Winant, *Racial Formation in the United States: From the 1960s to the 1980s* (New York: Routledge, 1986); V. Prashad, *The Karma of Brown Folk* (Minneapolis: University of Minnesota Press, 2000); R. Takaki, "Race as a Site of Discipline and Punish," in *Privileging Positions: The Sites of Asian American Studies,* ed. G.Y. Okihiro, M. Alquizola, D.F. Rony, and K.S. Wong, (Pullman, WA: Washington State University Press, 1995), 335–48.

23. Walters, "Blacks and American Super-Patriotism."

24. Ibid. News reports announcing that the Washington D.C., sniper, who "terrorized" residents during a two-week rampage, was John Allen Muhammad, an African American Muslim, who some claim committed his crimes to speak out on behalf of Islamic brothers whom he believed the U.S. government had mistreated since September 11, are likely to reopen familiar and draconian scenes of black villainy and criminality positioned in contrast to "Americans" imagined by extension as white. (See B. Knickerbocker and F. Bowers, "A Search for Motives in Sniper Shootings," *Christian Science Monitor,* 28 October 2002, p. 1.)

25. C. Strausberg, "War on Terror: From Birmingham to bin Laden," *Chicago Defender,* 5 January 2002, p. 1.

26. J. Tilove, "Black Americans' Issues May Suffer in Wake of Attacks," *Plain Dealer,* 30 September 2001, p. A6.

27. Ibid.

28. J.R. Barras, "Many Blacks Have Doubts," *Washington Post,* 28 October 2001, p. B3.

29. L. Aubry, "Urban Perspective: Flag-waving and Patriotism far from the Whole Truth Part 1," *Los Angeles Sentinel,* 6 February 2002, p. A7.

30. Ibid.

31. K.J. Carillo, "Interpreting the Terror: Activists Give Statements on WTC Attacks," *New York Amsterdam News,* 3 October 2001, p. 3.

32. R. Lee, "Black American Criticism is not Unpatriotic," *Philadelphia Tribune,* 28 September 2001, p. 7A.

33. A. Muhammad, "Askia-at-Large: Reconciling Islam, Peace and Terrorism," *Washington Informer,* 24 October 2001, p. 16.

34. Parenti, *Land of Idols,* 29–31.

35. G. Curry, "In My Opinion: Vernon Jordan Says Blacks Are No Strangers to Terrorism," *Washington Informer,* 1 May 2002, p. 11.

36. Ibid.

37. C. Strausberg, "Pincham Seeks U.S. Shrines for Blacks Who Died from 'Homegrown' Terrorists," *Chicago Defender,* 8 January 2002, p. 5.

38. Burns, 26 September 2001, p. 1.

39. R. Antoine, "Loud and Clear: US Government Originated the Terrorism Language," *Miami Times,* 13 November 2001, p. 4A; L. Clark, "Terrorism: The Melting Pot and American Hypocrisy," *Los Angeles Sentinel,* 17 October 2001, p. C8.

40. "The One Lone Vote That Made Us Stop and Think," *Baltimore Afro-American,* 5 October 2001, p. A16.

41. "Black History is America's History," *New York Voice/Harlem,* 20 February 2002, p. 4.

42. J. Fiske, *Media Matters: Everyday Culture and Political Change* (Minneapolis: University of Minnesota Press, 1994), 191

43. Carillo, "Interpreting the Terror."

44. "N.J. Poet Laureate Defends His 9-11 Work: State Officials Can't Force Resignation," *Washington Post,* 3 October 2002, p. C1.

45. Carillo, "Interpreting the Terror."

46. W. Raspberry, "America Puts Blacks in Dangerous Position," *Miami Times,* 20 November 2001, p. 10A. Raspberry explains that while the "terrorists" were foreigners, black Americans are patriots; the former declared war on this country, while the latter has repeatedly sought to make it live up to its solemnly enunciated ideals; and when black Americans have been involved in terrorism, it has been as victims rather than as perpetrators.

47. Ibid.

48. "Blacks React to Terrorism."

49. D. Jones, "An Open Letter to Colin Powell," *Miami Times,* 30 October 2001, p. 9A.

50. Fiske, *Media Matters,* 202.

51. Clark, "Terrorism: The Melting Pot and American Hypocrisy."

52. Barras, "Many Blacks Have Doubts."

53. J. Davidson, "Six Months Later Policies Are Examined," *Miami Times,* 19 March 2002, p. A6.

54. "PUSH Forum Focuses on Threats to Americans' Civil Liberties."

55. Walters, "Blacks and American Super-Patriotism."

56. Included here are such recent incidents as an unarmed black man being shot in the back by a Cincinnati policeman; Amadou Diallo, an unarmed African immigrant shot nine times by police officers in New York City; and Abner Louima, a black man who was sodomized by New York City police officers while being interrogated.

57. Jones, "An Open Letter to Colin Powell."

58. D.E. Murphy and D.M. Halbfinger, "9–11 Bridged the Racial Divide, New Yorkers Say Gingerly," *New York Times,* 16 June 2002, p. 25.

59. Ibid.

60. Ibid.

61. Walters, "Blacks and American Super-Patriotism."

62. S. Brooks Hodge, "Blacks Split on New Terrorism Legislation," *Tennessee Tribune,* 7 November 2001, p. 1A.

63. "The One Lone Vote That Made Us Stop and Think."

64. Curry, "In My Opinion: Vernon Jordan Says Blacks Are No Strangers to Terrorism."

65. Ibid.

66. *The Matrix,* dirs. Andy and Larry Wachowski, 1999; *The Green Mile,* dir. Frank Darabont, 1999; *The Legend of Baggar Vance,* dir. Robert Redford, 2000.

67. *New York Times,* 2 August 2001, p. A21.

68. *Ghost,* dir. Jerry Zucker, 1990; *Passion Fish,* dir. John Sayles, 1992; *Bulworth,* dir. Warren Beatty, 1998; *Black & White,* dir. James Toback, 1999; *Save the Last Dance,* dir. Thomas Carter, 2001.

69. N. Baroudi, "Rep. McKinney Delivers Passionate Plea for Arab-Black Alliance," *ADC Times,* 31 July 2001, p. 27.

70. Ibid.

71. Ibid.

72. T. Snow, "Attacks Change Attitudes to Racial Profiling: Debate Sparked by Need for Counter-Terrorism Measures," *Voice,* 8 October 2001, p. 15.

73. "Arab Dragnet Equals Profiling," *Portland Skanner,* 28 November 2001, p. 4. The same article also praised the actions of Interim Police Chief Andrew Kirkland of Portland, Oregon, who refused U.S. Attorney General John Ashcroft's mandate that city police forces should help in rounding up and questioning young Arab men not suspected of any crime.

74. D. Ward, "Media Roundup: Civil Rights Debate Stays Hot in Media Well after 9–11," *PR Week,* 26 August 2002, p. 13.

75. S. Crouch, "U.S. Must Stay Tough about Sealing Borders," *Daily News,* 14 March 2002, p. 41.

76. Snow, "Attacks Change Attitudes to Racial Profiling: Debate Sparked by Need for Counter-Terrorism Measures." The poll reported that 71 percent of blacks, compared with 57 percent of whites, believed at the time that Arabs and Arab Americans should "undergo special, more intensive security checks before boarding airplanes."

77. "PUSH Forum Focuses on Threats to Americans' Civil Liberties."

78. Davidson, "Six Months Later Policies Are Examined."

79. F.M. Beal, "The Right to Dissent: First Casualty of Terrorism?" *Black Radical Congress News,* 3 October 2001. Available at http://www.brc-news.org.

80. Ibid.

81. Barras, "Many Blacks Have Doubts."

82. Carillo, "Interpreting the Terror."

83. Such moves are entirely consonant with prevailing discourses of neoliberalism, the retreat from racial justice, as Stephen Steinberg (1995) puts it, which have enabled a series of assaults upon social and racial justice programs promulgated in the sixties. These assaults have mangled the character of the American sixties, positioning the social revolutions of the time as heroic but tidy and long-finished, and as having borne mutant progeny like affirmative action with troublesome constituencies of quota queens and token hires. See S. Steinberg, *Turning Back: The Retreat From Racial Justice in American Thought and Policy* (Boston: Beacon Press, 1995); A. Reed, Jr., *Stirrings in the Jug: Black Politics in the Post-Segregation Era* (Minneapolis: University of Minnesota Press, 1999); D. Roediger, "White Workers, New Democrats, and Affirmative Action," *The House That Race Built,* ed. W. Lubiano, (New York: Vintage, 1998), 48–65; J.D. Skrentny, *The Ironies of Affirmative Action: Politics, Culture, and Justice in America* (Chicago: University of Chicago Press, 1996).

84. D. Kellner, "September 11, the Media, and War Fever," *Television and New Media,* 32 (2002): 143–51; R.W. McChesney, "The Zillionth Time as Tragedy," *Television and New Media,* 32 (2002): 133–37.

85. Kellner, "September 11, the Media, and War Fever."

CHAPTER 4: COMMODIFYING SEPTEMBER 11

1. Polly Devaney, "Cheerful Super Bowl Ads Mask a Deeper Malaise," *Marketing Week,* 28 February 2002, p. 36.

2. Anheuser-Busch Vice President of Brand Management Bob Lachky is quoted in an article by Michael McCarthy, "Some Bowl Commercials Take on a Serious Tone," *USA Today,* 1 February 2002, p. 2B.

3. *Adweek* critic Barbara Lippert is quoted in an article by Greg Johnson, "Patriotism Barely Gets Off the Bench," *Los Angeles Times,* 4 February 2002, Business Section, p. 1.

4. Gail Pennington, "Light Touch Is the Right Touch on Ads," *St. Louis Post-Dispatch,* 4 February 2002, p. B18.

5. Bob Garfield, "Britney Bowl; Mad Ave Shows Some Restraint and, for the Most Part, Sticks to the Humor," *Advertising Age,* 4 February 2002, p. 1.

6. Joseph Campbell, *The Power of Myth* (Garden City, NY: Doubleday, 1988), 31.

7. Authors that address the concept of modern cultural myths include linguist/philosopher Roland Barthes, *Mythologies,* trans. Annette Lavers (New York: Hill and Wang, 1972); philosopher/historian Mircea Elliade, *Myth and Reality* (New York: Harper and Row, 1963); cultural anthropologist Glifford Geertz, *The Interpretation of Cultures* (New York: Basic Books, 1973); psychologist Carl Jung, ed., *Man and His Symbols* (New York: Dell, 1964); cultural anthropologist Claude Levi-Strauss, *Structural Anthropology* (Garden City, NJ: Anchor-Doubleday, 1967); and political scientist, literary and cultural critic Raymond Williams, *Television: Technology and Cultural Form* (New York: Schocken Books, 1975).

8. Roland Barthes, *Mythologies,* trans. Annette Lavers (New York: Hill and Wang, 1972), 11.

9. Stuart Hall, "Encoding/Decoding," in *Culture, Media, Language,* eds. Stuart Hall et al. (London: Hutchinson, 1980), 134.

10. Clifford Geertz, *Local Knowledge: Further Essays in Interpretive Anthropology* (New York: Basic Books, 1983), 84.

11. See, for example, S. Elizabeth Bird and Robert W. Dardenne, "Myth, Chronicle and Story: Exploring the Narrative Qualities of News," in *Media, Myths, and Narratives: Television and the Press,* ed. James Carey (Newbury Park, CA: Sage, 1988); Christopher P. Campbell, *Race, Myth and the News* (Thousand Oaks, CA: Sage, 1995); Richard Campbell, *60 Minutes and the News: A Mythology for Middle America* (Urbana, IL: University of Illinois Press, 1991); and Hal Himmelstein, *Television Myth and the American Mind* (New York, Praeger, 1984). The Summer 2002 edition of *Journalism and Mass Communication Quarterly,* 79, no. 2, was devoted to "Mythology in Journalism," and includes seven articles about the mythological role of journalism.

12. S. Elizabeth Bird and Robert W. Dardenne, "Myth, Chronicle and Story: Exploring the Narrative Qualities of News," in *Media, Myths, and Narratives: Television and the Press* ed. James Carey (Newbury Park, Ca: Sage, 1988), 70, 72.

13. Jack Lule, "Myth and Terror on the Editorial Page: *The New York Times* Responds to September 11, 2001," *Journalism and Mass Communication Quarterly,* 79, no. 2 (summer 2002), 286.

14. Martin Esslin, "Aristotle and the Advertisers: The Television Commercial as a Form of Drama," in *Television: The Critical View* ed. Horace Newcomb (New York: Oxford University Press, 1976), 271.

15. Hal Himmelstein, *Television Myth and the American Mind* (New York, Praeger, 1984), 62.

16. Sut Jhally, *The Codes of Advertising* (New York: St. Martin's Press, 1987), 141.

17. Sut Jhally, prod., *Advertising and the End of the World* (video) (Northampton, MA: Media Education Foundation, 1998).

18. Theresa Howard, "Americana Ads Help GM Salvage 2001 Sales," *USA Today,* 7 January 2002, p. 2B.

19. Ibid.

20. Bob Garfield, "Ads Fly Flag to Get Cash Registers Ringing," *Advertising Age,* 15 October 2001, p. 1.

21. Howard, "Americana Ads Help GM Salvage 2001 Sales," p. 2B.

22. Garfield, "Ads Fly Flag to Get Cash Registers Ringing," p. 1.

23. Henry Magenheim, "Ad Messages Focus on Patriotism, Reassurance," *Travel Weekly,* 18 October 2001, p. 4.

24. Pete Millard, "Patriotism Becomes Trendy Advertising Theme," *The Business Journal-Milwaukee,* 30 November 2001, p. 8.

25. Associated Press, "New United Ads Take Flight; But Carrier's TV Spots Draw Mixed Reviews," *Newsday,* 24 October, 2001, p. A51.

26. Ibid.

27. Ibid.

28. Shelley Emling, "It's a Red, White and Blue Shopping Season; Retailers Stress Patriotism, Family in Low-key Displays," *Atlanta Constitution,* 23 November 2001, p. 1E.

29. Lewis Lazare, "Patriotic Marketing, Right on the Nose," *Chicago Sun-Times,* 14 December 2001, p. 69.

30. Tom Siebert, "The Pimping of Old Glory," *Baltimore Sun,* 20 December 2001, p. 23A.

31. Dave Walker, "An Ad for America; Locally Produced Commercial Celebrates Pop Culture and Patriotism in the Wake of Sept. 11," *Times-Picayune,* 26 October 2001, p. 1.

32. Nancy Bell, Trumpet Advertising's vice president of communication and marketing strategies for The Oath, is quoted in Walker, "An Ad for America; Locally Produced Commercial Celebrates Pop Culture and Patriotism in the Wake of Sept. 11," p. 1.

33. Frank Witsil, "For Advertisers, It's Anything But Business as Usual," *Tampa Tribune,* 27 September 2001, p. 1.

34. Becky Ebenkamp, "Survey Says: Long May It Wave on the Airwaves," *Brandweek,* 29 October 2001, p. 20.

35. Chris Reidy, "Public Mood Challenges Advertisers," *Boston Globe,* 28 September 2001, p. C1.

36. Ibid.

37. Margaret McKegney, "Has Shopping Become the New Patriotism?" *Ad Age Global,* 1 November 2001, p. 6.

38. Donald L. Potter, "Letters to the Editor," *Advertising Age,* 22 October 2001, p. 24.

39. Marc Kempton, managing partner of Core Advertising Agency, is quoted in an article by Thomas Lee, "Sympathy and Patriotism are Agencies' Battle Cry; Firms are Forced to Refocus After Last Week's Attacks," *St. Louis Post-Dispatch,* 23 September 2001, p. F1.

40. Mike Flynn, senior director of planning and research for D'Arcy Masius Benton & Bowles ad agency, is quoted in Lee's "Sympathy and Patriotism are Agencies' Battle Cry; Firms are Forced to Refocus After Last Week's Attacks," p. F1.

41. Rick Boyko is quoted in an article by Stuart Elliot, "Madison Avenue Rides Wave of Patriotic Fervor," *New York Times,* 8 October 2001, p. C1.

42. Ibid.

43. Ibid.

44. Steve Laughlin, president of Laughlin/Consable Inc., is quoted in Mallard, "Patriotism Becomes Trendy Advertising Theme," p. 8.

45. Monty Phan, "Bowling Them Over; Advertisers' Big Goal on Super Sunday," *Newsday,* 1 February 2002, p. A54.

46. David Hinckley, "Government Messages on Drugs Lecture Us from on High," (NY) *Daily News,* 22 May 2002, p. 46.

47. Ibid.

48. Matthew Briggs is quoted in an unbylined article, "Debating the Drug Ads; Government's TV Campaign Linking Terrorism to Narcotics Trade Provokes Outspoken Reactions," *San Francisco Chronicle,* 5 February 2002, p. A2.

49. Susan Aschoff, "The Latest Weapons," *St. Petersburg Times,* 19 February 2002, p. 3D.

50. Office of National Drug Control Policy spokesman Tom Riley is quoted in Aschoff's "The Latest Weapons," p. 3D.

51. "Those Super Bowl Anti-Drug Ads," *Tampa Tribune,* 18 February 2002, p. 14.

52. Abigail Trafford, "Drug Users As Traitors," *Washington Post,* 12 February 2002, p. F01.

53. Himmelstein, *Television Myth and the American Mind,* 62.

54. Ibid., 218.

55. Hillary Chura, "The Player: Hill Holliday Lures Sweeney, and A-B Keeps Work Coming; Family Man Tackles Brewer's 'Impossible Tasks'," *Advertising Age,* 17 June 2002, p. 32.

56. Ibid.

57. Ibid.

58. Hall, "Encoding/Decoding," 134.

59. Bruce Horovitz, "Bud Light Rules Super Bowl," *USA Today,* 4 February 2002, p. 4B.

60. McCarthy, "Some Bowl Commercials Take on a Serious Tone," p. 2B.

61. Hall, "Encoding/Decoding," 137.

62. Ibid.

63. John Fiske and John Hartley, *Reading Television* (London: Methuen & Co Ltd, 1978).

64. Ibid, 41.

65. Ibid, 45.

66. Jhally, prod., *Advertising and the End of the World* (video).

67. William Leiss, Stephen Kline, and Sut Jhally, *Social Communication in Advertising: Persons, Products & Images of Well Being* (Scarborough, Ontario: Nelson Canada, 1990), 193.

68. Ibid.

69. Laughlin, quoted in Mallard, "Patriotism Becomes Trendy Advertising Theme," p. 8.

70. Hall, "Encoding/Decoding," 138.

71. Ibid.

72. Fiske and Hartley, *Reading Television,* 46.

73. See Antonio Gramsci, *Selections from the Prison Notebooks,* ed. Quintin Hoare and Geoffrey Nowell Smith (New York: International Publishers, 1971).

74. Todd Gitlin, "Prime Time Ideology: The Hegemonic Process in Television Entertainment," in *Television: The Critical View,* ed. Horace Newcomb, (New York: Oxford University Press, 1994), 518.

75. Jhally, prod., *Advertising and the End of the World* (video).

76. Fiske and Hartley, *Reading Television,* 50–58.

77. Judith Williamson, *Decoding Advertisements* (London: Marion Boyars, 1978), 13.

78. Ibid.

79. Leiss, Kline, and Jhally, *Social Communication in Advertising: Persons, Products & Images of Well Being,* 31–32.

80. Edward S. Herman and Noam Chomsky, *Manufacturing Consent: The Political Economy of the Mass Media* (Toronto: Pantheon Books, 1988), 14.

81. "The Money Game," *Age* (Melbourne), 31 January 2002, p. 3.

82. The president is quoted in Carolyn Lockhead, and Carla Marinucci, "Freedom and Fear Are at War," *San Francisco Chronicle,* 21 September 2001, p. A1.

83. Ibid.

84. Theresa Howard, "Ads Walk a Fine Line in Sensitive Times," *USA Today,* 25 September 2001, p. 3B. Several months after Maher's program was canceled by ABC, he was hired by HBO to host a late-night talk show that was scheduled to begin airing in February 2003.

85. A collection of interviews with Noam Chomsky in the weeks after the attacks was published in Noam Chomsky, *9–11* (New York: Seven Stories Press, 2001), 81.

86. James W. Carey, *Communication as Culture: Essays on Media and Society* (Winchester, MA: Unwin Hyman, 1989), 60.

CHAPTER 5: RITUALS OF TRAUMA

1. The author wishes to thank all those who have added to this article. This includes: Claudia Breger, Michel Chaouli, Steven Chermak, Peter Namyslowski, Bill Rasch, Faye Stewart, Marc Weiner, and the participants of my courses.

2. Michiko Kakutani, "The Information Age Processes a Tragedy: Books and More Books Analyze, Exorcise and Merchandise the Events of Sept. 11," *New York Times* 28 August 2002, p. B1.

3. Ruth Leys, *"Trauma": A Genealogy* (Chicago: University of Chicago Press, 2000), 2.

4. Chomsky writes: "we can think of the United States as an 'innocent victim' only if we adopt the convenient path of ignoring the record of its actions and those of its allies, which are, after all, hardly a secret." Noam Chomsky, *9–11,* (New York: Seven Stories Press, 2001), 35. For the number of deaths, see 39–54. Chomsky also points out another way in which the media construct a more convenient story of "9-11," namely that the extremists attack America "because its commitments of free speech, religious liberty, gender equality, and racial and ethnic diversity" (see Alan Wolfe, "The Home Front: American Society Responds to the New War," in *How Did this Happen? Terrorism and the New War,* ed. James F. Hoge and Gideon Rose [New York: Public Affair, 2002], 283–94, 284). Instead, Chomsky maintains that it is unlikely that the terrorists are concerned with how *we* live but rather reacted to what they perceived as U.S. terrorist interventions into *their* affairs (Chomsky, 41).

5. Reuters, *September 11: A Testimony* (New York: Pearson Education, 2002).

6. Thus, Jacques Derrida characterizes "archives" according to the Greek word *arche* by means of the duality of the memory of an origin and the ruling over something, *Archive Fever: A Freudian Impression,* trans. Eric Prenowitz (Chicago: University of Chicago Press, 1996).

7. Mitchell Fink and Lois Mathias, ed., *Never Forget: An Oral History of September 11, 2001* (New York: HarperCollins Publishers, 2002).

8. The data for such accounts are still being collected; in the meantime, see Jacques Steinberg, "The Fears of a Child, Reflected in the Clouds Above Any U.S. City," *New York Times* 11 September 2002, p. G4.

9. Herman writes: "The ultimate goal...is to put the story, including the imagery, into words." Judith Herman, *"Trauma" and Recovery: The Aftermaths of Violence—from Domestic Abuse to Political Terror* (New York: Basic Books, 1997), 177.

10. For the relationship of media and ritual, see Catherine Bell, *Ritual: Perspectives and Dimensions* (New York: Oxford University Press, 1997), 242–50.

11. Luhmann's German finds a single term for this function of rituals: "Kommunikationsvermeidungskommunikation," Niklas Luhmann, *Die Gesellschaft der Gesellschaft* (Frankford: Suhrkamp, 1997), 235.

12. See Der Derian, "9.11: Before, After and In Between," retrieved from the World Wide Web at http://www.ssrc.org/sept11/essays/der_derian.htm.

13. It is also remarkable how few and careful reports addressed the suffering of the enemy's side. While it was often reported that possibly less than ten members of al-Qaeda and maybe not a single member of the Taliban knew of the planned attacks, a full-blown war seemed inescapable. Civilian casualties on the side of Afghanistan trickled into the U.S. news usually by reference to foreign broadcasters, at least until the actual war was over. The surprising indifference of the suffering by innocent people does require explanation, and my best guess is that this is, in good part, due to the ritualistic rechanneling of empathy.

14. Or some phantasmic relationship to the U.S. superiority, see Jean Baudrillard, "L'Esprit du Terrorisme," trans. Donovan Hohn, *Harper's Magazine,* February 2002, 13–18.

CHAPTER 6: "AMERICA UNDER ATTACK"

1. Aaron Brown, CNN anchor, reacting to the first tower's collapse, 11 September 2001.

2. Pew Research Center, "American Psyche Reeling from Terror Attacks," 19 September 2001. Available on-line at http://people-press.org/reports/display.php3?reportID=3. Pew Research Center, "Terror Coverage Boost News Media's Images," 28 November 2001. Available on-line at http://people-press.org/reports/display.php3?reportID=143. Elizabeth White, "CNN Widens Lead in Terrorist Coverage," *Media Life Magazine,* 24 September 2001, 4.

3. Amy Reynolds and Brooke Barnett, "This Just In...How National TV News Handled the Breaking 'Live' Coverage of September 11" (paper presented at the annual meeting of the Association for Education in Journalism and Mass Communication, Miami, FL, 2002).

4. William A. Gamson, "Foreword," in *Framing Public Life: Perspectives on Media and Our Understanding of the Social World,* ed. Stephen D. Reese, Oscar H. Gandy, Jr., and August E. Grant (NJ: Lawrence Erlbaum Associates, 2001), ix-xi.

5. Ibid, x.

6. Robert Entman, "Framing: Toward Clarification of a Fractured Paradigm," *Journal of Communication* 43 (1993): 51–58.

7. Ibid., 52.

8. James W. Tankard, Jr., Laura Hendrickson, J. Silberman, K. Bliss, and Salma Ghanem, "Media Frames: Approaches to Conceptualization and Measurement" (paper presented at the annual meeting of the Association for Education in Journalism and Mass Communication, Boston, Massachusetts, 1991). This paper has frequently been cited in mass communication framing studies and was recently revamped and rewritten as a book chapter. The chapter is James W. Tankard, Jr., "The Empirical Approach to the Study of Media Framing," in *Framing Public Life: Per-*

spectives on Media and Our Understanding of the Social World, ed. Stephen D. Reese, Oscar H. Gandy, Jr., and August E. Grant (NJ: Lawrence Erlbaum Associates, 2001), 95–106.

9. Murray Edelman, "Contestable Categories and Public Opinion," *Political Communication* 10 (1993): 231–42; William A. Gamson and Andre Modigliani, "Media Discourse and Public Opinion on Nuclear Power: A Constructionist Approach," *American Journal of Sociology* 95 (1989): 1–37; William A. Gamson, "A Constructionist Approach to Mass Media and Public Opinion," *Symbolic Interaction,* 11 (1988): 161–74; Zongdang Pan and Gerald Kosicki, "Framing Analysis: An Approach to News Discourse," *Political Communication,* 10 (1993): 55–73; Robert Entman, "Blacks in the News: Television, Modern Racism and Cultural Change," *Journalism Quarterly* 69 (1992): 341–361.

10. Gamson, "Foreword," ix.

11. Pamela J. Shoemaker and Stephen D. Reese, *Mediating the Message: Theories of Influence on Mass Media Content.* (2d ed.) (New York: Longman, 1996); Stephen D. Reese, "Setting the Media Agenda: A Power Balance Perspective," in *Communication Yearbook,* ed. James Anderson (California: Sage) 309–40; Stephen D. Reese, "Understanding the Global Journalist: A Hierarchy-of-Influences Approach," *Journalism Studies* 2 (2001): 173–87.

12. Shoemaker and Reese, *Mediating the Message,* 28.

13. Dennis McQuail, *Mass Communication Theory, an Introduction.* (3rd ed.) (London: Sage, 1994).

14. See, for example, Herbert J. Gans, *Deciding What's News* (New York: Pantheon Books, 1979); David Weaver and G. Cleveland Wilhoit, *The American Journalist: A Portrait of U.S. News People and Their Work* (Indiana: Indiana University Press, 1991); David Weaver and G. Cleveland Wilhoit, *The American Journalist in the 1990s: U.S. News People at the End of an Era* (2nd. Ed.) (New Jersey: Lawrence Erlbaum Associates, 1996); Shoemaker and Reese, *Mediating the Message,* 63–102.

15. Shoemaker and Reese, *Mediating the Message,* 175–251.

16. Reynolds and Barnett, "This Just In…", 9.

17. Paul Messaris and Linus Abraham, "The Role of Images in Framing News Stories," in *Framing Public Life: Perspectives on Media and Our Understanding of the Social World,* ed. Stephen D. Reese, Oscar H. Gandy, Jr., and August E. Grant (New Jersey: Lawrence Erlbaum Associates, 2001), 215–26.

18. Ibid, 216. For more on this concept, see Paul Messaris, *Visual "Literacy": Image, Mind and Reality* (Colorado: Westview Press, 1994).

19. Ibid., 217. For more on indexicality, see Charles Sanders Peirce, *Peirce on Signs: Writings on Semiotics by Charles Sanders Peirce* (North Carolina: University of North Carolina Press, 1991) and Paul Messaris, *Visual Persuasion: The Role of Images in Advertising* (California: Sage, 1997).

20. Ibid.

21. Ibid., 219.

22. Maria Elizabeth Grabe, "The South African Broadcasting Corporation's Coverage of the 1987 and 1989 Elections: The Matter of Visual Bias," *Journal of Broadcasting and Electronic Media* 40 (1996): 153–79.

23. Walter Lippmann, *Public Opinion* (New York: Macmillan, 1922).

24. Maxwell E. McCombs and Donald L. Shaw, "The Agenda-Setting Function of Mass Media," *Public Opinion Quarterly,* 36 (1972): 176–187. For a detailed account of agenda-setting studies and expansion of the theory over the past three decades, see Maxwell E. McCombs and Amy Reynolds, "News Influences on Our Pictures of the World," in *Media Effects: Advances in Theory and Research* (2d ed.), ed. Jennings Bryant and Dolf Zillmann (New Jersey: Lawrence Erlbaum Associates, 2002).

25. Edward S. Herman and Noam Chomsky, *Manufacturing Consent: The Political Economy of the Mass Media* (New York: Pantheon, 1988).

26. Michael Parenti, *Inventing Reality: The Politics of News Media* (2d ed.) (New York: St. Martin's Press, 1993).

27. Ibid, 174.

28. J. Herbert Altschull, *Agents of Power: The Media and Public Policy* (2d ed.) (New York: Longman, 1995), 144.

29. Ibid, 145.

30. Robert W. McChesney, *Rich Media, Poor Democracy: Communication Politics in Dubious Times* (Illinois: University of Illinois Press, 1999), 281.

31. Grabe, "The Matter of Visual Bias," 163.

32. James K. Hertog and Douglas M. McLeod, "A Multiperspectival Approach to Framing Analysis: A Field Guide," in *Framing Public Life: Perspectives on Media and Our Understanding of the Social World,* ed. Stephen D. Reese, Oscar H. Gandy, Jr., and August E. Grant (New Jersey: Lawrence Erlbaum Associates, 2001), 139–61.

33. Ibid, 150–51.

34. See Brooke Barnett and Maria Elizabeth Grabe, "The Impact of Slow Motion Video on Viewer Evaluations of Television News Stories," *Visual Communication Quarterly* 7 (2000): 4–7. Their experiment shows that when viewers watch slow-motion video they perceive the images to be more intense.

35. CNN is owned by AOL/Time Warner.

36. McChesney, *Rich Media, Poor Democracy,* 281.

37. Gamson, "Foreword," x.

38. Howard Zinn, *Declarations of Independence: Cross-Examining American Ideology* (New York: Harper Perennial, 1990).

CHAPTER 7: INTERNET NEWS REPRESENTATIONS OF SEPTEMBER 11

1. The authors wish to thank Steven Chermak, Bruce Hoffman, and their students/classmates for their commentary and contributions to earlier drafts of this paper.

2. Walter Benjamin, "The Work of Art in the Age of Mechanical Reproduction," in *Illuminations,* trans. Harry Zohn (New York: Schocken, 1969), 217–51.

3. Nicholas Mirzoeff, ed., *The Visual Culture Reader* (New York: Routledge, 1999).

4. John Seely Brown and Paul Duguid, *The Social Life of Information* (Boston: Harvard Business School Press, 2000), 32.

5. Primary Sources: *CNN.com—War Against Terror* (www.cnn.com/SPE-CIALS/2001/trade.center); *Washington Post—America Attacked* (www.washington post.com/wp-dyn/nation/specials/attacked); *Time.com—America on Alert* (www.time.com/time/911); *Foxnews.com—America at War* (www.foxnews.com/war/main.htm); *MSNBC—America on Alert* (msnbc.com/news/attack_front.asp); *ABCNews.com—A Nation United* (www.abcnews.com/sections/us/DailyNews/WTC_SubIndex.html); *USNews.com—America Under Attack* (www.usnews.com/usnews/news/terror); *BBCi News—Attack on America:* (news.bbc.co.uk/hi/english/in_depth/americas/2001/day_of_terror). Secondary Sources and Comparison Packages: *The Atlantic Online—The War on Terrorism* (www.theatlantic.com/waronterror/); *The Nation—September 11* (www.thenation.com/special/wtc/index.mhtml); *New Yorker, The—From the Archives, September 11 & After* (www.newyorker.com/FROM_THE_ARCHIVE/PREVIOUS); *The Urbana-Champaign Independent Media Center—Terrorism Links* (www.ucimc.org/library/terrorism.html); *Znet—Emergency: Terror and War* (www.zmag.org/terrorframe.htm); *AlterNet* (www.alternet.org/); *Independent Media Center: 9–11: Peace and Justice* (indymedia.org/peace/); *Media Education Foundation: Beyond the Frame—Alternative Views on the Sept. 11th Atrocities* (mediaed.sitepassport.net/btf); *CBC News—U.S. Under Attack* (www.cbc.ca/news/indepth/usattacked/); *World Press Review—Special Report: Battle Without Borders: The War Against Terror* (www.worldpress.org/specials/wtc/mideast.htm); *Guardian Unlimited: Britain After September 11* (www.guardian.co.uk/ukresponse/0,11017,583503,00.html).

6. Funded by the Indiana University President's Summer Undergraduate Research Initiative. This study was conducted by undergraduate and graduate students as a companion project to a course introduced in Fall 2002 in Indiana University's American Studies Program. Special thanks to Elizabeth Holladay for participation in the data collection.

7. Data collection and analysis took place over the summer of 2002 (May 1 through August 31). The time span of the study was due, in part, to the nature of the funding (a summer grant) as well as a belief that at that point the Web sites had solidified into a fairly final design, still mapped from the news site's home page (the source of breaking news). After the one-year anniversary of September 11, most of these sites were moved into an archival format.

8. William A. Gamson, *Talking Politics* (New York: Cambridge University Press, 1992).

9. Katherine Beckett, "Media Depictions of Drug Abuse: The Impact of Official Sources," *Research in Political Sociology* 7 (1995): 161–82; Theodore Sasson, *Crime Talk: How Citizens Construct a Social Problem* (Hawthorne, NY: Aldine de Gruyter, 1995); Richard Ericson, Patricia Baranek and Janet B. L. Chan, *Representing Order: Crime, Law and Justice in the News Media,* (Toronto: University of Toronto Press, 1991); Erving Goffman, *Frame Analysis: An Essay on the Organization of Experience* (New York: Harper and Row, 1974); Murray J. Edelman, *The Symbolic Uses of Politics* (Chicago: University of Illinois Press, 1964).

10. S. Hall, C. Critcher, T. Jefferson, J. Clarke, and B. Roberts, *Policing the Crisis: Mugging, the State and Law and Order* (New York: Holmes and Meier, 1978); John Fiske, *Media Matters: Everyday Culture and Political Change* (Minneapolis: University of Minnesota Press, 1994).

11. Sasson, *Crime Talk;* Ray Surette, *Media, Crime, and Criminal Justice: Images and Realities* (Pacific Grove, CA: Brooks/Cole Publishing Company, 1992); Austin Sarat, *When the State Kills: Capital Punishment and the American Condition* (Princeton: Princeton University Press, 2001).

12. Stuart Hall, ed., "Encoding/Decoding," in *Culture, Media, Language* (London: Hutchinson, 1980); Fiske, *Media Matters;* Alison Young, *Imagining Crime* (Thousand Oaks, CA: Sage Publications, 1996).

13. Jakob Nielsen, *Hypertext and Hypermedia* (New York: Academic Press, Inc, 1990).

14. Mark Poster, *What's the Matter with the Internet?* (Minneapolis: University of Minnesota Press, 2001).

15. Brown and Duguid, *The Social Life of Information.*

16. Roy Rada, *Hypertext: From Text to Expertext* (New York: McGraw-Hill Book Company, 1991).

17. Nielsen, *Hypertext and Hypermedia,* 1.

18. Ilana Snyder, *Hypertext: The Electronic Labyrinth* (Melbourne, Australia: Melbourne University Press, 1996), ix.

19. Ibid.; Brown and Duguid, *The Social Life of Information.*

20. Michel Foucault, *The Archaeology of Knowledge and The Discourse on Language* (New York: Pantheon Books, 1972), 129.

21. Hall, "Encoding/Decoding," 129.

22. Nielsen, *Hypertext and Hypermedia;* Rada, *Hypertext: From Text to Expertext.*

23. Jacques Derrida, *Archive Fever: A Freudian Impression* (Chicago: University of Chicago Press, 1996).

24. Surette, *Media, Crime, and Criminal Justice.*

25. Alexis de Tocqueville, *Democracy in America,* rev. ed., (Westvaco's American Classics Series. New York: Westvaco, 1999); Robert Neelly Bellah et al., *Habits of the Heart: Individualism and Commitment in American Life* (New York: Harper & Row, 1986).

26. Benjamin Barber, *Jihad vs. McWorld: Terrorism's Challenge to Democracy* (New York: Ballantine Books, 2001).

27. Hall, "Encoding/Decoding," 137.

28. Brown and Duguid, *The Social Life of Information,* 179.

29. Thomas Valovic, *Digital Mythologies: The Hidden Complexities of the Internet* (New Brunswick, NJ: Rutgers University Press, 2000), 59.

30. Michael Heim, *The Metaphysics of Virtual Reality* (New York: Oxford University Press, 1993), 83.

31. Brown and Duguid, *The Social Life of Information,* 2.

32. Ibid.

33. Edward T. Linenthal, *The Unfinished Bombing: Oklahoma City in American Memory* (New York: Oxford University Press, 2001).

34. Michel Foucault, "What is an Author?" in *The Foucault Reader,* ed. Paul Rabinow (New York: Random House, 1984), 101–120.

35. Linenthal, *The Unfinished Bombing,* 2–3.

36. Snyder, *Hypertext: The Electronic Labyrinth,* 17.

37. Jorge Luis Borges, *Labyrinths: Selected Stories and Other Writings* (New York: New Directions, 1962).

CHAPTER 8: REPORTING, REMEMBERING, AND RECONSTRUCTING SEPTEMBER 11, 2001

1. The *Guardian* Review, 16 August 2002, p. 2.

2. Ibid., p. 4.

3. The *Guardian,* for example, publishes a Manchester edition, supposedly for the North of England, but it actually varies little, apart from the local television listings.

4. M. Bromley and S. Cushion, "Media Fundamentalism: The Immediate Response of the UK National Press to September 11," in *Journalism after September 11,* ed. B. Zelizer and S. Allan (London: Routledge, 2002), 160.

5. J. Tunstall, *Newspaper Power* (Oxford: Clarendon Press, 1996).

6. 18 March 1997.

7. T. O'Sullivan, B. Dutton, and P. Rayner, *Studying the Media,* (London: Arnold, 1998), 82.

8. S. Hall, C. Critcher, T. Jefferson, and J. Clarke, ed. *Policing the Crisis: Mugging, the State, Law and Order* (UK: Macmillan, 1978); S. Hall, ed., *Representations: Cultural Representations and Signifying Practices* (London: Sage, 1997); T. Trew, "Theory and Ideology at Work and Linguistic Variation and Ideological Difference: What the Papers Say" in *Language and Control,* ed. R. Fowler, B. Hodge, G. Kress, and T. Trew (London: Routledge Kegan Paul, 1979); C. Husband, *Social Identity and Race E3542* (UK: Open University, 1984), 5–6; T. Van Dijk, *Racism and the Press* (London: Routledge, 1991); R. Ferguson, *Representing Race: Ideology, Identity and the Media* (London: Arnold, 1998).

9. The *Guardian,* 24 March 1999.

10. M. Wykes, *News, Crime and Culture* (London: Pluto Press, 2001).

11. Ferguson, *Representing Race: Ideology, Identity and the Media,* 153.

12. Ibid., 138.

13. E. Herman and N. Chomsky, *Manufacturing Consent* (USA: Pantheon, 1988), 2.

14. Tunstall, *Newspaper Power.*

15. L. Christmas, *Chaps of Both Sexes* (Devizes BT Forum, 1997); L. Van Zoonen, "One of the Girls: The Changing Gender of Journalism" in *News, Gender and Power,* ed. C. Carter, G. Branston, and S. Allan (London: Routledge, 1998), 33–47; S. Allan, "(En)Gendering the Truth Politics of News Discourse" in *News, Gender and Power,* eds. C. Carter, G. Branston, and S. Allan (UK: Routledge, 1998), 121–37.

16. Allan, *News, Gender and Power,* 133.

17. Ibid.

18. C. Sparks and J. Tulloch, ed., *Tabloid Tales: Global Debates over Media Standards* (Oxford: Rowman and Littleman, 2000); B. Franklin, *Newzak and Newspapers* (London: Routledge, 1997).

19. Franklin, *Newzak and Newspapers,* 113.

20. Petley, December 06, 2001 http://www.cpbf.org.uk.

21. J. Galtung and M. Ruge, "Structuring and Selecting News" in *The Manufacture of News: Deviance, Social Problems and the Mass Media.* ed. S. Cohen and J. Young (1982 edition) (London: Constable, 1965).

22. See http://news.bbc.co.uk/1/hi/england/2255722.stm for details of the case.

23. S. Chibnall, *Law and Order News* (London: Tavistock, 1977).

24. Hall et al, *Policing the Crisis,* 66.

25. The *Daily Telegraph,* 1.

26. P. Scraton, ed., "Introduction: Witnessing 'Terror', Anticipating War" in *Beyond September 11: An Anthology of Dissent* (London: Pluto Press, 2002), 2.

27. Galtung and Ruge, "Structuring and Selecting News"; Chibnall, *Law and Order News.*

28. Trew, "Theory and Ideology at Work and Linguistic Variation and Ideological Difference: What the Papers Say"; Wykes, *News, Crime and Culture,* 138–63.

29. B. Gunter, J. Harrison, and M. Wykes, *Violence on Television: Distribution, Form, Context and Themes* (USA: Lawrence Erlbaum, 2003).

30. M. Foucault, *Discipline and Punish* (UK: Allen Lane, 1975); M. Foucault, *The History of Sexuality vol. 1* (UK: Penguin, 1979).

31. Foucault, *The History of Sexuality vol. 1,* 87.

32. A.C.H. Smith, E. Immirzi, and T. Blackwell, *Paper Voices: The Popular Press and Social Change* (London: Chatto and Windus, 1975).

33. Bromley and Cushion, "Media Fundamentalism: The Immediate Response of the UK National Press to September 11," 167.

34. E. Berrington, "Representations of Terror in the Legitimation of War" in *Beyond September 11: An Anthology of Dissent,* ed. P. Scraton (London: Pluto Press, 2002), 49.

35. The *Daily Telegraph.*

36. The *Guardian.*

37. Ibid.

38. The *Daily Mail.*

39. The *Guardian,* 20 December 2001.

40. P. Scraton, ed., "In the Name of a Just War" in *Beyond September 11: An Anthology of Dissent* (London: Pluto Press, 2002), 225.

41. Ibid, 228.

42. W.B. Yeats, "The Second Coming" in *Macbeth Poetry 1900–1975* (Harlow Longman, 1921).

CHAPTER 9: CREATING MEMORIES

1. The authors wish to thank William Alex Pridemore and Steven M. Chermak for comments on earlier drafts of this paper.

2. Barry Schwartz, "Postmodernity and Historical Reputation: Abraham Lincoln in Late Twentieth-Century American Memory," *Social Forces* 77 (1998): 63–103; Bill Rolston, *Drawing Support: Murals of War and Peace* (Belfast, NI: Beyond the Pale Publications, 1998).

3. Matti Bunzl, "The Politics and Semantics of Austrian Memory: Vienna's Monument Against War and Fascism," *History and Memory* 7 (1996): 7–40; Kirk Savage, "The Politics of Memory: Black Emancipation and the Civil War Monument," in *Commemorations: The Politics of National Identity,* ed. John Gillis (Princeton, NJ: Princeton University Press, 1994), 135–48.

4. Actually, the 9-11 attacks could be considered a continuation of the 1993 attack on the World Trade Center.

5. Steven Chermak, *Searching for a Demon: The Media Construction of the Militia Movement* (Boston, MA: Northeastern University Press, 2002).

6. John Gillis, "Memory and Identity: The History of a Relationship," in *Commemorations: The Politics of National Identity,* ed. John Gillis (Princeton, NJ: Princeton University Press, 1994), 3–24; Jon Reid and Cynthia Reid, "A Cross Marks the Spot: A Study of Roadside Death Memorials in Texas and Oklahoma," *Death Studies* 25 (2001): 341–56; Edward Linenthal, *Preserving Memory: The Struggle to Create America's Holocaust Museum* (New York: Columbia University Press, 2001).

7. Edward Linenthal, *The Unfinished Bombing: Oklahoma City in American Memory* (New York: Oxford University Press, 2001).

8. Cheryl Jorgenson-Earp and Lori Lanzilotti, "Public Memory and Private Grief: The Construction of Shrines at the Sites of Public Tragedy," *Quarterly Journal of Speech,* 84 (1998): 150–70; C. Haney, Christina Leimer, and J. Lowery, "Spontaneous Memorialization: Violent Death and Emerging Mourning Ritual," *Omega,* 35 (1997):159–71; John Bodnar, *Remaking America: Public Memory, Commemoration, and Patriotism in the 20th Century* (Princeton, NJ: Princeton University Press, 1992).

9. Linenthal, *The Unfinished Bombing.*

10. Edward Linenthal, *Preserving Memory;* Kari Watkins, personal communication, 2002.

11. Jorgenson-Earp and Lanzilotti, "Public Memory and Private Grief."

12. Schwartz, "Postmodernity and Historical Reputation," 64; Lawrence Langer, *Preempting the Holocaust* (New Haven: Yale University Press, 1998).

13. Linenthal, *The Unfinished Bombing*.

14. Technically, neither the chapel nor the statue are official parts of the memorial. Nevertheless, they are considered being part of the memorial because of their location.

15. David Smith, Elaine Christiansen, Robert Vincent, and Neil Hann, "Population Effects of the Bombing of Oklahoma City," *Journal: Oklahoma State Medical Association* (April 1999).

16. Linenthal, *The Unfinished Bombing*.

17. Jim Dwyer, "The Memorial that Vanished," *New York Times*, 23 September 2001.

18. Christy Ferer, "Lives Lost and the Renewal of Downtown," *New York Times*, 18 May 2002.

19. Editorial Desk, "Turning to Renewal," *New York Times*, 31 May 2002.

20. Roger K. Lewis, "Consider a Memorial of Moments, Not Monumental Proportions, in Lower Manhattan," *Washington Post*, 29 June 2002.

21. Gerald Zelizer, "Quick Dose of 9–11 Religion Soothes, Doesn't Change," *USA Today*, 7 January 2002.

22. David W. Dunlap, "Polished Marble and Sacramental Scuffs," *New York Times*, 25 August 2002.

23. Ellen Sorokin, "Mourners Memorial Rises Near Pentagon," *Washington Times*, 19 September 2001.

24. Eric W.R. Ollom, "What to Build?" The *New York Times*, 2 December 2001.

25. Eric Lipton, "Cleanup's Pace Outstrips Plans for Attack Site," *New York Times*, 7 January 2002.

26. Edward Wyatt, "Many Voices, but Little Dialogue on Memorial for Trade Center Site," *New York Times*, 26 January 2002.

27. Al Burrelli, "Rebuild Downtown And Remember," *New York Times*, 27 March 2002.

28. David Cho and Jamie Stockwell, "Pentagon Wreckage Lures Thousands: Victims' Families, Onlookers United in Tears, Prayer; Officials Award Contract to Rebuild Facility," *Washington Post*, 16 September 2001.

29. Ann McFeatters and Rachel Smolkin, "Flight 93 Memorial Takes Wing; Murtha Expects Congress to Easily Approve His Bill," *Pittsburgh Post-Gazette*, 9 March 2002.

30. Keota Fields, "What to Build?" *New York Times*, 2 December 2001.

31. Diane Cardwell, "In Final Address, Giuliani Envisions Soaring Memorial," *New York Times*, 28 December 2001.

32. Edward Wyatt, "Six Plans for Ground Zero, All Seen as a Starting Point," *New York Times*, 17 July 2002.

33. Elissa Gootman, "A Day of Somber Reminders Revolves Around a Broken Sculpture and Lights," *New York Times*, 11 March 2002.

34. Matt Assad, "Eeriness difficult to escape in Shanksville; Somerset County coroner regrets he couldn't bring closure to families of Flight 93 crash victims," *Morning Call,* 11 September 2002.

35. Bill Hough, "Toward a Shrine at a Solemn Place, " *New York Times,* 2 March 2002.

36. Ruth Burgess, "Ground Zero Rite: A Widow's Anguish," *New York Times,* 31 May 2002.

37. Sorokin, "Mourners Memorial Rises Near Pentagon."

38. Jim Abrams, "House Approves Memorial to Commemorate Flight that Crashed in Pa. on Sept. 11," *Associated Press State & Local Wire,* 23 July 2002.

39. Scott Pirrello, "A Fitting Tribute: Memorial Stadium," *New York Times,* 21 October 2001.

40. Paul Aster, "The City and the Country," *New York Times,* 9 September 2002.

41. Dinita Smith, "Competing Plans Hope to Shape a Trade Center Memorial," *New York Times,* 25 October 2001.

42. Bill Keller, "Remembering and Forgetting," *New York Times,* 22 September 2001.

43. Judy Lin, "Somerset County Curator Preserving Crash Site Tributes," *Associated Press State & Local Wire,* 4 December 2002.

44. Michael Miscione, "The Forgotten," *New York Times,* 23 December 2001.

45. Herbert Muschamp, "Leaping From One Void Into Others," *New York Times,* 23 December 2001.

46. Kirk Johnson, "In Bereavement, Pioneers on a Lonely Trail," *New York Times,* 8 September 2002.

47. Sorokin, "Mourners Memorial Rises Near Pentagon."

48. Abrams, "House Approves Memorial."

49. Jane Levere, "He Loves New York, Up to a Point," *New York Times,* 3 February 2002.

50. Kittridge White, "A Day to Pause, to Remember a Lost World," *New York Times,* 11 March 2002.

51. Kenneth Sandbank, "Majestic Memorial, Rising to the Sky," *New York Times,* 13 April 2002.

52. McFeatters and Smolkin, "Flight 93 Memorial Takes Wing."

53. Dan Barry, "From a World Lost, Ephemeral Notes Bear Witness to the Unspeakable," *New York Times,* 25 September 2001.

54. Chuck Nathanson, "A Trial at Ground Zero," *New York Times,* 23 November 2001.

55. John Tierney, "Beauty From Evil: Preserving Felled Tower Façade as Sculpture," *New York Times,* 25 September 2001.

56. Susanna Beacom, "The Tribute in Light," *New York Times,* 2 April 2002.

57. Maria Sanminiatelli, "Virginia Man Designs Attacks Remembrance Flag," *Associated Press State & Local Wire,* 10 September 2002.

58. Smith, "Competing Plans Hope to Shape a Trade Center Memorial."

59. Marylynne Pitz, "Process to Begin for Memorial to 40 on Flight 93," *Pittsburgh Post-Gazette,* 9 December 2001.

60. Laurie Kellman, "Thousands Apply to Design 9–11 Memorial," *Columbian,* 23 October 2002.

61. Emile Durkheim, *The Elementary Forms of Religious Life* (New York: The Free Press, 1915); see also Robert Bellah, "Civil Religion in America, " in *Beyond Belief: Essays on Religion in a Post-Traditional World,* ed. Robert Bellah (New York: Harper and Row, 1970), 168–89.

62. Cody Lyon, "A Memorial For All," *New York Times,* 14 October 2001.

63. Maurice Halbwachs, *Collective Memory* (New York: Harper and Row, 1950).

64. Barry Schwartz and Todd Bayma, "Commemoration and the Politics of Recognition: The Korean War Veterans Memorial," *American Behavioral Scientist* 42 (1999):946–67; Barry Schwartz, "Collective Memory and History: How Abraham Lincoln Became a Symbol of Racial Equality," *The Sociological Quarterly* 38 (1997): 469–96.

CHAPTER 10: STEP ASIDE, SUPERMAN . . . THIS IS A JOB FOR [CAPTAIN] AMERICA!

1. To date, there exists no standard manual of style for the citation of comic books. Most scholarly treatments of comic books include the title of the story, the title of the book in which it appears, the volume and series number of the issue, the publisher, and the issue's cover date. As comic books frequently have no pagination, direct quotes are not referenced with a page number (see William W. Savage, Jr., *Commies, Cowboys, and Jungle Queens: Comic Books and America 1945–1954* [Hanover, NH: Wesleyan University Press, 1998]; Bradford W. Wright, *Comic Book Nation* [Baltimore: The Johns Hopkins University Press, 2001]).

2. Steven T. Seagle (story), Duncan Rouleau and Aaron Sowd (art), "UNREAL," in *9–11 Volume 2* (NY: DC Comics, 2001).

3. Action Comics #1, "Superman, Champion of the Oppressed!" reprinted in its entirety in *Superman—The Action Comics: Archives Volume 1* (New York: DC Comics, June 1938 [1997]).

4. Action Comics #12, "Superman Declares War on Reckless Drivers," reprinted in its entirety in *Superman—The Action Comics: Archives Volume 1* (New York: DC Comics, May 1939 [1997]).

5. Captain America Vol. 2 #6, "Meet the Fang," reprinted in its entirety in *Captain America: The Classic Years*. Vol. 2 (New York: Marvel Comics, 1941 [2000]).

6. Captain America Vol. 2 #7 "Captain America and the Red Skull," reprinted in its entirety in *Captain America: The Classic Years*. Vol. 2 (New York: Marvel Comics, 1941[2000]).

7. Captain America Vol. 4 #1, "Dust," (New York: Marvel Comics, June 2002).

8. Jessica Evans and Stuart Hall, *Visual Culture* (Thousand Oaks, CA: Sage Publications, 1999).

9. Scott McCloud, *Understanding Comics* (Northampton, MA: Kitchen Sink Press, 1993).

10. Marshall McLuhan, *Understanding Media* (New York: McGraw-Hill, 1964), 164.

11. Orrin E. Klapp, *Heroes, Villains, and Fools* (Englewood Cliffs, NJ: Prentice-Hall, 1962), 27.

12. Ibid, 46, 47.

13. Jeff Williams, "Comics: A Tool of Subversion?" in *Interrogating Popular Culture,* ed. Sean Anderson and Greg Howard (Albany, NY: Harrow and Heston, 1998), 97–115.

14. Action Comics #2, "War in San Monte, Part 2," Summarized in *Superman— The Action Comics: Archives Volume* 1 (New York: D.C. Comics,. July 1938 [1997]); Action Comics #8 (January 1939 [1997]) "Superman in the Slums"; Action Comics #12, "Superman Declares War on Reckless Drivers"; Action Comics #11 "Superman and the 'Black Gold' Swindle," reprinted in its entirety in *Superman—The Action Comics: Archives Volume* 1 (New York: D.C. Comics. April 1939 [1997]).

15. Williams, "Comics: A Tool of Subversion," 102.

16. William W. Savage, Jr., *Commies, Cowboys, and Jungle Queens: Comic Books and America 1945–1954,* 5.

17. Superman #170, "Superman's Mission for President Kennedy," reprinted in *Superman in the Sixties* (New York: D.C. Comics, July 1964 [1999]).

18. Richard G. Powers, *G-Men: Hoover's FBI in American Popular Culture* (Carbondale: Southern Illinois University, 1983), 158.

19. Klapp, *Heroes, Villains, and Fools.*

20. Savage, *Commies, Cowboys, and Jungle Queens.*

21. Ibid.

22. Brian K. Vaughn (story), Pete Woods and Keith Champagne (art), "For Art's Sake." *9–11 Volume 2* (New York: D.C. Comics, 2001).

23. Wright, *Comic Book Nation,* 36.

24. Captain America Vol. 2 #6 "Meet the Fang"; Captain America Vol. 2 #7, "Horror Plays the Scales," reprinted in its entirety in *Captain America: The Classic Years.* Vol. 2 (New York: Marvel Comics, 1941[2000]); Captain America Vol. 2 #6, "Battle of the Camera Fiend and His Darts of Doom," reprinted in its entirety in *Captain America: The Classic Years.* Vol. 2. (New York: Marvel Comics. 1941[2000]).

25. Steve Duin and Mike Richardson, *Comics: Between the Panels* (Milwaukie, OR: Dark Horse Comics, 1998).

26. Captain America Vol. 1 #1, "Captain America Goes to War Against Drugs." (New York: Marvel Comics, 1990); Captain America Vol. 1 #405, "Dances with Werewolves" (New York: Marvel Comics, 1992).

27. Captain America Vol. 4 #1, "Dust."

28. Ibid.

29. Captain America Vol. 4 #2, "One Nation," (New York: Marvel Comics, July 2002).

30. Captain America Vol. 4 #3, "Soft Target," (New York: Marvel Comics, August 2002).

31. Captain America Vol. 4 #4, "Never Give Up," (New York: Marvel Comics, September 2002).

32. Captain America Vol. 4 #3, "Soft Target."

CHAPTER 11: OF HEROES AND SUPERHEROES

1. The author would like to thank Joe Gregov for his helpful comments on this manuscript.

2. Christopher Murray, "Superman vs. Imagio: Superheroes, Lacan and Mediated Identity," *International Journal of Comic Art* 4 (Fall 2002): 186.

3. Tom Sinclair, "Black in Action," *Entertainment Weekly,* 22 November 2002, p. 21.

4. Examples include works by the following creators: Ariel Olivetti, in *9–11: The World's Finest Comic Book Writers and Artists Tell Stories to Remember,* ed. DC Comics (New York: DC Comics, 2002), 148; Lee Bermejo, in *Stories to Remember,* 211; Dave Keown, in *Heroes,* ed. Marvel Comics (New York: Marvel Comics, 2001), 58; John Lucas, in *Stories to Remember,* 118; Neal Adams, "First Things First," in *Stories to Remember,* 176.

5. Examples include works by the following creators: Frank Miller, with Alex Sinclair, in *Heroes,* 9; Mike Deodata Jr., with Dennis Calero, in *Heroes,* 7; Rob Haynes, with Tim Townsend and David Self, in *Heroes,* 19.

6. Sam Keith, in *Heroes,* 1.

7. Examples include works by the following creators: Joe Kubert, in *Heroes,* 4; J. Scott Campbell with Hi-Fi, in *Heroes,* 23.

8. Examples include works by the following creators: Sean Chen, with Norman Lee and Pete Pantazis, in *Heroes,* 55; Richard Corbin, in *Stories to Remember,* 38; Lou Harrison, in *A Moment of Silence,* ed. Marvel Comics (New York: Marvel Comics, 2001), 39; Jepf Loeb (story), Carlos Pacheco and Jesus Merino (art), "A Hard Day's Night," in *Stories to Remember,* 71–73.

9. Examples include works by the following creators: Alberto Ponticelli, with Francesco Ponzi, text by John Figueroa, in *Heroes,* 45.

10. Alan Davis, with Robin Riggs and Pat Prentice, in *Heroes,* 3.

11. Carlos Pacheco with Jesus Merino and Tom Smith, text by Kurt Busiek, in *Heroes,* 13.

12. Christopher Moeller, in *Stories to Remember,* 147.

13. Steven H. White and Joseph E. O'Brien, "What Is A Hero? An Exploratory Study of Students' Conception of Heroes," *Journal of Moral Education* 28 (March 1999): 90.

14. Sal Velluto, with Bob Almond and Chris Dickey, in *Heroes,* 6.

15. Tim Sale, from an idea by Chuck Kim, in *Stories to Remember,* 70.

16. Eddie Berganza and Kyle Baker, "The Call," in *Stories to Remember,* 127.

17. Amy Kiste Nyberg, *Seal of Approval: The History of the Comics Code* (Jackson, MS: University of Mississippi Press, 1998), 6–7.

18. Examples include works by the following creators: Dave Gibbons, in *Stories to Remember,* 42; Marv Wolfman (story), Barry Kitson and Rich Faber (art), "This, Too, Shall Pass," in *Stories to Remember,* 137–40.

19. Steven T. Seagle (story), Duncan Rouleau and Aaron Sowd (art), "Unreal," in *Stories to Remember,* 15–16.

20. Dan Jurgens (story), Robin Riggs, Mike Collins and Mark Farmer (art), "If Only," in *Stories to Remember,* 149–52.

21. Matthew Pustz, *Comic Book Culture: Fan Boys and True Believers* (Jackson, MS: University of Mississippi Press, 1999), 29.

CHAPTER 12: NARRATIVE RECONSTRUCTION AT GROUND ZERO

1. Dorothy Holland, William Lachicoote, Jr., Debra Skinner, and Carole Cain, ed. *Identity and Agency in Cultural Worlds* (Cambridge, MA: Harvard University Press, 1998), 66–95. Holland et al. discuss how in Alcoholics Anonymous the drinker becomes an alcoholic in recovery by learning and internalizing the cultural narrative.

2. Ulrich Baer, *110 Stories: New York Writes After September 11* (New York: New York University Press, 2002), 3.

3. Dean E. Murphy, *September 11: An Oral History* (New York: Doubleday & Company, 2002); Susan Hagen and Mary Caroula, *Women At Ground Zero: Stories of Courage and Compassion* (Indianapolis, IN: Alpha, 2002); Mitchell Fink and Lois Mathias, *Never Forget: An Oral History of September 11, 2001* (New York: Harper-Collins Publishers, 2002); Chris Bull and Sam Erman, ed., *At Ground Zero: 25 Stories From Young Reporters Who Were There* (New York: Thunder's Mouth Press, 2002); Baer, *110 Stories;* Jill Gardiner, "A Detoured Commute," in *At Ground Zero: 25 Stories From Young Reporters Who Were There,* ed. C. Bull and S. Erman (New York: Thunder's Mouth Press: 2002), 107–118; David Paul Kuhn, "All I Hear is Silence," in *At Ground Zero: 25 Stories From Young Reporters Who Were There,* ed. C. Bull and S. Erman (New York: Thunder's Mouth Press, 2002), 65–80; Jennifer Smith, "The Lost," in *At Ground Zero: 25 Stories From Young Reporters Who Were There,* ed. C. Bull and S. Erman (NY: Thunder's Mouth Press, 2002), 381–401.

4. Smith, *At Ground Zero;* Gardiner, "A Detoured Commute."

5. Baer, *110 Stories,* 11, 5.

6. For example, for the young journalists "Overnight, the journalistic landscape changed for the better, opening careers and beats to previously unimaginable possibilities. But even this development pricked the conscience. These writers and broadcasters struggled to reconcile the opportunities this story afforded them with the

enormity of carnage and suffering they saw all around them. They recoiled against the image of tabloid journalists forcing microphones and tape recorders into the faces of grieving victims even when they felt obliged to engage in a gentler variation of the same practice." (Bull, *At Ground Zero.*)

7. Linda Fairstein, *Bloodletter,* monthly newsletter, Sisters in Crime, New York/Tri-State chapter, 9, no. 5 (2002). In another example, Linda Fairstein, speaking as an attorney, said: "I was at my desk, just a few blocks north of the World Trade Center, when the first plane hit, and actually saw the second crash and subsequent building collapses from my window. Although government offices were being evacuated, the District Attorney asked us to stay and work on since were part of the law enforcement efforts of that day and the months that have followed."

8. Jeri Fink, family therapist and mystery writer, interviewed by e-mail, 29 May 2002.

9. The views expressed in this chapter are exclusively those of the author in her private capacity and do not in any way represent the official views of the New York City Taxi and Limousine Commission or the City of New York.

10. Irene Marcuse and Marge Mendel, Untitled, in *Bloodletter* 9, no. 4 (2001).

11. Ibid.

12. Robin Hathaway, Untitled, in *Bloodletter* 9, no. 5 (2002).

13. Trish Stein, Untitled, in *Bloodletter* 9, no. 5 (2002).

14. Linda Fairstein, Untitled, in *Bloodletter* 9, no. 5 (2002).

15. Joyce Christmas, Untitled, in *Bloodletter* 9, no. 2 (2002).

16. Robin Hathaway, *Bloodletter.*

17. K.j.a. Wishnia, Untitled, in *Bloodletter* 9, no. 5 (2002).

18. S. J. Rozan, Untitled, in *Bloodletter* 9, no. 5 (2002).

19. Stein, *Bloodletter.*

20. Shelley Freydont, Untitled, in *Bloodletter* 9, no. 5 (2002).

21. Ellen Pall, Untitled, in *Bloodletter* 9, no. 5 (2002).

22. Leah Robinson Rousmaniere, Untitled, in *Bloodletter* 9 no. 5 (2002).

23. A legal anthropologist, speaking at the American Anthropological Association's annual meetings, November 2001.

24. Ibid.

25. Ibid.

26. David Rosen, interview by the author, telephone, 20 May 2002.

27. Susan Hirsch, a paraphrase from a discussion at the American Anthropological Association's annual meetings, November 2001.

28. Rosen, telephone interview.

29. "The New York City Taxi and Limousine Commission (TLC), created in 1971, is the agency responsible for licensing and regulating New York City's medallion (yellow) taxicabs, for-hire vehicles (community-based liveries and black cars), commuter vans, paratransit vehicles (ambulettes) and certain luxury limousines." For more information, see www.ci.nyc.ny.us/html/tlc/html/about.html.

30. Remarks made by an administrative law judge of the Taxi and Limousine Commission at the TLC court, in Long Island City, New York, several days after September 11, 2001 (and often repeated).

31. Remarks made by an administrative law judge, of the Taxi and Limousine Commission at the TLC court, in Long Island City, New York, several days after September 11, 2001 (and often repeated).

32. Administrative law judge, interview by the author, telephone, 21 May 2002. Not everyone appreciated the camaraderie. For example, one administrative law judge stated, "Most of the judges spoke about the inconvenience that it caused them but I didn't feel any spiritual bonding going on. The chief judges and administrators were annoying and self congratulatory and carried this air of superfluous self-importance.... It was like everybody wanted to use the tragedy to make themselves more important and in the know."

33. Jerome Bruner, *Actual Minds, Possible Worlds* (Cambridge, MA: Harvard University Press, 1986); Elinor Ochs and Lisa Capps, "Narrating the Self," *Annual Reviews in Anthropology* 25 (1996): 19–43.

34. Bakhtin, M.M., *The Dialogic Imagination: Four Essays by M.M. Bakhtin,* ed. Michael Holquist, trans. Caryl Emerson and Michael Holquist (1981; reprint, Austin: University of Texas Press, 1996); Michael Holquist, *Dialogism: Bakhtin and His World* (New York: Routledge, 1990).

35. Holland, Lachiotte, Skinner, and Cain, *Identity and Agency in Cultural Worlds.*

36. D. Graham Burnett, *A Trial By Jury* (New York: Alfred A. Knopf, 2001), 182–83.

CHAPTER 13: AGONY AND ART

1. Douglas Wolk, "Cliches for a Reason," *The Village Voice,* 23–29 January 2002.

2. Mikal Gilmore, "Bob Dylan," *Rolling Stone,* 22 November 2001.

3. Sean Wilentz, *American Recordings: On "Love and Theft" and the Minstrel Boy* (2001), retrieved from the World Wide Web http://bobdylan.com.

4. Greg Tate, "Intelligence Data," *Village Voice,* 26 September 2001.

5. Gilmore, "Bob Dylan."

6. Chad Palmer, *1927 Flood Spawned Flood Control Act* (2001), retrieved from the World Wide Web http://*USATODAY. com.*

7. See Robert Gordon (foreword by Keith Richards, 2002) *Can't Be Satisfied: The Life and Times of Muddy Waters* (Boston: Little, Brown, 2002); and http://archive.ncsa.uiuc.edu/Cyberia/RiverWeb/History/blues35.html.

8. Greil Marcus, "Bringing the Deep South Back Home," *Guardian,* 8 September 2001.

9. See Mark S. Hamm, *In Bad Company: America's Terrorist Underground* (Boston: Northeastern University Press, 2002).

10. All information on Holiday's song is drawn from David Margolick, *Strange Fruit: Billie Holiday, Café Society, and an Early Cry for Civil Rights* (New York: Running Press of America, 2001).

11. Information on the songs of World War II is drawn from wysiwyg://20http://libwww.syr.edu/digital/images/b/Belfer78/patriotic.htm.

12. Neil McCormick, "Sounds of Silence." The *London Telegraph,* 19 September 2002.

13. Alexis Petridis, "The Cultural Impact of September 11: Pop," *Guardian,* 29 September 2002.

14. Young's reading of "Imagine" was ultimately selected as one of the best cover tunes of all time, ranking alongside Jimi Hendrix's cover of Bob Dylan's "All Along the Watchtower" and Merle Haggard and Willie Nelson's cover of the great Townes Van Zandt's "Pancho and Lefty." *My Generation,* Jan.–Feb. 2003: 54.

15. See Stuart Hall, "What Is This 'Black' in Black Popular Culture?" *Social Justice* 20 (1993): 104–14.

16. Stanley Kurtz, "Those 9–11 Songs." *National Review,* 27 August 2002.

17. See McCormick, "Sounds of Silence."

18. Greg Kot, review of Neil Young's *Are You Passionate?, Rolling Stone,* 11 April 2002.

19. Howard Becker, *Outsiders: Studies in the Sociology of Deviance* (New York: The Free Press, 1963), 1–2.

20. Robert Christhau, "Attack of the Chickenshits: Steve Earle Practices Rock and Roll Leftism for Its Own Sweet Sake," *Village Voice,* 18–24 September 2002.

21. McCormick, "Sounds of Silence."

22. My comments on DiFranco's song are derived largely from Gene Santoro, in "Blowin' in a New Wind," *The Nation,* 16 December 2002. As he points out, "Self Evident" was also covered by rapper Chuck D, formerly of Public Enemy.

23. Frank Rich, "Mr. Ambassador," *New York Times Magazine,* 3 November 2002.

24. Matt Rubin, "Peace Movement in Pieces without Protest Music." *Phoenix Online,* 25 October 2001.

25. McCormick, "Sounds of Silence."

26. Tania Branigan, "George Michael Video Rages at US Policy in Middle East and Attacks 'Poodle' Blair." *Guardian,* 2 July 2002.

27. This information comes from a woman speaker I heard at an Indianapolis peace rally on October 26, 2002.

28. *9–11 News and Resources,* see http://Researchbuzz.com.

29. McCormick, "Sounds of Silence."

30. Josh Tyrangiel, "Bruce Springsteen," *Time,* 5 August 2002.

31. Kevin M. Cherry, "Come On Up for the Rising," *Village Voice,* 29 July 2002.

32. Gilmore, "Bob Dylan."

Index

About the Contributors

FRANKIE Y. BAILEY is an associate professor in the School of Criminal Justice, State University of New York Albany (SUNY). Her area of research is crime and culture, focusing on crime and mass media/popular culture, and crime history. She is the author of the Edgar-nominated *Out of the Woodpile: Black Characters in Crime and Detective Fiction* (Greenwood, 1991). She is the co-editor (with Donna Hale) of *Popular Culture, Crime, and Justice* (1998). She is the co-author (with Alice Green) of *"Law Never Here": A Social History of African American Responses to Crime and Justice* (Praeger, 1999). She is the co-author (with Donna Hale) of a forthcoming book, *Blood on Her Hands: The Social Construction of Women, Sexuality, and Murder.* Bailey is the author of a mystery series, featuring crime historian Lizzie Stuart in *Death's Favorite Child* (2000), *A Dead Man's Honor* (2001), and *Old Murders* (2003).

BROOKE BARNETT is an assistant professor of Communication at Elon University where she teaches broadcast journalism, freedom of expression, crime and the media, global studies' and mass media law and ethics. Her research interests include television news processes and effects and first amendment law.

FRITZ BREITHAUPT teaches in the Department of Germanic Studies at Indiana University, Bloomington. He is the author of a study on Goethe *(Jenseits der Bilder. Goethes Politik der Wahrnehmung)* and a forthcoming book on the question of why economics became the leading paradigm to explain the world, to be entitled *The Ego-Effect of Money.* He also works on the public reception of notorious crimes since the eighteenth century.

MICHELLE BROWN is an assistant professor in the Department of Sociology and Anthropology at Ohio University. Her primary research interests include the sociology of punishment and risk, the administration of justice, media studies, and cultural theory. These interests are at the center of her dissertation which explores shifts and contests in the meanings and justifications of imprisonment in the post-rehabilitation United States. Through case studies of inmate experiences, examinations of media portrayals, and an analysis of the science surrounding imprisonment, this study interrelates various levels of cultural production in an effort to better understand the contrmporary patterns of incarceration.

CHRISTOPHER P. CAMPBELL, PH.D., is the director of the Scripps Howard School of Journalism and Communications at Hampton University. He is the author of *Race, Myth and the News* (1995). He writes frequently about issues of cultural diversity and the media for *Television Quarterly.*

STEVEN CHERMAK is an associate professor in the Department of Criminal Justice at Indiana University. Professor Chermak's primary research interest is the representation of crime and criminal justice in the news media. He is the author of *Victims in the News: Crime and the American News Media* (1995) and *Searching for a Demon: The Media's Construction of the Militia Movement* (2002). His recently published book explores how the media presented the militia movement before and after the Oklahoma City Bombing in 1995.

KELLY R. DAMPHOUSSE is an associate professor in the Department of Sociology and director of the department's Center for the Studies of Crime and Justice. He has been the Associate Director of "The American Terrorism Study" since 1994. He is also the Site Director of the Oklahoma City and Tulsa Arrestee Drug Abuse Monitoring (ADAM) program. His research areas include terrorism, city-level homicide, drugs and crime, the anti-Satanism movement, media and crime, gangs, jails, and prisons. His recent research has been published in *Criminology, Criminology and Public Policy, Social and Behavioral Personality, Crime and Delinquency, Homicide Studies,* and in several book chapters.

LEIA FUZESI graduated from Indiana University with a triple major in Criminal Justice, Psychology, and Sociology. She is working as a case manager at the Salvation Army Social Service Center in Indianapolis. Her past research involvement includes work at the IU School of Medicine in the Neonatal Research Department.

MARK S. HAMM is the author of *In Bad Company: Inside America's Terrorist Underground* (2002) and *American Skinheads: The Criminology and Control of*

Hate Crime (1993), among other works on terrorism and hate violence. He is a professor of criminology at Indiana State University.

KRISTEN S. HEFLEY is a Ph.D. candidate in the Department of Sociology at the University of Oklahoma. Her research interests include criminological theory, adolescent and juvenile crime, feminist legal and crime theory, gender and sexuality, and media depictions of crime and deviance. Her current research involves content analysis of popular film for the contexts surrounding the sexual double standard and the changes in its application over time.

RANDY FRANCES KANDEL is an adjunct associate professor in the Department of Anthropology, John Jay College of Criminal Justice of the City University of New York. Her current research interests include the anthropology of legal experience, the vernacularization of human rights, the comparative ethnography of proceedings concering children, and the sociolinguistics of law and dispute conversations. She has written numerous articles and book chapters and her most recent book is *Family Law: Essential Terms and Concepts* (2000).

KARA KITCH is a graduate student at IUPUI (Indiana University-Purdue University Indianapolis).

JARRET LOVELL is assistant professor of criminal justice at California State University, Fullerton. His research interests focus upon critical theory, media ideology, and the administration of justice. His most recent publication examines true-crime comic books published during the early years of J. Edgar Hoover's FBI, and he is currently completing work on a book examining the influence of mass media on police practices. In addition to his position at the university, professor Lovell is also a founding member of the Orange County Peace Coalition and the host of a weekly radio program discussing social activism and progressive politics.

ROOPALI MUKHERJEE is assistant professor of media studies at Queens College of the City University of New York. Her research interests include critical policy studies and race/ethnicity. She is currently finishing a book, *The Racial Order of Things: U.S. Public Policy and the Cultural Imaginary.*

AMY KISTE NYBERG is an associate professor of media studies in the department of communication at Seton Hall University. She is the author of *Seal of Approval: The History of the Comics Code,* a study of comic book regulation and censorship. In addition, she has written many book chapters and articles on various topics related to comic books. She was the 1996 recipient of the M. Thomas Inge Award for Comics Scholarship, presented by the Comic Art and Comics Area of the Popular Culture Association.

AMY REYNOLDS is an assistant professor in the School of Journalism at Indiana University. Reynolds' research focuses on dissent and the First Amendment, including the abolitionists' conceptualization of their free speech/free press rights in the early nineteenth century. She has had articles published in *Communication Law and Policy* and the *Journal of International Communication* and has contributed chapters to several books. Reynolds is currently editing a book that focuses on multidisciplinary approaches to the study of communication law and is conducting several studies that focus on the contemporary conceptualization of dissent in America as well as mainstream media coverage of dissent.

BRENT L. SMITH served two years in the U.S. Army as an instructor in the Department of Military Police Operations and the Counterterrorism Course at the U.S. Army's Military Police School. He served as chairman of the Department of Justice Sciences from 1994–2003. Since 2003 he is a member of the faculty at the University of Arkansas. Dr. Smith's research has focused primarily upon social movements and governmental response. Additionally, terrorism—and how the polity responds—has been of continuing interest throughout his career. His publications on terrorism have appeared in *Criminology, Justice Quarterly, Criminology and Public Policy, Terrorism: an International Journal,* and *Studies in Conflict and Terrorism* and in Congressional testimony. He is the author of *Terrorism in America: Pipe Bombs and Pipe Dreams* (1994). Dr. Smith directs the American Terrorism Study, a project involving the analysis of federal criminal cases resulting from indictment under the FBI's Counterterrorism Program from 1980–present.

CRYSTAL SPIVEY attends law school at DePaul where she has recently been named a dean's scholar. With strong interests in both international and criminal law, Crystal has worked at a criminal law firm and for the probation department of the City of Bloomington, conducting fieldwork on juveniles.

JOHN STRAWSON directs the Encountering Legal Cultures research group at the University of East London and works on law and postcolonialism with special reference to Islam, the Middle East and International Law. His publications include, editor of *Law after Ground Zero* (2002).

MAGGIE WYKES has been a lecturer in criminology in the Law Faculty, University of Sheffield, since January 2001. She was previously with the Department of Journalism Studies, University of Sheffield. She teaches in the areas of criminological theory, policing and deviance and is course leader for the BA in Law and Criminology. Her research focuses on issues of representation, identity, criminalization and power. Publications include a book about journalism and crime in late twentieth century Britain *News, Crime and Culture* (2001).